Big Money Thinks Small

COLUMBIA BUSINESS SCHOOL PUBLISHING

JOEL TILLINGHAST

BIG MONEY
THINKS
SMALL

Biases, Blind Spots, and
Smarter Investing

Columbia Business School
Publishing

Columbia University Press
Publishers Since 1893
New York Chichester, West Sussex
cup.columbia.edu
Copyright © 2017 Joel Tillinghast
All rights reserved

Library of Congress Cataloging-in-Publication Data

Names: Tillinghast, Joel, author.
Title: Big money thinks small : biases, blind spots, and smarter investing / Joel Tillinghast.
Description: New York : Columbia University Press, [2017] | Includes index. |
Identifiers: LCCN 2016048351 (print) | LCCN 2017011170 (ebook) |
ISBN 9780231544696 (electronic) | ISBN 9780231175708 (cloth : alk. paper)
Subjects: LCSH: Investments. | Stocks. | Portfolio management. | Finance, Personal.
Classification: LCC HG4515 (ebook) | LCC HG4515 .T55 2017 (print) | DDC 332.6—dc23
LC record available at https://lccn.loc.gov/2016048351

Columbia University Press books are printed on permanent
and durable acid-free paper.
Printed in the United States of America

COVER DESIGN: Noah Arlow

Contents

Contents

Foreword

PETER LYNCH

I have been an active stock picker for virtually my entire life, so it pains me when critics conveniently lump everyone into the same bucket and say "active managers cannot beat their benchmarks." Well, I am here to tell you that is simply not true. Investors need to know that not all active managers are created equal. There are many skilled investment professionals whose funds have beaten their benchmarks over time—and Joel Tillinghast is right up there with any of them. Joel has now successfully managed the Fidelity Low-Priced Stock Fund more than twice as long as I had managed Fidelity Magellan.

There are a lot of books out there that purport to help you become a better investor. But few mesh the human aspects of investing and business with the numbers side, and even fewer do that by drawing on the experiences of arguably one of the most successful stock pickers and active mutual fund portfolio managers over the past three decades. Whether you are a professional investor or a beginner, *Big Money Thinks Small* can help you better understand how to avoid common investing tricks, traps, and mistakes.

I have been investing for over fifty years and have had the pleasure of working with and meeting some of the greatest minds in investing, from Mario Gabelli and Sir John Templeton to Warren Buffett and Will Danoff. Simply put, Joel is up there with all of them. I can say this with a great deal of confidence, not only because I've known Joel for over thirty years but also because I hired him at Fidelity. Since then, I have witnessed Joel's growth as an investment professional, and I continue to be amazed by his almost unworldly ability to consume mountains of information about hundreds of companies at a time, analyze it, distill it, and use it to find long-term winners while avoiding many of the losers.

It is this analytical ability, combined with his customer-first mindset, that got me to take Joel's cold call more than thirty years ago when he was looking for a new professional challenge. I remember he got through to my assistant Paula Sullivan, who told me, "You have to talk to this guy. He keeps calling and is so sweet. He is from the Midwest and I think he might be a farmer." I told Paula, "I can give him five minutes." So Joel got on the phone and I was immediately impressed by him. He was a stock hound and had so many great ideas, like Puerto Rican Cement. Then he started talking about a savings and loan I had never heard about that got me excited. We talked about more companies, like Chrysler and Armstrong Rubber. I ended up talking with him for well over an hour. Once we hung up, I immediately called the head of Fidelity's investment division and said, "We've got to hire this guy. He is unbelievable. He is as strong as anyone I have ever met." This was September 1986, and the rest is history. While past performance is no guarantee of future results, Joel has delivered impressive results for the shareholders of his fund over his nearly twenty-eight-year tenure.

In my book (not literally, of course), Joel is one of the greatest, most successful stock pickers of all time. He is truly a shining example of an active manager who has been able to beat the street. If you were to look up "alpha" in the dictionary, I would argue there should be a picture of Joel. He is a unique, one-of-a-kind investor, so there is no recipe for replicating his success. That said, Joel clearly embodies the qualities and characteristics that I believe are critical to being a great investor. He is patient, open-minded, and flexible. He also has the ability to ignore the worries of the world long enough to allow his investments to succeed, and he has a willingness to do independent research and an equal willingness to admit when he is wrong and exit. He is persistent, but not stubborn. While good investors have some of these qualities, great investors like Joel have all of them.

Another quality that truly separates Joel from the rest of the professional investing pack is his ability to find value where no one else, or at least very few, might be looking. In his book, Joel talks about water utility stocks. Water stocks are boring. And when you add in strange names like Dwr Cymru (Welsh Water), Severn Trent, and Northumbrian Water, it is almost a given that very few people are looking at them . . . certainly not to the degree of analysts covering companies like Google or Apple. Those who do look usually do not have the patience and commitment to doing the deep fundamental research needed to understand the stories and find opportunities. I remember talking with Joel about these water utilities, and the fundamental story was really compelling. Who else but Joel would look at these?

Joel also has shown a consistent ability to find long-term growth stocks before they experience their big run-ups. After all, it is the ones you miss on the way up that hurt the most. In this book, Joel highlights a few of the companies he found early in their growth cycle that ended up being big contributors to past performance of the Fidelity Low-Priced Stock Fund—names such as Ross Stores, AutoZone, Monster Beverage, Ansys, and numerous others. The tendency of most investors is to cash out after a stock moves up 10 or 15 percent and move on to something else. But just because a stock goes up 10 or 15 percent doesn't mean there isn't room for significantly more growth. A successful investor is one who holds on for the long term and continues to monitor the fundamental story, and if it remains in place you stay, and if not you move on. It is that and his other skills that made Joel such an incredibly successful investor over his career.

In *Big Money Thinks Small*, Joel draws on his experience as a seasoned active equity mutual fund manager to illustrate how certain investment theories can succeed . . . and fail. While he has proven a keen ability to succeed over his career, Joel, like all investors, is not infallible. Stock picking is hard work, and over nearly three decades, even the best investors, like Joel, are going to make mistakes. It is what you do over your complete body of work that matters. In this book, Joel does an exceptional job of examining some of his major sources of investment regrets and suggests ways readers can potentially avoid the same mistakes.

Joel argues that while you cannot learn to be a great investor, you can learn to shy away from mistakes and be a successful one. Persuasive stock promoters and others can lead the average investor into overconfidence and rash decisions. Joel writes that acting cautiously, avoiding mistakes, and being patient are far more likely to pay off than a few bold investments.

In his book, Joel introduces five key principles for avoiding investment mishaps. Depending on whether your glass is half-full or half-empty, these principles can be seen as things to avoid or things to do. For example:

1. Do not invest emotionally, using gut feel / Do invest patiently and rationally
2. Do not invest in things you don't understand, using knowledge you don't have / Do invest in what you know
3. Do not invest with crooks or idiots / Do invest with capable, honest managers
4. Do not invest in faddish or fast-changing, commoditized businesses with a lot of debt / Do invest in resilient businesses with a niche and strong balance sheet
5. Do not invest in red-hot "story" stocks / Do invest in bargain-priced stocks.

Big Money Thinks Small is not another book about how to "play the market," a phrase that has always bothered me. The verb "play" is very dangerous in the context of investing. Investing in stocks is not easy, but it should not be painful. Plain and simple, it requires work and an understanding that stock prices tend to follow company earnings over time. There is an incredible correlation here. For example, Ross Stores' corporate earnings are up seventy-one-fold over the past twenty-four years, and not surprisingly, its stock price is up ninety-six-fold over that same period. And Monster Beverage's corporate earnings are up 119-fold over the past fifteen years; not surprisingly, its stock price is up 495-fold over that same period. It is important to note that the same correlation exists when earnings go down. History is littered with them.

The vast majority of stocks are fairly priced. I have always said that if you look at ten stocks, you will find one worth the investment. If you look at twenty you will find two; look at one hundred and you will find ten . . . and so on. It is the person who turns over the most rocks who wins. To further torture this metaphor, Joel not only turns over the most rocks, he is also a great geologist!

Joel has proven his commitment to doing the work. He does not try to time the market. He puts in the time and effort to research each and every stock, and not just before he buys them, just as importantly, while he owns them. I would argue that Joel works as hard as any of the best professional investors, and the success he has delivered on behalf of his fund shareholders shows this.

Lots of people have the brainpower to make money in stocks. Not everyone has the stomach. Joel has both, and through sensible instruction, he masterfully guides readers through each step of his investment process, showing how to ask the right questions and to think objectively about the condition of your portfolio.

There is so much great information in this book that I am going to stop here and simply tell you to read it. *Big Money Thinks Small* is a must read . . . it is a ten-bagger!

Acknowledgments

This book could not have been written without the assistance and guidance of numerous people. Without Peter Lynch, I might never have come to work at Fidelity Investments, and thus never have had the experiences and discussions that produced this book. More broadly, Fidelity has given me the freedom to learn and grow, with Abby Johnson continuing in the tradition of Ned Johnson and his father before him. Huge thanks for endless comments from Tom Allen, Justin Bennett, Richard Beuke, Elliott Mattingly, Peter Hage, Emily McComb, Maura McEnaney, Derek Janssen, Arvind Navaratnam, Leslie Norton, F. Barry Nelson, Brian Peltonen, and Charles Salas, and the entire Fidelity small-cap team. Thanks also for technical expertise from Jeff Cathie, Daniel Gallagher, Sean Gavin, Scott Goebel, Salim Hart, Mark Laffey, Joshua Lund-Wilde, Chris Lin, Sumit Mehra, Karen Korn, Ramona Persaud, Doug Robbins, Ken Robins, Jeff Tarlin, and John Wilhelmsen. I also appreciate the encouragement I received from Myles Thompson of Columbia University Press, as well as the editing, proofreading, and advice from Jonathan Fiedler, Meredith Howard, Ben Kolstad, Leslie Kriesel, and Stephen Wesley. Above all, I am grateful to my parents, and Anne Croly, Erick Montgomery, and Valerie Tillinghast for supporting me and putting up with me during the writing process.

PART I

Sleight of Mind

1

It's a Mad, Mad World

Your beliefs become your thoughts, your thoughts become your
words, your words become your actions, your actions become
your habits, your habits become your values, your values become
your destiny.

—MAHATMA GANDHI

DO YOU WANT TO BE RICH? Economists consider the question absurd, because the answer is so obviously YES! Unless the notion of building wealth appealed to you, I doubt you would be reading a book about investment decisions. Still, it's unwise for me, or anyone, to assume too much about motives, beliefs, and decision-making. A key theme of this book is that in the investment world reality is not as it appears, and often the ideal differs from both appearances and reality. Nor do we actually choose in the rational way that we think we do. And our choices aren't perfect—we all make decisions we later regret.

This book is about succeeding in investing by avoiding mistakes. The organizing framework of this book, in five parts, is that we will reap pleasing investment rewards if we (1) **make decisions rationally,** (2) **invest in what we know,** (3) **work with honest and trustworthy managers,** (4) **avoid businesses prone to obsolescence and financial ruin,** and (5) **value stocks properly.** While the stories in this book about my mistakes will be most readily grasped by readers who have made their own investment mistakes, I hope this book offers a wider audience an opportunity to learn from the mistakes of others and provides some entertainment value.

I have run the Fidelity Low-Priced Stock Fund (FLPSX) with an intrinsic value approach since 1989, and it has outperformed both the Russell 2000 and Standard & Poor's 500 indexes by 4 percentage points a year.

Over twenty-seven years, a dollar invested in FLPSX grew to $32, while a dollar invested in the index grew to $12.

However, the world of businesses and stocks changes constantly. What's worked in the past may not continue to work. More importantly, investors are diverse, with different emotional constitutions, aptitudes, knowledge, motivations, and goals. One size decidedly does not fit all. And because we've just met, I shouldn't leap to conclusions about you.

"What Happens Next?" *and* "What's It Worth?"

Most investors seek to answer two questions: "What happens next?" and "What's it worth?" Our minds naturally leap to reply to the first question, often before we realize that it was even posed. The stock price has been going up, so what happens next is that it will go up some more—unless, of course, it goes down. A company reports catastrophic financial results. Then earnings forecasts get slashed. The stock price dives—that is, unless the market knew it was going to be a bloodbath and is relieved that management's guidance wasn't more dismal. Unavoidably after whatever happens next, something else will happen, and you may not be ready for it. The question of what happens next is an endless treadmill of, "And then what?" Many of those answers will be wrong.

The longer your time horizon, the more likely you are to be a step ahead of other investors. Mindful investors will look out for at least a few iterations of what happens next. The answer to the second instance of "What happens next?" depends somewhat on the first, and the third on the second and possibly on the first too. And so it goes. Suppose, for example, a company has developed a marvelous new product. This often leads to strong sales and high profits. But high profits draw competitors, and that means . . . Sometimes, the first company to launch a product is the winner and takes it all. Other times, the pioneer is the one with arrows in its back, warning where not to go. Correct or not, I don't know how to convert these answers into investment decisions.

"What's it worth?" is an even more involved question. Many ignore the question of value because they think it's too tough to answer. Others don't ask it because they assume a stock's price and value are the same.

They suppose a stock is worth exactly what it can be sold (or bought) for. If you must sell in a hurry, you will receive market price, not value. However, the central idea of value investing—of which I am an advocate—is that price and value are not always equal, yet should be at some date in the future. Because the date is unknown, patience is mandatory.

Proof of worth arrives years later, long after the decision to buy or sell. Value can be shown only indirectly, never precisely, as it is based on projections of earnings and cash flows into the unfathomable future. Forecasts will always be guesses, not facts. In many cases, the actual outturn will depend more and more on what happens over time. If this year's losses are particularly horrific and the firm goes under, well, it really was a terminal value. Most people don't have the patience to muddle through anything as slow and sketchy as valuation.

Answering "What's it worth?" demands patience and low turnover. but the seemingly easier path of constantly buying and selling based on "What happens next?" doesn't work for most investors, even professionals. A portfolio's turnover is defined as the lower of purchases or sales, as a percent of assets, so a portfolio with 100 percent turnover would change its holdings completely every year. Mutual funds are directed to file data on their holdings and turnover with the U.S. Securities and Exchange Commission, so their behavior is a matter of public record.

Broadly, most studies show that the higher the turnover, the worse the fund does (see table 1.1). Every study I've seen shows that mutual funds

Table 1.1
Mutual Fund Turnover and Excess Returns

Turnover Quintile	Avg. Turnover Rate	Annual Excess Returns
High 1	128%	−0.24%
2	81%	−0.31%
3	59%	+0.07%
4	37%	+0.33%
Low 5	18%	+0.10%

Source: Salim Hart (Fidelity), Morningstar-listed active equity funds with more than $0.5 billion in assets.

with portfolio turnover greater than 200 percent perform badly. Those with turnover above 100 percent fare a bit better, but not much. The studies *don't* agree about whether the best level of turnover is moderate or as close to zero as humanly possible. Mutual funds with turnover below 50 percent are more likely to be using a reasoned, patient approach—like value investing.

Folklore and Crowds

Historians, psychologists, and economists describe behavior in stock markets differently. For centuries, the folklore of stock exchanges has depicted them as crowded, anonymous carnivals of mass delusion and mayhem, with a whiff of sin. In a venue where avarice and envy are constants, no one expects decisions to be morally ideal. Financially, the greatest dangers stem from misunderstanding reality, which leads to endless cycles of boom and bust. These include the Dutch tulip mania, the South Sea Bubble, the Great Crash, Japan's asset bubble, and dozens more—including, yes, the tech and housing bubbles. Investors believed they were taking part in adventures that would reinvent the world. When the bubbles popped, investors were left with wasted capital, scams, and crushing debt.

French polymath Gustave Le Bon wrote *The Crowd* in 1895 as a rant on French politics, but his observations also describe how stock market manias occur. Under the influence of crowds, individuals act bizarrely, in ways they never would alone. Le Bon's key theme is that crowds are mentally unified at the lowest, most barbaric, common denominator of their collective unconscious—instincts, passions, and feelings—never reason. Being unable to reason, crowds can't separate fact from fiction. Crowds are impressed by spectacle, images, and myths. Misinformation and exaggeration become contagious. Prestige attaches to true believers who reaffirm shared beliefs. Crowds will chase a delusion until it is destroyed by experience.

British investors couldn't resist the image of cities of gold in the New World, inflating the South Sea Bubble. Today, El Dorado might be imagined as no-stick blood tests, colonies on Mars, or solar-powered driverless cars. Investors can be as ardent about stocks like Facebook, Amazon, Salesforce.com, or Tesla as about religion or politics. Professional fund managers *should* be less susceptible to pressures to fit in and conform than individuals, but . . . We have quarterly and annual critiques of our relative performance and deviations from benchmarks, and clients who yank their accounts when we are behind in the derby.

The South Sea Company was launched in 1711 as a scheme to privatize British government debt. The Crown granted South Sea exclusive rights to trade with South America. Holders of government annuities (bonds) could swap them for South Sea shares, and South Sea would collect the bond interest. Interest income was to be South Sea's *only* source of net earnings. While international trading provided speculative sizzle, South Sea never made a profit from it, even after it added slaves to its cargo. Nonetheless, over half a year, its share price vaulted eightfold to a peak near £1,000 in June 1720. King George I was honorary governor of the company, and much of London society was sucked into the mania. Shares were offered on an installment plan. Others borrowed money to buy shares. South Sea shares plunged to £150 over a few months and dipped below £100 the following year, ruining many who had used leverage.

There were five categories of mistakes made during the South Sea Bubble, in which investors did the **opposite** of the five key tenets of this book. First, *make decisions rationally*. The decision to invest in the South Sea Company reflected a shared hallucination about cities of gold in South America. True, commerce with English-speaking North America had been lucrative, but South America was mostly Spanish territory. When the facts can't be readily ascertained, we go with the (often erroneous) judgments of those in authority. The king's share ownership and position at South Sea was surely counted as an endorsement. The fear of missing out (FOMO) sounds laughable until you've witnessed folks around you pocketing unearned windfalls. FOMO can be overwhelming! Sir Isaac Newton, the renowned physicist, is reported to have lost money on the South Sea Bubble and then to have said, "I can calculate the motions of the heavenly bodies, but not the madness of the people."

Second, *invest in what you know*. Nothing in the experience of most investors in the South Sea Company equipped them to quantify the benefits of trade with South America. Ocean journeys were long and slow, and few had been outside England or spoke Spanish. Investors may not have grasped that it was in Spain's interest to monopolize trade with its own colonies. Royals and the landed gentry were at the top of the social order, where too much familiarity with business was considered a demerit. The only English people who might have had any idea of how profitable voyages to South America might be were pirates.

Third, *work with honest, capable management.* The promoters of the South Sea Company had no experience at, or interest in, operating shipping routes and were bent on making money off of shareholders, not with them. Then, as now, government-granted monopolies eliminated competition and were typically lucrative—but some might sense a criminal aspect. Share options had been given to members of the ruling class, including King George I, his German mistresses, the Prince of Wales, the Chancellor of the Exchequer, and the Secretary to the Treasury. The promoters of the South Sea Company issued shares at inflated prices. In its largest offering, shares were swapped for government annuities with a notional value three times as great. In the aftermath, John Aislabie, the Chancellor of the Exchequer, and others were impeached and imprisoned, and dozens were disgraced.

Fourth, *avoid competitive industries and seek stable financial structures.* The nature of the South American trade and the financial structures around shareholdings made failure inevitable over time. The English Crown was not free to grant the monopoly, as it was in Spain's interest to maintain control over trade with its colonies, and England was no ally. France had ambitions as well, leaving the long-run prospects for South Sea routes murky. Purchases of South Sea shares were also funded in ways not built to last. Many government officials received shares without paying cash up front, which could be seen as an option—or a bribe, as they could simply collect the net gain. Shares were offered publicly on installment terms, with an initial payment and two later payments, while others borrowed money to buy shares. When the bills came due, many sold shares to raise cash.

Finally, *compare stock prices with intrinsic value.* The market price of South Sea stock was totally disconnected from any realistic estimate of value. **Intrinsic value is the "true" value of a stock, based on** the dividends it is expected to pay over its entire remaining lifetime. Archibald Hutcheson, a Member of Parliament who opposed the scheme, calculated in the spring of 1720 that the shares were worth £150, while the market price was many times that. Hutcheson's estimate of value was based largely on South Sea's interest income. Over previous years, South Sea's expeditions had produced losses (and would continue to do so in the future), so it might have been fair to say that those operations had no value. In 1720, South Sea paid a dividend that—unsustainably—exceeded its net income, making its yield an unreliable indicator of value.

The madness of crowds explains some of the misjudgments in the South Sea Bubble, but not all of them. On their own, people are perfectly capable of not knowing what they don't know. As investors, we're trying to assess the decisions and durability of organizations, which isn't quite crowd psychology. The process of estimating a stock's value requires reasoning with probability and statistics, and here we need a different sort of psychological knowledge.

Thinking Fast and Slow

How should we think about investing? In psychologist Daniel Kahneman's stylized account of decision-making, there are two systems of mind: System 1, which thinks fast, and System 2, which thinks slowly and deeply. System 1 (called the "lizard brain" in popular science) recognizes patterns automatically, quickly, and effortlessly—telling you what will happen next. System 2 grudgingly allocates attention to complex thoughts like estimating a stock's value, and understanding Kahneman. Although choice, agency, and attention are associated with System 2, our decisions often originate in System 1. We often believe that our decisions were arrived at rationally, using step-by-step logic, when actually they arrived through emotionally driven pattern recognition, that is, intuition. When those intuitions are about probability and statistics, we shouldn't trust them.

System 2 would have nothing to work with if the lizard brain wasn't constantly suggesting cause-and-effect relationships and inferring intentions, even though many hints turn out to be bogus. Because our intuition generates feelings and predispositions so effortlessly, it often provides the illusion of truth and unjustified comfort in its beliefs. Confidence comes more often from ignorance than from knowledge.

System 1 ignores ambiguity and muffles doubt with a tunnel-vision focus on the evidence that is immediately visible. Kahneman calls it *What You See Is All There Is*, or WYSIATI. Often, instead of answering a difficult question, our minds will answer an easier one using *heuristics*, or shortcuts. System 1 is more attentive to surprises and changes than to what's normal, average and recurring. It overweights low probabilities, frames decisions narrowly, and is more sensitive to losses than to gains.

How Do Investors Really Behave?

Kahneman observed that humans don't behave the way economists assume *rational* economic men do. As the word rational is commonly used, most decisions are reasonable. Economists add the requirements that choices are logically consistent and maximize economic well-being. No one I know, even the greediest of bastards, single-mindedly maximizes anything (except misery) in a logically consistent manner. *The* most rational might be Warren Buffett, the great value investor and CEO of Berkshire Hathaway. Rather than being so one-dimensional, most people trade off two or more opposed goals at the same time. They optimize. Consider return *and* risk: economic man isn't risk averse, but I am. When I am baffled by the choices others are making, I consider other motives behind their decisions.

When I look at how economists assume economic man behaves, I am reminded that I am a flawed, fallible human, even though I strive constantly to improve.

- *Perfect information*: Everyone knows all relevant information about all securities, even if it's hidden or private, and no misinformation.
- *Perfect foresight*: We know exactly how the future will turn out.
- People calculate and compare the odds and expected utility of everything.
- Everyone will interpret news correctly.

- Tastes do not change. (Investing in teen retailers is a snap!)
- Everyone is infinitely greedy. (Is it really rational to want more money than you need?)
- Hired hands will do the same things that owners would do.

Economists study investment risk from on high, tossing all sorts of risk into one pot. They take an *outside view* of the market, categorizing the outcomes for an *entire* group of statistical subjects, and so look for the net effect on the overall system, not individual outcomes. If, for example, oil prices rise, and the profits of airlines and truckers fall by the same amount as the rise in profits of oil companies, it doesn't matter to the system—so there's no net systemic risk. Risk has been diversified away. In this view, it does not matter whether risk stems from inept or crooked executives, obsolescence, or too much debt; it's **all** "market risk."

Investors, however perceive a multitude of types of risk—some more attractive than others, and greater risk overall. I am watchful of the risk of overpaying, but in the system view it doesn't matter because my loss is your gain. The outside view is also unnatural because, unlike most securities analysts, it ignores the story and details of the case at hand and does not try to forecast its unique outcome. But the outside view can be useful in estimating a base rate of probability for the proper statistical reference class.

A *base rate* is the frequency of an attribute in a statistical population. For example, perhaps 2 percent of biotech research projects develop into a profitable drug. Going back to the features of the case, I might redefine the reference class as well-funded biotechs that are further on in the Food and Drug Administration approval process. By using too broad a reference class, the outside view can turn everything—including mixed games of chance and skill like tennis, chess, or investing—into pure games of chance.

Aren't Markets Efficient?

The efficient market hypothesis (EMH) builds on a series of behavioral assumptions that are more true than not. In the real world, no individual has perfect information on all the securities in the market, and everyone is not equally well informed, but fairly good information is available for those who want it. Not everyone interprets the information identically, but many do. No one has perfect foresight, but the market does look ahead. Investors do try to rationally value stocks, but not all buyers are investors. People shouldn't trade except when a stock is mispriced, but many do. Transactions costs are not zero, but have fallen to low levels. Anyone who takes the assumption of no taxes too seriously is going to have a problem with the Internal Revenue Service.

The EMH arrives at conclusions that are more true than not, such as: At all times stocks will be fairly priced, omnisciently reflecting all information everywhere. Prices will fluctuate randomly as news arrives or interest rates change. All stocks will offer the same risk-adjusted return. (So why pick stocks?) No one should expect any stock or portfolio to beat the market. While returns can't be improved, volatility can be diversified away by holding a portfolio that tracks the entire market—an index fund. Your only lever for improving returns—in the real world, where there are fees and taxes—is to avoid those expenses. The EMH was so compelling that it led John Bogle, founder of mutual fund giant Vanguard, to launch the first low-fee S&P 500 index fund.

I see the EMH as a cautionary tale. It's true that the average person will earn average results, but as in any other endeavor, some are more skilled and interested than others. In every competitive game, winners are paired with losers. That does not mean the game is not worth playing. However, looking at the average result for the entire category alone, everyone should "set it and forget it" with an index fund. Your competition is also smart and diligent, so you need more than that to have an edge.

Are you more economically rational and emotionally even-keeled than the average person? Do you have financial commitments that could limit your ability to be patient as your investments grow? Are you more interested in joining crowds in doing things that you don't understand or in understanding why people do things? Your answers will help determine whether you belong in a different statistical group than the broadest category of investors.

Interest comes before ability, so if you see stock-picking as a great game of skill and the stock market as a fascinating puzzle with more angles than a Rubik's Cube, I'm with you. Conversely, if investment research seems like a chore and the stock market a game of chance—then an index fund is best for you.

Index investors believe they are rewarded for taking overall market risk, while value investors think they are also paid for doing the opposite when others behave badly. If you aren't interested in the question of what good and bad behavior might be, you won't see it as a source of profit. It isn't always either/or; some people find that owning an index fund *and* an actively managed fund *and* individual securities works for them.

Regrets

Whether you invest in individual stocks, an actively managed fund, or an index fund, the sources of your regrets are likely to fall into our five **inverted** (mistake) buckets, which we explore in this book:

1. Allowing emotions, not reason, to guide decisions
2. Thinking you know more than you actually do
3. Trusting capital to the wrong people
4. Choosing businesses prone to failure because of obsolescence, competition, or excessive debt
5. Overpaying for stocks, most frequently those with vivid, striking stories

In part I of this book, we explore how the impulsive lizard brain causes predictable decision biases, which become fatal when distinctions between investing, speculating, and gambling are poorly understood and when investors fail to learn from mistakes. People who don't reflect before acting will fail to notice that there are some subjects which they know deeply, others which they don't, and still others in which no one really has the answers.

In part II, we search for investment blind spots, which can be small details of the dynamics of investment advice, exotic securities, or certain industries. Or they can be cosmic questions about cross-cultural misunderstandings or how economic statistics relate (or not) to specific stocks.

Study your own strengths and limitations, and you'll understand those of the agents to whom you entrust your capital.

Part III is about assessing management's honesty and capability. Skilled managers keep businesses focused on doing something uniquely valuable to customers, and apply capital where it will earn the best returns. Scammers do leave clues, many of which can be found in corporate accounts.

Even capable managers will struggle in tough businesses, so part IV explores why some industries are more durable and resilient than others. Proprietary products, few competitors, evolutionary change, and low debt all extend corporate longevity.

An asset's value is a function of its income, growth, longevity, and certainty, so in part V, we put the pieces together. To estimate a discount rate, we examine historical return patterns for stocks. To be sure we are discounting the right cash flows, we look at earnings quality. Even when we have correctly identified a stock as undervalued, it often proceeds to become even more so.

Diversification and Indexes

So, should you pick stocks or diversify in a fund? Diversification can spread, reduce, and transform risks—more so for those related to the companies, less so for risks related to you. While an S&P 500 index fund is a very complete form of diversification, actively managed funds and portfolios of individual stocks are also diversified. If you are impulsively trading like a whirling dervish, it hardly matters whether you do it with the S&P 500 or with specific stocks. Diversification won't help there, but it would avoid concentrated investments in areas that you don't understand. Index investors can rely on more general rules and general economic knowledge than stock-pickers, who need to understand the growth and competitive picture of specific industries and companies.

An index fund takes an outside view of the risks of corporate fraud—waste, obsolescence, bankruptcy, and stock valuation. Some company management teams will include idiots or crooks. However small the average frequency of awful management is, you'll get it with the index fund. But you'll also get some brilliant innovators and exemplary stewards, in line with those base rates. Some industries are fading away and some companies are financially strapped; the index holds them in proportion to their market values. The index is bailed out by holding the rising stars and cash cows, also in proportion. Index investors don't need to sweat the details, only whether the balance is more favorable than negative. Unless a country's whole economic system is corrupt or outmoded, the net is usually positive.

The valuation and returns of an index fund are again sorts of group averages for the entire group of stocks, with spectacular bargains offsetting grotesquely overvalued blimps—that is, if you admit that bargains and bubbles exist, which the EMH denies. For those of us who aren't true believers, it's possible for the index itself to sell for more than its intrinsic value, and for expected stock returns to be comparatively unattractive. Here, I'd ask you to meditate on the expected returns of a broader opportunity set. You can put your money into domestic and foreign stocks, various classes of bonds, real estate, cash, art, gold, Spam™, and munitions. Typically, but not always, stocks are the savvy alternative.

Index investors will minimize regrets differently than stock-pickers, focusing most on curbing unnecessary activity and expanding their knowledge base. They tend not to dwell too much on intrinsic value, although I think they would have fewer regrets if they did. Fiduciary misconduct and financial failure are, for them, bolts from the blue. In contrast, concentrated stock-pickers can be blown up on any of these fronts: emotional decisions, gaps in understanding, working with bad dudes, unexpected disruption, too much debt, or just paying too much. Although they would love to minimize all of these risks simultaneously, they can't. The good news is that stock-pickers can outperform simply by cutting out the stuff that drags down returns. They seek out undervalued stocks of companies they understand in growing industries with honest, capable management.

How to Think About Investing

In investing, everything begins with decisions. There's a hall-of-mirrors quality to it as we are assessing the decisions of others. We're dealing with the unknown future, and the facts are not in evidence. So, as social animals, we seek other opinions, which can be wrong, sometimes dramatically. As individuals, the best we can do is make decisions mindfully, using our System 2 (thinking slowly), aiming for fewer but better choices. Most directly, this means avoiding excessive turnover and trying to invest based on "What's it worth?" rather than "What happens next?" It also means choosing a format for investing that works for you—whether stocks, index funds, actively managed funds, or something else altogether.

2

Silly Human Tricks (Decision Biases)

The degree of one's emotion varies inversely with one's knowledge
of the facts—the less you know, the hotter you get.

—BERTRAND RUSSELL

PSYCHOLOGISTS CLAIM THAT HUMANS systematically make predictable errors of judgment—particularly in complex, ambiguous situations like the stock market, where the problems are not clearly structured (unlike casinos) and the answers are draped in randomness. Investing forces you to reach conclusions with inadequate data. No wonder we choose based on the information right in front of us, neglecting evidence we can't see, or latch onto a well-told story rather than digging into complexity. Stories are about unique events, not statistical groups, so we either don't calculate odds or else miscalculate them, using the wrong reference point. This chapter covers the ways psychological biases misinform our investments, and how the stock market charges us for certain emotions and behaviors and pays us for others.

We tend to weight information based on its *availability* (ease of recall), because our System 1 thinks *What You See Is All There Is*. This WYSIATI means that it's the recent, dramatic, unexpected, and personally relevant images that jump to mind. What doesn't come to mind is historical, statistical, theoretical, and average. Even with work, a stock's value is opaque. Instead, the shortcut is: today's news is good, so buy the stock. Such investors blow with the wind, claiming their actions are "data dependent." Every reasoned decision is based on data. Which data? Why?

After a crash, the risks of stocks are front and center, whereas late in a bull market, the stellar returns of risky glamour stocks are more prominent. Extrapolating the recent past leads to buying expensive stocks and selling cheap. Likewise, the funds and asset classes that have done well this quarter make headlines; the fact that stocks have typically out-earned Treasury bills over most long periods does not. During industrial booms, the record profits of deeply cyclical businesses are reported, without remarking that not so long ago they lost money, and will again. The emissions scandal and car recall plaguing Volkswagen in 2016 sent its stock plummeting. The scandal may bear on the question of whether Volkswagen was well positioned and well managed, but is so shocking that it overwhelms any attempt to answer it. A different question was substituted and answered: Sell the stock! *Now*!

Instead, shine a spotlight on the evidence that is silent. Lurking in the background are unexamined assumptions about society and institutions. To fix recency bias, study history—the longer and broader, the better. To envision the future, investors need some idea of the normal baseline. Discover which things change and which endure. Statistics, probability, and the outside view are key. History is especially important because people repeat what works, but in the stock market we don't get timely feedback on our decisions—and what we do get is mostly noise.

The downside of history is the *narrative fallacy*. In *The Black Swan* (2010), Nassim Taleb wrote:

> The narrative fallacy addresses our limited ability to look at sequences of facts without weaving an explanation into them, or, equivalently, forcing a logical link, *an arrow of relationship*, upon them. Explanations bind facts together. They make them all the more easily remembered; they help them *make more sense*. Where this propensity can go wrong is when it increases our *impression* of understanding.

In other words, a problem arises when we see causation where there is none.

If we're more inclined to believe dubious stories when they're palpable, visible, personal, emotionally appealing, unusual, and confirm what we already believe, then we should move in the opposite direction. Push toward longer, multiple histories, comparative history, statistical history, and theory generally. Still, data mining is a growth industry, and it's never been easier to come up with spurious correlations between the prices of Amazon stock and silver, or the S&P 500 and butter production in Sri Lanka. Investors need an explanation that holds up over time, plus numbers, plus skepticism throughout.

It *Wasn't* Inevitable

One outgrowth of the narrative fallacy is *hindsight bias*, the revisionist history tendency to think that an outcome was inevitable and predictable all along. But, really, the needed information wasn't available. Personally, I combat hindsight bias by keeping company files, intermittently noting reasons for my trades. Others keep an investment diary. This might include a *premortem*, in which one mentally time travels, finds that one's decision has turned out poorly, and conjectures the reasons for the flop. Often when I refer back to notes, I find that the original reason for buying has been replaced by a new one, which can be even stronger, or may be a sell signal. I was originally interested in Monster Beverage for its natural fruit drinks, but the stock's gains were being driven by explosive growth in its energy drink. Conversely, energy company asset values based on $110 oil looked silly when the oil price was $45.

Anchoring

Because stories are appealing, we often begin with the wrong (statistical) reference point, which is called *misplaced anchoring*. Sometimes people are highly suggestible and, when prompted with an irrelevant number, anchor on it. For example, investors often can't bring themselves to sell a stock for less than their cost, hoping to get back to even. (Instead, they should decide based on the intrinsic value of the stock today.) For stocks that have rallied sharply from an absurdly undervalued price, Fidelity fund manager Peter Lynch advised "mental whiteout" of the gains you have missed, in order to focus on today's opportunity for further gains.

Any single number can be a misplaced anchor—be it a stock's previous highs, a historical valuation ratio, or estimated earnings. It usually isn't relevant to compare today's price/earnings ratio (P/E) for a small-cap or growth stock to its five-year average, because its growth profile and market conditions may have shifted radically. Instead, care about what its P/E should be today, based on what you know, perhaps by comparing it to similar opportunities. It also helps to look at a mosaic of data in assessing value, rather than reducing decisions to one single ratio.

By using the outside view on the proper reference set, you can anchor on better estimates of probabilities. The correct statistical reference category includes all the cases that were similarly placed when the group was formed, including the ones that are no longer around. More data usually produce more reliable predictions. But when you know that a group contains apples and oranges, a narrower reference class is better. Here we must avoid survivorship bias, or studying only the examples that successfully made it through. Later we will investigate why some industries and companies are more prone to failure than others.

More broadly, incorrect anchoring and WYSIATI can lead us to skip steps, thinking we're nearer to the conclusion than we are. Growing companies are worth more than melting ice cubes. Top-quality businesses can be valued more accurately than junky commodity firms, but identifying an outstanding blue-chip grower doesn't prove that it's a buy at any price.

Seek Refuting Evidence

Confirmation bias is the tendency, when you think something is true, to seek evidence to confirm it and ignore refuting facts. The lizard brain makes quick decisions about urgent physical dangers. But when we invest, we need an independent, accurate answer—not a quick one. With everyone digitally connected, it is increasingly hard to avoid the echo chamber. Social networks and other media explicitly try to feed you content that you like and presumably agree with. Investment management has always been a clubby occupation—asset managers have similar backgrounds and shared habits of mind. When a stock goes up after I buy it, and colleagues congratulate me on the score, it's hard not to take this as proof that I was right. Instead, I should be asking whether I was wrong but lucky and the stock is now overvalued.

Seek out the refuting evidence or bearish story. Invert. Consider whether the opposite story also makes sense. For example, low or negative interest rates are said to stimulate the economy. Inverted: Low interest rates depress the economy by signaling that the government is panicked about the economy (and you should be too)! Savers will have less interest income and so will need to spend less to meet their financial goals. Everything has a shadow side. Find it. Except near bear market lows, every investment usually has some defect, even if it's just that it's overpriced. Also, absence of evidence isn't evidence of absence; just because fraud can't be proved doesn't mean it didn't take place.

Bull

By shutting out refuting evidence, we become vulnerable to *overoptimism* that our chosen stocks will flourish. Wall Street encourages this tendency because anyone can buy a stock, while only owners can sell. Buy recommendations far outnumber sells. For estimates of a company's earnings more than a year out and long-term growth rates, reality chronically falls short. Declining earnings are rarely forecast but often occur. This does not apply to predictions of the next two quarters, which, if anything, are slightly low. Companies and analysts tacitly collude to create quarterly "upside surprises." Skepticism and a comparison of forecasts with past results can counter overoptimism.

Some people can't handle the truth and are in denial. When there's a loss, unsuccessful investors try to shift blame. In small doses, we all claim our skill produced good outcomes and blame luck for bad results. But it's your fault, so sort out what happened. Don't let loyalty to coworkers or an organization interfere with the search for truth. You can fix a problem only if you recognize and diagnose it correctly. Ask yourself whether there are things that you do not want to know. When the problem is that you don't know the answer, but no one else does either, accept that. Set out in search of questions you can answer. People who can't handle the truth should let someone else manage their money.

Highly Overconfident

Investment institutions are rife with *overconfidence* that *their* answer is right. Wall Street is a magnet for alpha males and people born on third base who think they've hit a triple. Seriously, being cocksure helps careers. In fields where ability is easily measured, self-assurance and skill usually go hand-in-hand. Attempts to detect investing skill are thrown off by noise and streakiness, but clients still flock to a coherent story, told confidently. Overconfidence might even be *rational*, in that economic man fearlessly takes any risks that will maximize wealth. Chickens like me won't take risks unless we're paid. From the cheap seats, it looks like some triumphant, bold risk-takers were just lucky.

Confidence becomes overconfidence when you seriously miscalculate the odds and take risks that leave you uncomfortable. To believe that your analysis is right and the market wrong, you need confidence, which, without a valid reason, is arrogance. You *should* be confident in proportion to your own skill, knowledge, consistency, and patience, even if that's not the signal that the market is giving you today. It also helps to know the boundaries of your knowledge and skill. I am more confident with stocks than bonds, for example, and the long term over the short term. Be wary of topics at the edge of your expertise (like, for me, the nuances of psychology).

Decisions can also be affected by whether trade-offs are *framed* as losses or gains. For example, framed as a recurring, certain loss of a premium, no one would buy insurance. Instead, it's sold as gaining certainty that policyholders will not suffer from a catastrophic loss. When something is presented as a gain, people usually choose the guaranteed or safer option. When presented as a loss, they pick the riskier option, which in this case would be going uninsured for a devastating event. Investing is all about trade-offs between risk and return, and among diverse risks, such as fiduciary dishonesty, mismanagement, obsolescence, and financial failure. Unless you really are getting something for nothing, comparisons shouldn't be framed as losses or gains, but as trade-offs.

Recognize Mistakes *Quickly*

Investors are often said to be *myopically loss averse* because they are quicker to sell to take profits than they are to recognize losses. They are pulling the flowers and watering the weeds. However, if the intrinsic value of a stock is unchanged, it isn't a mistake to hold a fallen stock. I might even buy more. It is a mistake to anchor on an old value when the situation has deteriorated severely and the stock is now overpriced. It's also a mistake to sell if the stock's value has surged faster than the price. Be quick to recognize mistakes, not necessarily losses.

Profit from Mistakes of Others

Given all of these oh-so-human frailties, some argue that rules-based investing by the numbers is the solution. I don't fully agree. Algorithms, bots, and screens do take the emotion out of investing. Increasingly used by quantitative investors ("quants"), these tools often function like idiot savants, doing complex things extraordinarily well while making a mess of simple tasks. For example, "flash crashes" have caused prices to briefly plunge to levels far below any commonsense estimate of value.

System 1 reflects our species' hardwired wisdom from earlier times and makes simple tasks simple—for humans. I worry that quants forget that stocks are not just numbers but part ownership of businesses, run by people. For now, I think humans are better at gauging whom to trust and visualizing how societies, institutions, and technology might interact and evolve. My ideal is Spock: half human, half Vulcan.

One last run at rescuing (rational) economic man: The stock market charges us for certain emotions and behaviors, and pays us for others. Consumers pay money to buy goods and services that make them feel a certain way. Even for ridiculous purchases, like Vegas gambling sprees, the consumer is said to be king. If investors can select stocks that make them feel the same way, shouldn't they be willing to give up an equivalent amount of money to do so? With volatile glamour stocks, you get the same kick as a trip to Vegas, and your losses are tax deductible. Investors often don't realize that there is a hidden cost for everything that normal persons desire: action, excitement, fun, comfort, social acceptance, popularity, and social exclusivity. There's also shadow income from patience, boredom, worry, courage, pain, loneliness, being a nerd, and looking like an idiot.

The most expensive emotions are seeking comfort and panic, which induce unplanned purchases and sales. "Oh crap, how could I lose half my money in a conservative stock? The doommongers were right. I must destroy the evidence now." Followed by, "I was right to panic, and can't go back." Hanging out with the celebrity stocks is snazzy fun while it lasts. Conversely, value investors worry that the market might be right and that the situation may truly be pitch black when we think it's overcast gray. When our facts prove out, being a nerd can be quite rewarding.

While I believe that patient people make better decisions than hyperactive thrill-seekers, taxes guarantee that even if they hold the same stocks, patience will win. Commissions and fees accentuate this, but ignore them for now. Consider four investors, all of whom face tax rates of 35 percent on short-term trades and 15 percent on holdings of a year or longer. They all buy the same stock, which appreciates 8 percent every year, compounded, and doesn't pay a dividend. The only difference is how often the investors sell their stock and immediately buy it back. One does it every six months; the others do it at intervals of one, ten, and thirty years. Over thirty years, the lethargic trader accumulates almost twice the value of the frequent trader (table 2.1).

Table 2.1
Effect of Taxes on Thirty-Year Compound Return

	Trade every:			
	6 Months	1 Year	10 Years	30 Years
Pretax Return	8.0%	8.0%	8.0%	8.0%
$1,000 Compounds to	$4,576	$7,197	$7,822	$8,703
After Tax Return	5.2%	6.8%	7.1%	7.5%

Note: The tax rate for stocks held less than one year is 35%; long-term holdings are taxed at 15%.

Similarly, trading costs and fund management fees drag down net returns and compound over time. Suppose you invested in a hedge fund charging 2 percent of assets and 20 percent of gains. The fund happened to be the six-month trader described above. Assume transactions costs of 0.03 percent of assets per year. After taxes, your return would be 3.1 percent a year. Over thirty years, your $1,000 would grow to $2,499. All of this is in praise of doing nothing, or choosing a seemingly slothful manager with moderate fees.

It's easier to be patient with boring stocks. When I'm paid for accepting boredom, they are among my favorites. Stable, low-volatility stocks have historically done better than theory would predict, and exciting, risky stocks have fared worse. In theory, investors are paid for accepting volatility, but historical returns suggest that risk may actually be an *amenity* for some speculators. Constant motion is fun, especially when it's upward. If you could exactly time when a bull market would start and end, you would want the shares with the maximum possible beta (a measure of relative volatility).

I doubt the intermediate future will be like the past for stable, boring stocks. Quants, having noted that low-volatility ("low-vol") stocks have done well, now are marketing portfolios based on the low-vol "factor," pushing up their prices. The factor worked before because historically this class of stocks was undervalued. The other reason for the popularity of low-vol is that savers who normally put cash in their savings account or money market fund now earn almost nothing. To earn income, they must invest in stocks but wish they could regain the stable value of a savings account. Barring a crash, I'd expect returns on low-vol shares to support the theory that investors should be paid more for taking risk.

Social acceptance is perhaps the most universal comfort. Of all the motivations of those who make millions they don't need, social acceptance, popularity, and respect are surely near the top. Some firms are more accepted, popular, and respected than others, and this reflects on their owners. Shares of the most popular and respected companies tend to sell at higher valuation multiples than others, and historically, expensive stocks have underperformed on the market. Usually, businesses are popular and respected because they, and their stock, have done very well. But having set a very high bar, many can't keep it up, and for them, the penalty is steep.

It's uncomfortable, but investors do much better with shares that are temporarily in the doghouse. Stocks that aren't popular, respected, or even socially acceptable usually sell at depressed prices. In the 1980s and 1990s, cigarette stocks were shunned as selling socially unacceptable, noxious products that kill. Even though earnings were compounding rapidly, for decades tobacco stocks had sold at discounted P/Es compared to the overall stock market (with only brief exceptions as in 1972–1973). Since then, even though smoking remains a health hazard, and fewer cigarettes are sold every year, the stocks have beaten the market hugely over time, and their P/Es have expanded.

Almost by definition, the biggest mispricing will involve a glaring, hideous defect that popular opinion thinks cannot be overcome. That's when your lonely, preferably well-researched conclusion that it either can be resolved, or isn't so bad, will be rewarded. In principle, we would always buy understandable, well-run, durable franchises at bargain prices, but in practice the market must think that some element is missing. On average, you are paid for being a nerd and sorting out the true situation. Even more, you are rewarded for the courage to act on an unpopular opinion that made you look like an idiot, provided it turns out to be correct. Before then, there's endless pain and worry that, indeed, the crowd is right.

Are you are willing to do the digging and endure the pain, loneliness, and worry that go with superior returns? Economic man is willing, but many are not. Personally, I tolerate boredom well but am not eager to take pain. If it all seems too much for you, your best options are to invest in an index fund or a low-cost fund in a well-resourced fund complex whose managers take a long-term horizon. Even then, your impatient trading may destroy the benefit of your manager's patience.

About economists: Their goofy, surreal psychological assumptions are coded advice. Invest where you have an edge through superior information. Consider the popular interpretation, but also variant perspectives. Estimate the value of stocks; don't trade for other reasons. Try to look out as far into the future as possible. Be (calculatingly) bold. Minimize taxes, fees, and transaction costs; this is done most easily by trading infrequently. Above all, don't underestimate your rivals. If you are average, don't count on superior results. The perfect-competition assumption—that in competitive markets firms earn only a fair profit—means go where competition isn't.

Psychologists advise that you broaden your horizons beyond the easily available information to include social context, historical statistics, and some notion of baseline and normal. Be skeptical if you think you've fallen for the narrative fallacy. To correct a misplaced data anchor, use the outside view. Focus on what a stock is worth today. Counteract confirmation bias by seeking refuting evidence and asking whether the opposite thesis is also true. Frame trade-offs as trade-offs, not as losses or gains. Think for yourself.

The aim of mindful decisions is to ensure that things that matter are never slaves to the trivial. By widening your perspective and reflecting, you can avoid unforced errors and being backed into tough choices. Separate the idea from the person, and let ideas fight, not people.

3

Gamblers, Speculators, and Investors

CAPTAIN RENAULT: I'm shocked, shocked to find that gambling is going on here.

CASINO ATTENDANT: Your winnings, sir.

—CASABLANCA (MOVIE, 1942)

Gambling, Speculation, and Investment

IN THE PUBLIC EYE, it all looks like gambling, and sometimes it is. Wall Street confuses things further by calling all of its customers "investors." Awkwardly, every investment involves some form of speculation about future events. More dangerously, many who believe that they are investing are actually speculating. The distinctions matter because investors gather information and manage risk and uncertainty differently than speculators.

My aim in this chapter is to warn you away from unintentional gambling and from speculating on prices, psychology, and topics that are unknowable. Unlike at casinos, most of the people who gamble on Wall Street aren't aware that that's what they are doing. Some categories of speculation deserve their bad reputation, while others are necessary for our whole capitalist system to exist. People speculate to prepare for the future when vital information is missing and sometimes unobtainable. In my opinion, you'll invest more profitably if you speculate on factors that affect the stream of profits generated by an enterprise, rather than on market prices or crowd psychology.

The spectrum splits along two dimensions. First, event or holistic? Are you looking for an identifiable trigger or catalyst to produce a winning

Table 3.1
Possible Combinations of Levels of Research and Focus of Research

	Event	Holistic
Thorough research	Shrewd speculation	Investment
Sloppy research	Reckless speculation	Risky investment
No research	Gambling	Gambling

trade, or rather for a holistic (comprehensive, long-term) sense that capital and income are secure? Second, is this well-researched or not? Have you done thorough research, sloppy research, or none at all?

The possible combinations of an event-based trade with diligent, slapdash, and no investigation into whether the odds are favorable, are mapped out in table 3.1. I would call an event-based trade based on careful research a *shrewd speculation*. With casual research, it becomes a *reckless speculation*. With zero research, it's gambling. Likewise, the same range of depth of research can be mapped out for holistic trades. An *investment* is the product of thorough research that indicates that capital is broadly secure and an adequate return should be earned. Cursory research and a holistic approach add up to a *risky investment*. A generalized faith that somehow everything will come up roses, without supporting evidence, is gambling.

Know the Odds

Once you have grasped probability and statistics, gambling usually loses its charm. There's a famous story about a team of card counters from MIT, but they *weren't* gambling—because they had analyzed their chances. When you don't know your odds, or care about them, gambling truly is a tax on ignorance. For example, suppose collectively lottery players get back only 65 percent of the proceeds from ticket sales. Probabilistically, you lose 35 percent of your money the second you buy the ticket. The final outcome is typically a complete loss.

I did once gamble in financial markets, but at the time I thought I was speculating on interest rates. I'm sure most stock market gamblers do it unwittingly, as I did. As I discuss later, I quickly made, and lost, what was then a huge amount of money to me, bullheadedly thinking that my early victory proved that I was right. Some telltale signs of gambling include betting on discrete events, near-instantaneous timelines, use of leverage, overcommitment to one story, and no way to gauge whether the odds are in your favor.

Unwise Speculations

Speculation, properly done, isn't gambling. Like sex, speculation has a shady reputation but is universally practiced, often enjoyed, and none of us would be here without it. Going back to the Latin root word, *speculare* means "to observe or look out as from a watch tower." The only way we can prepare for and possibly shape what fate brings us is if we observe and try to imagine it. Businesses must somehow anticipate what customers might want, where materials will come from, and the quantities required. Investing can't be done without conceiving when and how capital might be in danger, or where it might be super-productive. The process of envisioning and creating the future can never be flawlessly logical, but without it rational economic man has no basis for his calculations.

Investors must unavoidably speculate, but many of the most popular topics of speculation are not amenable to research that gives them an edge. Among the most treacherous speculations are on share prices, commodity prices, and crowd psychology—unless you have something that can tell you that you are wrong, like a notion of fair value. If markets are efficient, past price movements should tell you nothing about the future path of prices. If true—and it is true *enough*—this means that research into historical price changes won't be rewarded.

The logic of price momentum is shifting and fickle. Numerous studies have shown that in the short term, rising prices *do* accurately predict further gains, and declines accurately predict further losses, sometimes even more powerfully than indicators of value. About a year or so later, momentum starts to reverse, so traders must be nimble. In the Internet age, it seems utterly ridiculous that momentum reflects slow dissemination of information or underreaction to news. More likely, momentum reflects overreaction to news, social proof, and piling on. That said, companies often dribble out bad news, and the issues that cause falling profits are often slow to fix. Value buyers must ensure that their expectations have been shaken down enough.

Momentum is a fast-paced game with a complex interplay between how far out you look, and how far out you think the crowd is looking. Consider a game in which each participant enters a whole number between zero and one hundred. The winner is the one who chooses the number, rounding down, nearest to half the average guess of the other participants. So have you picked a number yet? Some people might enter fifty, which is the average of numbers between zero and one hundred. But if you are aiming for half of the average guess, you might divide fifty in half and pick twenty-five. Knowing that your opponents might also do that calculation, it might be better to guess twelve. Long-term investors try to look out as far as the eye can see. Further iterations would indicate six, three, and one. A mathematician would say that at the limit, the endgame is zero.

When this game is played in real life, the winners gaze a step or two ahead, but no further. Those who answered fifty or twenty-five weren't thinking enough about second-order effects, the reactions to events. For example, a sharp spike in a commodity price will bring on more supply, which might blunt price momentum. Look slightly ahead and ask: If these are the obvious facts, how are others likely to respond? Because it's a game, it all depends on who else is playing. Conversely, zero never wins in these games because other participants rarely consider how it ends. Still, to me, speculating on how long others will remain shortsighted verges on gambling.

Research into group behavior can pay off, but usually not with the exact date and number sought by speculators. Stock market bubbles occur when traders latch onto a compelling initial premise and extend the logic too far. Speculators take rising prices as proof that they were correct. Their error becomes apparent to them only in the fullness of time. People avoid reason until they have tried everything else. If you fancy that there will be clear signs as to *when* the party will wind down, as most speculators do, you will surely be drawn into the thundering herd, despite knowing the inevitable result.

The other set of impossible inquiries lies in the distant haze. For example, the current dividend yield of the S&P 500 is 2 percent. At that rate it would take you fifty years to recover your purchase cost in dividends. Should we therefore handicap whether in decades hence the economy will be in a boom, chugging along, or depressed? I don't know enough to say. Instead, I look for situations in which it is less absurd to visualize the distant future and steer away from speculations that would be upended if I somehow did know the state of the economy decades out.

Speculations of Enterprise

Topics that are worth speculating on include whether management will make the right decisions when the time comes, whether an industry is prone to failure because of commoditization, obsolescence, or financial overreach, and what a security's value might be. Because we're anticipating responses to challenges and opportunities that have not yet presented themselves, no one really knows. However, the track records of executives and industries can provide useful indications. For example, bricks-and-mortar retailers will have to sell on the Internet, or risk being destroyed by Amazon. My speculations center on which categories of merchandise will move more slowly to the Internet, how Internet and in-store transactions might combine, and which chains have the systems and adaptability to serve customers in both formats.

It's impossible to invest successfully in early stage biotech and Internet companies without speculating on whether the science works, whether customers will like the product, and how large the potential market might be. If you're clueless about beta agonists or B2B CRM wave analytics, and why customers might want them, and you buy the shares anyway, you're gambling. But for savvy insiders who are close to the industry, the payoffs can be incredible. Without the specialized category of extreme speculators called venture capitalists, many of these science projects would never get the cash needed to turn ideas into products. Progress depends on this sort of speculation, in which income and certainty about the future are afterthoughts.

Investors focus on the cash that can be paid out as dividends by a business over its whole life, while speculators key off discrete events. When a stock is pitched as a play on anything, stop. We are being offered a speculation that will succeed only if other factors are less decisive than the one in focus. For example, airline stocks are touted as plays on falling oil prices, but this trade might fail on weak traffic, fare price wars, labor disputes, or bungling management. In betting parlors you can pick identifiable risks, but with stocks the attractive risks are bundled with less attractive risks.

Certainty That Capital Is Safe and Returns Are Adequate

Ben Graham, the father of value investing, wrote, "An investment operation is one which, upon thorough analysis, promises safety of principal and an adequate return." This opens up the issues of (a) what an adequate return would be, (b) how we judge that principal is safe, and (c) how much analysis is enough.

An adequate return is the greater of the rate currently available in the market or whatever you think is acceptable. While expected yields on bonds are readily quoted, for stocks they must be inferred, with a wide margin of error. Just because you require a higher return does not give it to you. In 2017, some bonds in Japan and Europe carried a negative yield, meaning bondholders get back *fewer* yen or euros in the future than they invested. Ugh! The alternatives are to hold cash or another asset, which may also offer lousy returns. An investment is always rooted in price and current circumstance; today, some investment-grade bonds (despite the label) are no longer investment vehicles.

If shares are partial interests in enterprises, not just numbers on a screen, the certainty we seek must emanate from the business itself. Training our minds on businesses rather than stock prices moves us in the right direction. We're not equally equipped to analyze every security or industry, but if we focus on spots where we are conversant, we'll be more certain that we've put together the evidence properly. By entrusting our capital only to honest and capable executives, we reduce the risk of malfeasance. Some industries are brutally competitive and change relentlessly, and some companies depend on the kindness of bankers. Go elsewhere, where there's more safety.

With stocks, the certainty that the principal value is safe is more metaphorical than with bonds, but is quantitative in both cases. Buying a one-dollar security for sixty cents provides a wider *margin of safety* than paying eighty cents. However, value is a forecast, so my dollar might be your seventy cents. Other than cash, many accounting numbers are estimates, so one company's dollar of earnings might be reported as a different number elsewhere. With stocks, safety of principal consists of an ample margin of safety calculated using prudent forecasts on a company following conservative accounting principles.

Diligent research increases certainty, both real and perceived. It also reaches a point of diminishing returns. Repeated exposure to variations on the same news can lead us to exaggerate its importance. Some information has a short shelf life and can become stale before a decision is reached. Our minds can handle only a limited number of facts at the same time—the consensus is around seven—so more inputs don't improve decision-making. It's more about recognizing patterns than about solving a polynomial equation. Above all, because we're trying to foresee the remote future, some answers must remain forever murky.

Too many investors don't think enough about information just slightly out of view and spend too much time on news that has been endlessly retweeted. After reviewing the quarterly earnings reports of a company for many years, I get a feel for which drivers matter. Getting that feel will take much longer if you review the reports only as they arrive rather than studying those that came before. Of course, news is available 24/7, and history takes digging. For the present-minded, a crooked or inept executive is newsworthy only if he or she has done something outrageous lately. Businesses that are overextended or suffering from changing times or competition draw attention only when they're actively crashing.

Tilt the odds in your favor by viewing data over longer time horizons and through the lens of large statistical groups. For example, I can't predict the day-to-day fluctuations of the market a year in advance, but I find it useful to know that, measured from their daily highs to their lows, there have been twenty-five 20 percent bear markets since 1928. Most unnerving! Oddly, the S&P 500 has had a total return loss worse than 20 percent in only six of those eighty-seven years. Many bear markets had been preceded by blow-off spikes or were followed by sharp snapback rallies that offset the worst of the damage within the year. Statistically, as observations are added over time (or more members of the group are observed), the central tendency is likely to emerge. Instead of making point estimates, I think of ranges.

Diversification can increase the certainty that unforeseen events won't blow up your portfolio. The fortunes of some industries, like airlines, rise as those of others fall, like oil producers. If you really don't want to speculate on oil prices, you might buy shares of an airline and an oil producer. While diversification reduces risk, it doesn't go away, even when you diversify across the entire market. Investors in an S&P 500 index fund bear only that unavoidable market risk and not the idiosyncratic risks of specific stocks. However, if you are any good at judging value, over time you should expect to beat the market, and diversifying across a portfolio of undervalued stocks should reduce the chances of a total bomb.

Distracted from Value

Technology is an extension of human behavior, and while in some ways it makes us better investors, it is an even greater boon to gambling and pulls us toward it. The good news first: Modern search and screening software is a massive timesaver for locating statistically attractive securities. Google also makes it easier to find news articles, industry information, and competitive analysis. The EDGAR system, the federal online library of corporate annual reports, is a miraculous and underused resource. Earnings conference calls are usually now open to everyone, everywhere on the Web.

The Internet is also an advertising and news medium that competes for your attention, usually by appealing to your lizard brain. The commercial intent of the Internet is to distract you with ads; attention-grabbing items of doubtful provenance make great clickbait. All of this distraction leads to multitasking. If you're doing multiple things at once, they all have to be pretty mindless. In that vein, here's a vivid, probably apocryphal story: A New York investment analyst, while attending to her iPhone, stepped into traffic and perished. Don't multitask while investing!

The average holding period for New York Stock Exchange–listed stocks has fallen from around seven years in 1960 to four months in 2016. These statistics are doubtless distorted by the most hyperactive traders, but I suspect median holding periods are shorter too. High-speed computer networks have made online trading cheap and super-easy, and now there's an arms race among algorithmic traders. With dedicated on-exchange servers and data lines, high-speed traders have cut trade execution times to milliseconds. The ease, speed, and cost of trading are terrific, but they make it too easy to dart in and out of securities on a whim. Treasury bonds change hands several times a year, on average.

Keep Your Thinking Cap On

Speculation can appeal to us because it involves identified catalysts, specific situations, and finite timelines—but these can also be drawbacks. With equities, a specific play like fuel prices and airlines is occasionally derailed by factors that speculators had pushed to the background. Also, when you limit your ability to patiently wait until your idea bears fruit, your investments become more speculative. For example, options have a preset expiration date, and margin debt must be paid back, which involuntarily shortens your time horizon.

Here's a quick checklist to be sure you actually are investing, not gambling:

1. Are you thinking about the profits of the enterprise as a whole, over time?
2. Have you investigated enough to feel fairly certain about your conclusions?
3. Will the business remain stable enough to say that your capital is secure?
4. Is it reasonable to expect an adequate return?

Investors in index funds will interpret these questions differently than stock-pickers. For indexers, the profits are for all five hundred of the companies in the Standard & Poor's index (S&P 500), not a specific enterprise, so a different sort of investigation is required. Many of the sources of uncertainty for an individual stock—including crooked or inept management, obsolescence, and financial failure—are reduced by diversification. While the index is a very complete form, you can also diversify through individual stocks. Part V of this book looks more at the topic of what returns to expect, both for indexes and for specific stocks.

4

Mind Over Money

The things we admire in men, kindness and generosity, openness, honesty, understanding and feeling, are the concomitants of failure in our system. And those traits we detest, sharpness, greed, acquisitiveness, meanness, egotism and self-interest, are the traits of success. And while men admire the quality of the first they love the produce of the second.

—JOHN STEINBECK

Businesspeople and Investors

NEARLY ALL OF THE ENTREPRENEURS on *Forbes* magazine's list of 400 richest billionaires founded firms that grew exponentially for decades. Think of Microsoft's Bill Gates, Alphabet's Larry Page, and Walmart's Sam Walton on the one hand. Most top investors on the list are value investors who became businesspeople along the way. Think of Warren Buffett, Charlie Munger, and Carl Icahn. It seems paradoxical. Investors invest in businesses, so shouldn't both entrepreneurs and investors benefit from growth or value? However, growth is not opposed to value. Rather, future growth is a component of value. While investors benefit from thinking like businesspeople, they play by different rules, define opportunity differently, and have distinct characteristics. This chapter explores the psychological traits of successful investors.

Entrepreneurs typically focus all their capital and energy on a single business venture. When that one business flourishes, it's glorious. Investors diversify, either on their own or through mutual fund managers mandated to hold at least twenty securities. Anyone who gets on the *Forbes* list must have extraordinary skill *and* luck (or the right parents). Diversification reduces the effects of luck for investors. To magnify the effects of skill, investors must carefully select for outstandingly favorable odds, bet heavily on them, and skip mediocre opportunities. Concentrating portfolios also amplifies the effect of luck, but this can hurt or help.

Warren Buffett took the idea of focused portfolios to an extreme, proposing an investment punchcard limited to only twenty opportunities in a *lifetime*. Like marriage, ownership of a business is an enduring commitment. If investing worked the same way, investors would set lofty standards and patiently wait for the right one. Mutual fund managers use up all twenty punches on their first day by necessity. Still I am intrigued by the idea of a punchcard. Unless you consider his Berkshire Hathaway one big punch, Buffett has used his billions to buy a few more cards.

It is the natural order of things that the most extreme outliers will mostly be undiversified businesspeople. But there are also undiversified investors who failed big. Yale University's endowment, for example, was wiped out in 1825 after it put almost the entire sum into Eagle Bank, which went under.

Shareholders need to appreciate how and why businesspeople think and act. That's because they are betting on both the cards and the player and do not hold the hand themselves. Professional investors are also businesspeople, in that we sell advice and management services. We are also like movie critics who trash films that they could not have produced themselves; the best of us have reviewed enough superior productions to judge appropriately. And while entrepreneurs hunt for customers that competitors have neglected, investors look for value that others have missed, which is sometimes the same thing, but often not.

Of course, not all successful investors are value investors. There are countless ways to make money in the stock market, each favoring a different personality type. Lucky reckless speculators and gamblers can do well, too, but for how long? The traits that help value investors often hurt shrewd speculators, and vice versa. Unless you are a rare stock biathlete (I'm not), I'd caution against jumping between investment and speculation. One can't play chess and tennis at the same time. But don't force the value approach; if it doesn't work for you, find one that does.

Patience is a virtue for investors, but speculators must worry about ideas and information going stale. It's only worthwhile to be patient with businesses with enduring strengths, a topic we'll come back to later. Calm emotional detachment helps investors, but speculators can make emotional sensitivity and worry work for them. Investors need a thorough, durable sort of decisiveness, while speculators need a more flexible kind.

Trained Intuition

In business, every personality type has a way to make money. But in successful investors, two traits stand out: what psychologists label as *thinking* and *intuitive*, or rational analysts. (Note that intuitive is not used here in the popular sense of "trust your gut." *Intuitive* is defined as attuned to pattern recognition, meaning, abstract theory, and the invisible, including the future.) Thinking people tend to make decisions based on logic (that is using their System 2), as opposed to *feeling* people, who decide based on people and feelings. Everything about the stock market is abstract—trying to guess what the future will bring, and what it means. Without theory, you'll get nowhere. I would call the combination of thinking and intuitive—grappling with the invisible in a logically consistent way—trained intuition.

Emotionally Aware But Let Reason Decide

Good analysts tend to favor thinking over feeling and to think rationally. They're alert to the biases and distortions of the sort described in chapter 2 and make an effort not to see facts selectively, overemphasize their importance, or overgeneralize. Where they can, they test hypotheses. They don't assume their prediction is an absolute fact.

Stoic detachment combined with emotional awareness is the perfect combination for stocks. Feel the fear, but let reason decide. The most *frequent* blunders come from those who believe everything their gut tells them. The *biggest* catastrophes come from people who are emotionally unaware when their gut is growling out a correct warning of something amiss. Worrying can be a good thing, if you don't stress out or feel too intensely. As a value investor, I like to worry when things *aren't* going wrong, because the emotional cost is lower. Most importantly, worry only if it will help you to work through the alternatives and find a better path. When the sky is predicted to fall and you can't save it, relax. Reduce news intake. Be happy.

Curious Skeptics

Every skilled investor I've met has been curious and a lifelong learner. They read broadly and constantly. For anticipating the future, it's more important to understand why things happen than what happened. By studying historical examples, I often find that some factors exert more, or less, influence than I would otherwise have thought. And when things happen that have never happened before, I study how others have handled unprecedented events in the past.

Curiosity needs to be balanced with skepticism. Everyone needs a spam filter and a crap detector—some way of classifying and throwing away redundant or wrong information. Things are often not as they seem in finance. Be skeptical and willing to challenge ideas others take for granted.

Independent Thinking

On the whole, students with high grade point averages achieve them through curiosity and diligence, but it's also possible to get high marks by gaming the system, sucking up to professors, and regurgitating whatever they want to hear. In investing, where doing nothing often prevents blunders, a certain style of laziness is adaptive, but mental laziness isn't, and not thinking independently is absolutely toxic. The entire game is about figuring out what others have missed. The largest prizes go to those who think differently and correctly. Some investing ideas will look stupid or crazy, and a few will be, but the alternative is mediocrity. Depending on the results, you will be called courageous, or arrogant and foolhardy. Don't be ashamed of error, only of failing to correct it. While university courses are evaluated on, perhaps, three quizzes and a term paper, the stock market never tells you which questions to work on, how to approach them, and whether you're out in left field.

Optimism for Solutions

Optimism is a powerful ally of entrepreneurs, but only one specific type helps investors: the optimism that with effort you will learn, grow, and find solutions to current dilemmas. In any endeavor in which you influence the outcome, optimism sustains you. Apple's Steve Jobs would not have been Steve Jobs without his "reality distortion field." If you believe that problems can be solved and solutions implemented, success *will* happen.

In many ways, investors do not control their fate, so *over*optimism only blinds them to risks and uncertainties and distorts the relative estimates of payoffs. Investors can determine the time and amount of a purchase or sale but cannot determine the price, except adversely. Undue pessimism causes one to miss opportunities and is exhausting to boot. The typical optimism of value investors consists of the lame belief that for a specific stock the outlook is overcast but is priced for pitch black. Perversely, when widespread panic sets in, value investors' sun comes out.

Discipline—*What* You Don't *Do*

Discipline can be shown by what you *don't* do or by what you *must* do. Investors need more of the first variety; speculators need more of the second. Staying within Warren Buffett's twenty punches implies not acting on scores of fairly attractive opportunities. Dividing an adult life span by twenty, an investor would lounge for years doing nothing, which might disturb clients or employers. It would look like analysis paralysis—and for a speculator, it would be. Conversely, an event-based trader whose event fails to materialize must sell. Ditto for momentum traders who use a rule that stocks that have fallen 12 percent must be sold. They can't convert to value investing for the day.

Agreeing to Disagree

Successful investors flout the social convention that if people do not agree, they do not like each other. Social life generally flows more easily when viewpoints are shared. However, in investing and science, discovering the truth comes first, so friendship is not undermined by variant perceptions when the facts aren't self-evident. You should also know that open-minded, analytical people will try out all sorts of quirky ideas that turn out to be bogus. They come around to the truth eventually.

Accepting Mistakes

Call it humility, call it honesty with yourself, but failing to admit to investment mistakes means failing investing. When you separate luck from skill, your skill improves. It's better to be good than to look good. From some perspective, every investor makes mistakes all the time. When I hang tough with a long-term holding when a slump is predictable, I have to concede that a nimble speculator might have spotted my mistake. While speculators' logic is usually short term, it may be correct for the long run. Psychopaths in investing benefit from not caring about other people, but usually their downfall is their inability to recognize when they are wrong. The ability to admit mistakes can be a barometer of overall truthfulness.

Shrewd speculators and investors study their experience to understand where their hits and misses are coming from and why they might win overall. For example, after being too adventurous with industries I didn't understand, I now stay away from some and keep positions of others tiny until I know more. My gut identifies many more people as shifty than really are; when I study their corporate accounting, I'm much better at spotting the *real* bad dudes. Being a coal analyst made me avoid businesses prone to competitive dogfights and obsolescence. In investing, being a cheapskate, and not paying up, helps—a lot. So I win by focusing on simple businesses, with honest management and proprietary products, bought cheaply. But during raging, thematic momentum bull markets, I lag pathetically.

Coping with Failure

Fidelity generally hires very bright, hardworking, ambitious, analytical types with a track record of success so when analysts wash out, it's rarely for technical reasons; usually it's because the stock market isn't a university and they haven't yet learned to cope with failure. Even with grade inflation, 55 percent wouldn't be a passing grade, but in the stock market, being right 55 percent of the time is as good as it gets. Stocks go down when they should go up and go up when down is forecast. For me, every market day brings a mosquito bite of failure, and some days, more serious bloodletting. I once suggested that we consider recruiting people with a track record of failure but was told there are better ways to hire resilient people with grit.

Comfort with Ambiguity

Good investors accept that they constantly work with ambiguous situations. Except for a few gifted finance professors, no one ever has perfect information. For someone to buy a stock, someone else must sell, presumably because that person thinks there's something wrong with it. Who's right? During bull markets, the air of mystery can be sexy and seductive, but during plunges, we assume the worst. It's a difficult trick to keep a relatively steady, or even countercyclical, tolerance for ambiguity. At the moments when you are stinging from ambiguous situations that cratered, and shedding risk as fast as you can, superb opportunities appear under shrouds. When frolicsome ventures have paid off more than you deserved, curb your enthusiasm and tilt toward well-defined earnings streams.

The Right Stuff

While investors must understand businesses and businesspeople, and often are in business themselves, they diversify across many holdings and must think probabilistically. The most successful investors tend to be rational, analytical sorts—*intuitive* and *thinking* in the psychological typology. The future can be understood only theoretically, because it is not yet reality. Reason is a better guide to stock decisions than emotions, so an emotionally detached but aware approach works best. Investors need to be resilient, because the stock market dishes out a lot of failure. They need to think independently, be willing to stand outside the crowd, and agree to disagree. The market rewards tolerance for ambiguity most when it is in short supply, so investors should aim to keep a constant or countercyclical tolerance.

PART II
Blind Spots

5

Need to Know?

Real knowledge is to know the extent of one's ignorance.

—CONFUCIUS

OUR MINDS ARE RESOURCEFUL in quickly reaching judgment based on scant information. Without this faculty, we would bog down in endless research and never make timely decisions. But it comes at the cost of skipping details that we later discover to be vital. For example, potential returns grab our attention, but not topics like risk control, incentives, and costs. We apply in new contexts shortcuts that work in a specific industry or country, not always successfully. Some people believe they can accurately predict economic statistics and, through them, interest rates, stock market fluctuations, and even prices of individual shares. Good luck! Until something gets lost in translation, we ignore cultural and institutional differences abroad, assuming that money is a universal language.

We overlook points because they don't fit with the story we had in mind. One remedy is to widen our horizons. I think bigger and then smaller, zooming out to theory and zooming in to finicky details. We can know facts, but also people, or how things get done. Some truths are objective, others are subjective. To contrarians' frustration, in finance many things are conventions, true when enough other people concur. But reflection takes time.

Here is the story of "Fred," who wasn't quite clear about his goals, how advisers work, and the mechanisms of complex securities like exchange-traded funds (ETFs).

"My portfolio is all ETF'd up," Fred grumbled. About four years earlier, Fred had hired a financial adviser who had invested his money mostly in ETFs. ETFs are investment pools that constantly create and redeem shares like mutual funds, but trade on exchanges as stocks. He knew his adviser had underperformed because his account had returned less than an S&P 500 index fund that he had hung onto. It also turned out to have trailed the Barclay's Bond Index as well. Something was wrong, but Fred couldn't put his finger on what.

Goals and Risk Tolerance

Some of the factors that determine your financial plan are objective, like age, income, and assets, but others like your risk tolerance and goals are best known to you. Before you hire expensive help, you must be clear about what you want to achieve. The adviser's job is to figure out *how* to reach your goals with a reasonable plan (and stick with it), not *what* your goals are. My bias is that you are an intelligent person and should do your own thinking. At the same time, recognizing that you don't know everything and need help can save you a lot of pain.

When people ponder their goals, they rarely imagine themselves in circumstances different from today. For example, younger people tend to close out their individual retirement accounts and spend down their savings when they change or lose jobs. People are more likely to lose their jobs during recessions when stock prices are low. One unfortunate event leads to another. Perhaps it's not really possible to plan for the unexpected, other than by saving more. The tricky part is choosing in prosperous times a mix of assets that will serve you when your income is lower. Fred couldn't, for example, reach his retirement income goals without stocks, but preferred nothing too racy.

Costs and Incentives

Fred was focused on what his adviser could do for his finances, and it didn't occur to him that his adviser was focused on what Fred could do for *his* finances. Investors' costs are someone's incentives. I suggested that Fred should ask *who* pays him. How much and for what? Is he in a position to put Fred's interests first? Or is he conflicted? Watch out for anything with a big sales load. His adviser's firm charged a fee based on the value of his account plus commissions on trades, a portion of which was paid to his adviser. The more trading his adviser did in his account, the more money he would make. Sure enough, looking through Fred's statements, he was totally swapping his holdings every eight months. The fees and commissions took a bite out of Fred's returns.

Investors unavoidably put their capital in others' hands—and prefer hands that deserve trust. An adviser may be only the first strand in a web of trust. He, in turn, relies on the honesty and ability of executives at funds he engages, who depend on the talents of the leaders of the businesses they own, who count on subordinates and business partners. Normally, officers are eager to provide indications of ability, albeit open to interpretation. Managers should be able to explain clearly what they are doing uniquely, why it succeeds, and show some numbers to back it up. But we are left to guess at motivation and ethics. I find clues by studying incentive schemes and choices of accounting principles. Later in this book, we return to the topic of avoiding betrayal by scoundrels and inept managers.

Why Does the Strategy Work?

You should not expect an investment strategy to beat the market unless you can identify how it proposes to do so, why the market isn't using these decision rules, and produce evidence that it is a fruitful approach. Index investors aim only to match the average, which is easily attained, excluding fees. Fred's adviser was doing something with "thematic sector rotation" and "factor investing," but the why was elusive. His adviser would catch shifts in economic momentum, jumping into the most dynamic factors and hottest industries. But he couldn't catalog the decision rules he used to trade ETFs or offer any proof that his strategy was effective.

I buy stocks for less than I think they are worth and hold them until they are fairly priced. This usually takes years. But if I have chosen well, their intrinsic value will have appreciated over time, earning not only an average return, but also the gap between price and value. Bargains appear only when investors sell shares with no regard for value, perhaps distraught by current prospects, or they are bored. My theory can't be proved directly, because value is a subjective forecast. But most estimates are grounded in historical financial data; the evidence is overwhelming that cheap stocks outperform, no matter whether measured by earnings, cash flow, or assets. My missteps usually arise when events move rapidly and unexpectedly, or I fail to separate the less certain elements of a forecast from the more certain.

Risk Control: Diversification

Managers and advisers are hired based on returns, but their essential job is to recognize and manage risk. Investors can't control returns, but they can decide which risks, and purchase and sale prices, are acceptable. There are two main ways to control investment risks—diversification and careful selection—that tug in opposite directions. Diversification across contrary and uncorrelated risks reduces the volatility of overall results, especially compared with a benchmark. The cheapest, easiest way to diversify is by indexing, but stock-pickers can also diversify by choosing opposed and uncorrelated risks. Stock selection reduces risk by eliminating unattractive risks, especially the risk of overpaying, and choosing attractive risks. In markets with a great dispersion of returns, selection is the more powerful tool.

Realistically, investors in a fund can't understand every one of its holdings, and they don't have to. But they should grasp how securities are chosen, and how flexible managers' marching orders might be. Some funds aim to match an index, while *actively managed* funds aim to beat it. For index funds, which criteria or formulas are used to determine the constituents of the index? What are the investment reasons for using this index or formula? For an actively managed fund, why does the manager think he might beat the market? Can his knowledge advantage be reduced to a trading algorithm? Is he surfing trends or taking a long-term view?

Because the S&P 500 index is widely used as the benchmark of the American market, funds that track this index are considered optimally diversified. If you view risk as the chance of lagging the benchmark, an S&P index fund is by definition very safe. It can be expected to exactly track the index, minus some (low) fees. But indexing doesn't allow you to control risk by avoiding overpriced securities and specific risks that you don't want. And when the overall market crashes, absolute performance matters. You still lose a bundle.

The outside view of expected returns for the category or index of stocks is the main focus of research for diversified investors. For stock-pickers it is just the first step. Both require a narrative to explain the data and provide an investment rationale. Both count on the law of large numbers to produce something like the recurring patterns of the past. It's not always straightforward or easy to define the right statistical reference class for the overall market or an investment strategy, and how long a time period suffices. The S&P 500 index fairly represents major American stocks, but not stocks universally. If you use different starting and ending points, you will often find that history contradicts itself about central tendencies.

Taking the widest possible outside view, considering all stocks globally, large and small, investing only in the S&P 500 is an **active** decision to deselect small and international shares. Beyond stocks, there are many other asset classes. The British FTSE 100, MSCI Developed World index, and perhaps three dozen other ETFs also provide low-cost, broadly diversified exposure to large companies. An S&P index fund *plus* a FTSE 100 index fund is better diversified than the S&P tracker alone. The purpose of broad, major market index funds in a portfolio is to earn average returns in global stock markets, not to make an exotic side bet. Stay away from stuff you don't know: foreign specialty, foreign currency, and commodity ETFs.

Comparing long histories of stock market returns from many nations, stocks have generally outearned bonds, with more price volatility, and the United States has fared better than many other countries. The facts seem to bear out the theory that stocks earn higher returns because they are riskier. So, for forecasting American stock returns, should we look at the record of all developed markets globally, or is the United States somehow exceptional? My guess is that America can maintain the part of its luck that comes from having rule of law, democratic institutions, relatively free markets, and great universities. But arguably some of the advantage was due to pure luck, or transitory factors.

Fred's adviser bought the Large Cap China ETF as a play on China's surging economy, but he missed something. The ETF is based on the FTSE China 50 index, which is heavily tilted toward state-owned enterprises (SOEs). Just over half of the index is in banks and financials, making it much less diversified than one might think. In China, full employment comes ahead of profits, so banks lend to inefficient SOEs with questionable finances. The most profitable, dynamic parts of China's growth story—small and private enterprises and technology—are barely represented in the index.

When a category's overall results are driven by outliers, indexing fails to produce the expected results. For some asset classes, like venture capital, junk bonds, and biotechnology, the distribution of returns looks nothing like the statistical bell curve. Depending on the mix of extreme losers and winners in the index, these categories will lurch between looking atrocious and fabulous; hence, I felt that Fred would have been better served with an actively managed fund rather than the high-yield bond index ETF. The companies with the most debt outstanding are the most important in the index. As a bond's yield falls, its price increases, boosting its weighting in the index. By contrast, for a given yield, live humans favor the strongest credits.

Selection: Themes Without Numbers

Stock-picking works best when you focus on areas in which it is not so arrogant to envision the future. Usually, your knowledge edge is greatest with details that are not cosmic, exciting, or fast moving. Unless you can recognize which of your forecasts are worthless or identical to the consensus, and *stop making them*, you won't succeed. Warren Buffett, for example, rejects businesses he doesn't understand; mediocre executives; cyclical, commoditized, and fast-changing industries; and stocks that aren't bargain priced. Almost no stocks remain, but Buffett has eliminated the possibility of severe disappointment.

Most ETFs are trading vehicles for targeting a narrow group, not diversifying. They're proposed as ways of getting away from single stock risk, but there's an art to combining the facts of various stocks. Suppose that two stocks make up an index, each trading at $50, with one earning $5 and the other losing $4 per share. Counting only the profitable company, the average price/earnings ratio (P/E) is ten. Summing both, the average P/E is one hundred. Or, for example, is the average of a dominant competitive position and a mediocre one average? Competitive rivalry is often the biggest risk to an industry, and that can be understood only by studying all of the major players.

His adviser's pitch for the smartphone ETF was that "everyone's getting one." But themes without numbers are hazardous, because you can't appraise value without them. Weirdly, suppliers to Apple and Samsung were far more important in the smartphone index than Apple and Samsung themselves. When many suppliers sell to gigantic customers, the suppliers hold the weaker hand. Also oddly, money-losing High Tech Computer and Blackberry had bigger weightings than Samsung, which earns billions. Much of the industry's growth is coming from selling cheap phones in Asia, often made by Huawei, which isn't in the ETF. Pricing pressure has meant that industry profits have sometimes fallen even as sales grew. Having identified the winners in an industry, I would want to invest only in them *at the right price*.

Data Without Understanding

Factor investing, or "smart beta," is the current trend with financial advisers and ETF promoters. Instead of viewing stocks as bundles of inseparable risks, they construct portfolios of stocks that score very high, or very low, in attributes like market capitalization, stock price volatility, stock price momentum, or measures of growth or value. Studies show that stocks with small market caps, low volatility, high momentum, and high value have outperformed, albeit sometimes erratically. For growth, the evidence is patchy and inconclusive. These factors had earlier been used to create taxonomies of funds and stocks, including the famous mutual fund "style box." My funds have always tilted toward small caps, value, and low volatility.

The experts don't agree on **why** these factors work, how to tell whether an earlier judgment about a factor was wrong, or how to identify decision rules for buying and selling. Although small caps have outperformed large over very long stretches, domestically and abroad, they have also had periods of lagging for multiple years. Perhaps small caps are discounted because information and analysis are harder to come by, but I'd argue this is less true than in the past. Small caps may indeed be riskier with less diversified, more cyclical, commoditized businesses often with greater customer concentration. But I can't refute the claim that the small cap effect is an artifact of a time before globalization and more relaxed antitrust enforcement.

Fred was baffled by the TVIX ETN and couldn't understand why it had been purchased in his account. TVIX, or Velocity Shares 2X Long VIX Short Term Exchange Notes, is a derivative based on the VIX. In the short term, the VIX is Wall Street's fear gauge. The VIX is an index of the implied volatility of stock index options, looking out over the next month. Traders' expectations of future share price volatility can't be directly observed and must be inferred from options' prices. Legally, TVIX is a structured note based on a rolling forward start variance swap. Volatility has no intrinsic value. Other than noting that the VIX is somewhat mean reverting, there's no way to take a long-term view about it. Despite abundant data, it's unanalyzable. It gets worse: TVIX is levered.

Devilish Details of Debt

Triple-levered funds go up and down three times as fast, but investors may not understand the implications of that. The ETF constantly borrows twice the shareholder's investment to enable it to hold three times that amount of the underlying index, such as the VIX. Thus if the underlying index drops by 25 percent, the triple-levered ETF will drop 75 percent. Whenever the value of the ETF drops, the ETF must sell enough of its index to reduce borrowings to twice the value of the ETF. Then suppose the index immediately rose by 33.3 percent, snapping back to its original level. As shown in the figure on the following page, the triple-levered ETF

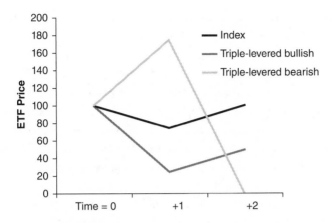

FIGURE 5.1 Inverse and triple-levered ETFs.

would double in value but, having fallen 75 percent, would end at half its starting value. This is shown in figure 5.1.

Borrowed money shortens investors' time horizons, and by maintaining constant leverage, funds embed a harmful algorithm: Buy high and sell low. In our example, the index round-tripped, ending where it started, yet the triple-levered ETF would have lost half its value. The chronological order doesn't matter. A rally first followed by a crash would produce the same end result. Whether long or short, investing more (using borrowed money) as things go your way guarantees whipsaws. You will be forced to exit at the least opportune moment.

Meanwhile, bearish (or "inverse") ETFs bet against an index without going through the mechanics of borrowing shares to sell short. Selling short is a dangerous proposition. Most long investments have unlimited upside with downside limited to −100 percent. When you sell short, your upside is capped at 100 percent and your potential losses are unlimited. Consider our previous example in which the index zigged from 100 to 75 and zagged back to 100, for percentage changes of −25 percent and +33.3 percent. For a short seller, the results would be reversed to +25 percent and −33.3 percent. Triple-levered short ETFs produce diabolical results. Tripling a loss of 33.3 percent would wipe out the bearish fund, even though the index was cumulatively unchanged.

"Why do they invent ETFs like that?" Fred asked angrily.

Derivatives and bonds are contracts, not part ownership of a business; your legal obligations and protections, if any, are lurking in the fine print. Their issuers are not otherwise duty bound to act in your best interests, unlike the senior executives of corporations you own. But Wall Street invents financial contraptions with features that are too complicated for many buyers to evaluate properly. For those who understand them better than others, these *inefficiencies* are profitable precisely because they dupe the unwary victims. Customers may know that a fund is leveraged but not realize that this feature makes it a wasting asset. The perfect targets think in terms of a story without numbers, rather than what a security is worth. Knowledgeable participants who do understand how the securities work will take advantage of the ill-advised trades offered by those who do not understand.

The purpose of this chapter has been to sensitize you to situations in which you ignore details and assume untruths. Fred's blind spots and unwarranted leaps almost certainly differ from yours or mine, but likely share some common ground. If we don't know our goals, no one else will. Many people don't want to ask how and why strategies work. Costs, incentives, whom to trust, and risk control seem like distractions from the task of maximizing expected returns, but in fact are central to it.

The best investment risks are those that you are aware of, that you can analyze, and that offer favorable odds. With smaller, simpler, more stable businesses, it's easier to assess all of these. Unless you have taken the time to understand the details, complexity is your enemy. Diversification protects you against risks you're unaware of and can't analyze. The best of both worlds is to diversify among stocks with superior odds. Anything that interferes with your ability to take a long-term view, like financial leverage, should be avoided.

6

It's the Simple Life for Me

People who think they know everything are a great annoyance
to those of us who do.

—ISAAC ASIMOV

INVEST IN BUSINESSES THAT YOU UNDERSTAND and know well. This is great
advice, but it bears explanation. To understand a business, you must
understand what every segment does and how they all make money. You
must identify the factors that will produce its future earnings and be
able to make a more or less accurate stab at forecasting them. Not all
industries are equally easy to understand. Some, like biotech, are just
impossible for most laypeople. After a little study, you'll find that some
industries are brutally competitive and unprofitable while others are consistently lucrative.

Google has done a great service by making information on any topic
instantly available, but there's also a downside: It encourages the illusion that you know more than you actually do. You lack certain crucial
knowledge but are sure you could gather it in seconds. People have always
been susceptible to that illusion, especially if they are bright and curious. The sort of information that you can retrieve instantly is far more
likely to help you answer the investment question "What happens next?"
than answer the question "What's it worth?" This can lead to a perilous
combination in investing: a bit of overconfidence and a short-term focus.

Familiarity isn't the same as knowledge, but they often go together.
Fidelity's Peter Lynch famously suggested that observing his wife Carolyn's shopping habits provided a good starting point for stock research.

Carolyn knew why *L'eggs* stockings were superior to competitive brands of panty hose. She would also know if and when a competitor launched a much better product. To understand a company, you need to know why customers buy their products. If you are uncertain about which industries you know best, Peter and I would both advise you to begin with consumer products.

Familiarity can also work against investors. If you continuously invested in the single largest S&P 500 stock by market value between 1972 and 2016, your compounded returns would have been less than 4 percent, while the index earned over 10 percent. A similar but smaller effect was seen with the ten largest S&P 500 stocks. Companies with large market values aren't always large businesses and aren't always familiar to investors, but it usually lines up that way. Facebook's market value dramatically exceeded Walmart's in 2016, despite having less than one-twentieth of the revenues, perhaps exactly *because* it is so familiar. Widely known names feel safer. Familiarity, or at least size, also gets reflected in bond ratings and yields. Smaller, lesser-known companies borrow at higher interest rates than popular large companies with equivalent credit ratios.

What Do You Need to Know?

Unless you were a philosophy major, you have probably spent roughly zero time thinking about what you don't know. Former U.S. Secretary of Defense Donald Rumsfeld was onto something important when he spoke of "known unknowns" and "unknown unknowns," but to people who had never thought about it, it sounded like drivel. If there's a quick way to figure out what you know and what you don't, it wasn't part of my education. Philosophers might enjoy the paradox: If I knew what I don't know, then I would know. But that doesn't help me as an investor. I just want to avoid areas where I don't know enough.

When I say "know" and "understand," I have some very definite criteria in mind. Do I understand why customers buy the company's product and why they might stop buying it or switch to a competitor's product? What, specifically, makes the company better than its competition? How does this business make its money? Why does its profitability rise and fall? What drives its growth? How does this sort of business fail? Do I know anything about where the company will be in five years and the factors that will determine the outcome? Can I spot a great opportunity in this industry? Is this an area where I will make wise decisions?

Some investors call it knowing your circle of competence. I not only agree with this idea, but I want to state it in the strongest possible terms. The difference is on the order of your four thousand Facebook friends versus your two or three lifelong friends—more a difference of kind than quantity. You don't want nodding acquaintances cutting into time with your besties. My point is that "circle of competence" should mean circle of special skill or insight. I may be competent in all industries, but some are easier to master, and I'm better in some spots than others. The rank order matters.

Successful people simplify their lives by focusing on the facts and actions that matter most. If you don't, you will find yourself either on a hamster wheel or bogged down in trivia. The trickiest part is staying open to new and contradictory information that affects your goals, while cutting out the clutter. *One test for noise is to ask whether a piece of information will still be useful in a year or two,* leaving out plenty of fussy details about quarterly results.

The facts I seek often look like stale background information; they have been, and will continue to be, true for a long time. I'm searching for important facts with a long shelf life; for example, a description of a company's competitive position or how management has historically used its cash flow. You'll rarely hear these topics on Fox News or CNBC, because they aren't news. For me, considering these facts in depth is much more valuable than reading six reports about recent quarterly results.

Avoid Difficult Industries

I am a sincere advocate of circle of competence despite a personal history of repeated lapses. My fund usually holds some eight hundred securities. I'm trying to balance "circle of competence" and "casting a wide net." For me, opening up endless possibilities is the fun part of the job, while deliberately limiting myself isn't. However, failing to exert willpower in service of an important objective leads to disaster.

There are thousands of stocks to choose from, and even narrowing the field to their circle of skill leaves most investors with ample opportunities. I have to turn down the lion's share of possibilities, including many that are perfectly good. Some approaches, such as buying only stocks that are featured on financial TV programs, actually direct you to less attractive opportunities. Most methods are somewhat random, like starting with the A's and working through the alphabet. Focusing on stocks you know might produce an improved set of possibilities. At the very least, you will be better able to spot *great* opportunities.

The choice of which industries to investigate and which to ignore depends on your existing knowledge, your goals, and the attractiveness of the industries. If you work in an industry, obviously you know more about it than most people. If you need current income, you should focus on stable industries where high dividend yields are common and stay away from those that don't pay dividends. After a bit of research, most investors will find that some industries have abundant opportunities for long-term investors and others have few. Short-term traders can make money playing the swings in stocks in erratic industries as they move from losses to profits. But longer-term investors will find that their returns look more like the average rate of profit; if that is mediocre, their results will be mediocre as well.

To scope out industries, I use print copies of the *Value Line Investment Survey*, which now has an online version. Value Line has two services, each covering about 1,700 stocks, organized by industry groups. Every three months there is a one-page report on each company with about fifteen years of historical numbers plus current commentary. In addition, there's an industry report that sums up the financial results for each group. When I flip through the pages on steel or airlines, it's easy to see that most firms lost money in at least a few years. On the company pages, I see that American, Delta, United, and US Airways have all gone bankrupt, sometimes multiple times. If I don't discover a company that is earning outstanding profits and remaking the industry, I move on.

Expectations of lousy long-term profitability and no growth in an industry do not mean its shares will lag the market, according to the efficient markets theory. All of that bad stuff should be baked into stock prices so low that a fair return will still be earned. Stocks generally trade at low prices relative to earnings or assets because the outlook is drab, at least near-term. On average, cheap stocks have beaten the market despite actual earnings gains that lagged the market, hinting that expectations were too low. But don't go looking for lousy outlooks alone. As a category, money-losing companies have generally lagged the market, suggesting that expectations weren't low enough.

When you narrow your universe of possible investments, tilt the odds in your favor. The EMH posits that all stocks and industry groups have identical risk-adjusted returns. If true, cutting out categories of stocks makes one's investment universe smaller and less diversified but shouldn't hurt expected return. I'd suggest that excluding a truly random industry doesn't hurt my odds and might improve them if I know little about the industry. Fund managers are hired for their knowledge, so we avoid admitting that we're pathetic in some industries. I also avoid decision rules that tend to cut out stocks that I think might have favorable attributes, such as low price/earnings ratios or small market capitalizations.

Dendreon's Unpredictable Journey

Unprofitable biotech stocks have always been way beyond me. But that hasn't stopped me from trying to learn from doctors that I know socially. Medicine is absolutely in their circle of competence, not mine. So I listened when "Dr. Rubin," a medically trained psychiatrist serving cancer patients, got excited about Dendreon when its stock was trading at $4. Dendreon was developing Provenge, an immunotherapy for prostate cancer. I shared Dr. Rubin's fascination with the development of a new, more-humane cancer treatment, but didn't buy Dendreon stock. I couldn't handicap Food and Drug Administration (FDA) approvals and estimate future earnings.

To estimate Dendreon's profitability five years out, one clearly needed to know the odds of Provenge's being approved by the FDA and brought to market, and then the size of its market. The FDA new drug approval process consists of three stages, and at each one the odds are against approval. The process took ten years for Provenge: seven for the FDA to rule that the initial trials had proven the drug was safe and effective, two more for a second round of trials, and another for final approval. After approval, Dendreon stock hit $56, up more than tenfold in just over a year, earning Dr. Rubin a not-so-small fortune on paper. Some analysts anticipated that Provenge sales could hit $4 billion by 2020.

Before the fact, I never would have predicted all the twists and turns in Dendreon's development of Provenge. Often with young businesses, investors assume that once a major milestone is reached, such as FDA approval, everything is golden. For Dendreon, FDA approval was not the end of the rainbow. Six weeks after Provenge was approved, Medicare proposed a cap on reimbursement for prostate cancer drugs. Provenge cost $93,000 for a course of treatment, but some other cancer drugs were even more. Private insurers also held back on reimbursement. Each Provenge patient receives medicine customized to his immune system, so manufacturing ramped up slowly. A researcher published a report suggesting that the clinical data on the survival benefit of the vaccine was skewed by the age of the patients. As with any drug, some patients suffered side effects.

Dendreon had to withdraw its first-year sales forecast as actual sales were about half of its earlier forecast of $400 million. Then, Johnson & Johnson launched Zytiga, which could be taken in combination with Provenge or positioned as a competing therapy. Zytiga and the other competing therapy, Medivation's Xtandi, are taken orally, while Provenge is injected; many patients prefer oral dosing. Provenge was a scientific success but a commercial flop. In 2014, on a conference call originally meant to be an earnings update, Dendreon announced that it had filed for bankruptcy.

Investors should change their opinions when the facts change, but if you know a company and its industry well, that shouldn't happen too often. Even now, I can't say whether Dr. Rubin's insight that the science was pretty good answered the question "What happens next?" or "What's it worth?" Not even a superhuman securities analyst would have been able to foretell all the ups and downs at Dendreon. If they had had perfect foresight, they would have concluded that ultimately Dendreon's value was zero, which for many years would have seemed absolutely wrong.

Insurance

One of the first industries I covered was life insurance, which can seem boringly predictable. Insurance works on the principle that if large numbers of similar but uncorrelated risks are aggregated, the outcome will be close to the theoretical average, or central tendency. Term life insurance, in principle, is a straightforward business. Oversimplifying, for example, an insurance company might cover a million lives, each for a premium of $1,000 a year or $1 billion in premiums. Actuaries might determine that 1 percent of their insured population passes away each year. Barring an epidemic or war, one person's death is usually statistically independent of other deaths. One million lives is a large enough number that probabilities average out, and the actuarial estimate of ten thousand deaths should be roughly accurate. Assuming death benefits of $65,000 each and selling and administrative costs of 25 percent of premiums, the insurance company would incur annual expenses of $900 million. It should earn an underwriting profit of about $100 million a year plus investment income on its reserves.

You can reasonably project what a conservative life insurer will look like in five or ten years; indeed, reported earnings *depend* on assumptions about the future. But the forecast itself is drab. Life insurance probably won't become obsolete, but it's a minimal growth market. Profits won't be awful because everyone uses similar mortality tables and has a good fix on costs. But profits also won't be thrilling because basic life insurance policies all look the same, leaving companies to compete on price. Insurers that start price wars to gain market share will give up profitability, so most will take a middle path. Investment income will vary because of changes in stock prices and interest rates. If you really could predict stock prices and interest rate changes, your best use of those forecasts wouldn't be in any earnings model.

For life insurance companies that issue annuities and other income policies, those shifting assumptions about investment income are crucial. Rather than trying to outguess financial markets, prudent insurance companies match the timing of cash flows from their bond portfolio with the timing of payments to annuitants. Because the annuitants are risk-averse, prudent insurance companies stick to top quality bonds. But policyholders have a variety of options—including lapsing their policy—that can throw off the balancing act. Unlike mortality, human behavior is shifting and not always predictable. Also, insurance companies are sometimes tempted to buy junk bonds or mismatch maturities to earn higher interest rates.

Property and casualty (P&C) insurance deals with uncertainty as much as with risk. For catastrophe reinsurance in particular, there is no such thing as a normal year; instead, most years will be good, but a few will bring massive losses. A company that insures a small number of highly valued properties in a concentrated geography will have wildly lumpy and unpredictable claims. In the short term, insurers can't know whether they have set premiums to reflect the true future odds, and it hardly seems to matter. Eventually the law of averages prevails, but quarterly and yearly results are futile to predict. If your company has written billions in wind cover on buildings in Miami, during hurricane season you will be glued to the Weather Channel.

Insurance company failures usually result from concentrations of investment and insurance risk that turned out badly. First Executive failed in 1991 because it had invested heavily in junk bonds that weren't actively traded, suffering huge losses when it was forced to dump them. Fremont Indemnity became insolvent in 2003 because it had written too much workers' comp in California. The workers' comp market had become intensely competitive in the 1990s, causing premiums to be set too low. Then, changes in benefit laws brought an epidemic of abusive claims and litigation. For P&C insurers, the true future odds do not mirror past history; they are unknown and unstable. The lurking danger is that when risks are infrequent and clustered, and haven't happened lately, underwriters set premiums too low.

AIG

Between my knowledge of some of its insurance businesses and an AAA credit rating and reputation, I thought in 2007 that American International Group (AIG) was within my circle of competence. Unwittingly, I had moved far outside it. For decades, AIG's track record of almost uninterrupted growth was unmatched, allowing it to become the largest insurer (by market value) in the world. Founded in Shanghai in 1919, AIG was a leading insurer in Asia, where insurance is still growing strongly, and around the globe. AIG offered all lines of business insurance, workers' comp, reinsurance, auto insurance, mortgage insurance, individual and group life insurance, accident and health, fixed and variable annuities, aircraft leasing, financial products, financial guarantees, guaranteed investment contracts, and more. With global diversity and varied lines of business, trouble in one area should have been offset by strength elsewhere.

During 2007, AIG stock had slipped about 20 percent from its highs partly because of controversy about its Financial Products (AIGFP) division. I mistakenly imagined I knew something about the situation because AIGFP had been founded by my former associate Howard Sosin in 1987. Before joining AIG, Sosin had worked at Drexel Burnham Lambert, where he ran the financial swaps desk. But this personal connection had nothing to do with AIG's situation in 2007. Sosin had left AIG in 1993. While the Drexel swaps desk acted mostly a broker (matching buyers and sellers for a fee), AIG was taking a risk position in financial swaps, treating swaps as insurance.

AIGFP was dealing in increasingly complex swaps unlike the ones that I had once known peripherally. Credit default swaps (CDS), which insure against default on risky debt, had become one of AIGFP's key products. Defaults on mortgages and corporate debt had been uncommon in recent memory, so the fees were set too low. Often the annual fees were less than one percent of the risk insured. Many buyers of CDS protection weren't insuring risky bonds but betting on default. AIG lost.

With hindsight, treating CDS as an insurance product is an absolutely terrible idea. Bond issues can run into the billions of dollars, so insuring them could create enormous, chunky risks. Insurance works by pooling multitudes of small risks. CDS were more like catastrophic coverage, but unlike property insurance, the catastrophes depend on human behavior, not natural events. Even worse, credit disasters are correlated with the business cycle and each other. Defaults might even be contagious!

By insuring risky credits, AIG effectively had large concentrations of investment risk that went bad simultaneously. As the CDS liabilities surged, AIG had to post more collateral, which strained its liquidity. To stanch the bleeding, AIG closed out some swaps at inopportune times, making losses that might have been temporary, permanent. For 2007, AIG reported a loss of $99.7 billion. The stock crashed 98 percent from its highs and the U.S. government stepped in to avert insolvency.

One advantage of investing in simple businesses is that if outsiders can diagnose the issues, skilled managers already know whether they can be fixed, and how. Clearly I had strayed beyond my competence and was in over my head, but maybe AIG management was as well. I tell myself that I wasn't the only one who considered only the brief recent history of CDS and did not conceive a broader analogy with taking large aggregates of highly correlated catastrophic risk for minimal premiums. Only AIG employees know for sure, but that's what I'll tell myself. Ignorance feels better when it's shared.

I constantly seek to learn new things, so it isn't always easy to stick to my circle of competence, let alone my circle of expertise. Even though I thought I had a decent grasp on the insurance business, AIG had evolved. I missed familiar sources of disaster in insurance because they occurred in an unfamiliar context. I had allowed prior commitments and knowledge to slip-slide into areas that I didn't understand. Generally, I favor smaller, simpler businesses. Now, instead of a complex conglomerate like AIG with a dozen business units, two of which are black boxes, I will often invest in ten smaller, more transparent stocks.

I remain strangely attracted to the potential for blockbusters in biotech, but I know I can't handicap the frequency of duds. I now know that I can't predict macroeconomic variables or the overall market, thanks to a disastrous experience trading futures, which I'll discuss in the next chapter. After investing abroad, I now recognize the dangers of not fully understanding local institutions, not to mention not knowing the language. When you stay close to your sweet spots, these sorts of errors don't happen.

7

Thinking Small

The curious task of economics is to demonstrate to men how little
they really know about what they imagine they can design.

—FRIEDRICH VON HAYEK

I'm only rich because I know when I'm wrong.

—GEORGE SOROS

Big Questions

GROSS DOMESTIC PRODUCT (GDP) reflects the sales of businesses throughout the economy, which indicates the direction of their earnings, which
are related to their stock prices—but macroeconomics is shockingly inef-
fective in predicting the stock market. New economic data are released
daily, which tends to shorten our horizons. More critically, the links
between different big-picture numbers, specific companies, and stock
prices are weak, dynamic, and often poorly understood. Data report the
past; stock prices reflect future expectations. The chain of intermittent
connections makes it hard to spot where we went wrong, or even know
that we erred. Most economic forecasts are meant to suggest the trend of
stock prices but never pause to estimate their fair value.

Beyond intellectual curiosity, the siren call of big-picture investing
is that it *looks* easy, because a deluge of pertinent information arrives
daily in the news. It might even appear that macro inquiry takes less
research than specific stocks. Furthermore, the value of perfect foresight of changes in GDP or the S&P 500 would be gargantuan compared to foresight about an individual stock. Macro investors deal in
massive, liquid markets, so there's never a worry about quickly entering
(or exiting) a position of the desired size. Positions can be scaled up,

because margin requirements for futures and derivatives based on stock indexes, bonds, commodities, and foreign currencies are minuscule compared with individual stocks. Selling short is no hassle in derivative markets, unlike stocks.

While most investors using a top-down approach make a hash of investing, a few have made spectacular fortunes with big-picture decisions. Roger Babson correctly called the 1929 stock market crash and left a fortune to endow Babson College. George Soros and John Paulson made billions shorting the British pound and subprime mortgages, respectively. When I was younger, I was convinced that macro mavens must have a great universal theory of everything economic in their heads. I now believe that their common features are first, openness to contradictory information; second, some way of testing whether they are incorrect; and third, a willingness to change their minds.

Almost from the start, economists have conceived of the economy as a machine. The economist William Phillips built a sculpture of the economic machine, which he called MONIAC. My grandfather William had an amazing talent for taking cars apart and reassembling them in working order. Once, I wanted to do the same thing with the economy. But I doubt that I can take apart the economy, let alone reassemble it.

Here's the problem: Every one of the parts in economics is abstract. What constitutes the economy or the market, or any piece of it, depends on your definitions. The "market" could be defined as all of the four thousand or so stocks listed in the United States, or just the five hundred in the S&P's 500, or the thirty in the Dow Jones Industrials. Is the economy made up of just the companies in a stock index? Shouldn't private companies and other organizations count as well, not to mention the self-employed?

Change definitions, and you change numbers. During the global financial crisis in 2009, some European countries struggled to meet targets for national debt based on GDP. By changing the definition to include revenues from prostitution, illicit drugs, and other activities, reported GDP was boosted by a couple of percentage points. With economic knowledge built on such abstract, shifting definitions, the idea of a perfect model with perfect foresight seems laughable.

During the Great Depression, John Maynard Keynes wrote *The General Theory of Employment, Interest and Money*, the most famous book ever written on macroeconomics. This theory is what most universities teach and many governments practice. While Keynesian theory has defects, there aren't yet any coherent, comprehensive alternatives, leaving open the question of whether it is better to be guided in error or unguided. Keynes created most of the key definitions used in macroeconomics, such as GDP equals consumption, capital investment, and government spending, plus exports minus imports.

The most volatile component, which often leads the other components and usually triggers booms and recessions, is capital investment. Businesses need to build capacity only when demand is growing. If demand tumbles, businesses won't add plant capacity and often don't even replace worn-out equipment. When businesses decide to invest, they have to consider the profits over the entire life of the equipment, not just the year ahead. But future profits are only projections, not yet facts. Therefore, investment depends on businesspeople's general outlook, which Keynes called "animal spirits." Forecasts will be wrong because animal spirits are elevated or depressed. Keynes's model sounds more like a living thing than a machine.

People forecast for many reasons other than to accurately predict the future; on Wall Street, estimates are primarily used to sell something and never look back. For example, a projection that Internet currencies will be widely accepted may be meant to spur actions to cause this forecast to come true. Conversely, Al Gore admitted that his forecast of global warming was meant to prompt action to avert disaster. Keynes's model was intended to influence government policy more than to make predictions. When animal spirits were low, his forecast was that the economy fared better if governments ran larger budget deficits. Governments have acted accordingly.

The economist Milton Friedman claimed that economic models need not use assumptions that look anything like the real world; they need only predict accurately. Really? Scientists start by observing and describing everything as precisely as possible, especially how pieces fit together into systems. Then they develop a model to explain things. They don't (and can't) make predictions until they can explain what's going on. Although physicists often begin with simple models and ideal assumptions that they know are unrealistic, they later add back the frictions and complexity that they had earlier ignored.

Importantly, physics models actually have to predict accurately; economics has lower standards of proof. When testing his general theory of relativity, Albert Einstein said, "If a single one of the conclusions from it proves wrong, it must be given up." Just one counterexample is enough to show a scientific theory is invalid. Economists don't work that way. If they did, nothing would be left of macroeconomics. Show me a model with ridiculous assumptions that predicts perfectly, and I'll accept ridiculous assumptions.

Everything in economics and investing is tendencies, probabilities, and situations; nothing is everywhere and always. Most economic events reflect a long chain of events and probabilities. The only way I can follow that chain is to be as accurate and precise as possible in describing reality and start with realistic assumptions. Economic theories that describe simple actions and transactions are usually more reliable than those that describe complex systems. Even robust theories have counterexamples, so economists cling to theories with dreadful predictive records, unable to prove their validity either way.

When explaining stock prices through macroeconomics, the thread is often lost. Economic logic reminds me of the childhood game of telephone, in which a statement as simple as "Miss Du Bois planted a geranium near her house" could be twisted into something as unlike as "I saw Mr. Shapiro and Miss Du Bois smooching in her yard." Similarly, there's distortion and slippage with every link in a chain of economic and financial events. Often the end result is totally different from the starting point, especially because some economic actors are thinking short-term and others long-term. Investors have to imagine the many possible stories that could happen, not just the one that actually will.

Wassily Leontief's GDP input-output model is the most precise model of a complex economy that I know of. The input-output matrix catalogs all of the inputs needed to produce everything the economy makes. Suppose an average auto uses 2,400 pounds of steel, 325 pounds of aluminum, and so on. The equipment to make the car might require another 600 pounds of steel per car. Based on auto production of 16 million vehicles, you could calculate how many millions of tons of iron ore would be needed. Predicting GDP should be a breeze, right?

But business economists don't forecast GDP with an input-output model. The things the economy produces change constantly. Businesses will always look for ways to produce the same output with fewer inputs, and new products with old inputs. The input-output model works poorly for knowledge industries such as software, movies, or pharmaceuticals, where the bottlenecks and costs are in developing the first copy. Additional copies are cheap to make. With most economic growth now coming from knowledge industries, the input-output model has become a lousy way to estimate GDP growth. (Don't write the model off entirely, though; the advent of Big Data may give it new life.)

Working at Drexel

When I worked as a research economist at Drexel Burnham Lambert in the 1980s, clients had no use for elaborate models or theories of everything. They simply wanted to know "the number" before a key economic statistic was reported or, failing that, explanations of what just happened.

We never looked very far, or very boldly, into the future. Traders played the statistics to be reported in the next month or quarter. Nailing the number was a favorite pastime, then and now. When my boss, Dr. Norman Mains, assigned me coverage of economic statistics, he advised me never to give a number and a date at the same time. I think he was joking, but his point was that frequently released numbers reflect a lot of noise, and there's a lot we can't know. Some economic policy makers and investors believe they can predict and control near-term events, while others aim for generally favorable long-term outcomes, accepting randomness or even pain in the interim.

To make guesses on economic statistics that weren't too wide of the mark, I had to learn how the sausage is made. Many statistics are calculated with data that have already been released, adding some new information. Industrial production numbers feed into the calculation of GDP growth but are released earlier, giving a hint of the latter number. The government uses electric power consumption to estimate industrial production. Heating and cooling degree-days can be calculated before the electricity consumption numbers are released. When it was very hot or cold, more electricity would be used. But with every step, there's some slippage, so you can't leap from degree-days to GDP growth, let alone market impact.

I could make a decent stab at monthly figures by taking the average change over the last year. When consumer prices had been up an average of 0.2 percent a month, my estimate might be 0.2 percent. If earnings per share had risen 10 percent over the last year and the year ago quarterly earnings per share was 50 cents, my forecast was 55 cents. Sometimes there would be flaky data or unusual events in a period, and I would tweak the numbers a bit. I'd also adjust for the components that had already been reported. To make sure I hadn't missed something, I would check out other economists' predictions.

Eventually, Dr. Mains encouraged me to share my predictions with journalists and clients, but one customer told me he never read my daily comments because he couldn't make money from them. My forecasts were accurate enough, he told me, but they were copycats of everyone else's. The client only cared about the size of the market reaction, not the data itself, so consensus forecasts and minor statistics like capacity utilization were distractions. A correct prediction also had to be important and unexpected. The client was a fan of economists with forceful views and a persistent tilt that happened to match his own. Economists don't forecast because they want to, but because they are asked.

High Taxes = Strong Economy?

My most frustrating project at Drexel was attempting to show that President Reagan's tax cuts had been a great boon to the economy. Many clients and all of the senior people at Drexel were in the top income tax bracket, so the desired conclusion was self-evident. Even though I was far from the top bracket and wary of the intersection of economics and political beliefs, I believed the answer that we favored was actually correct. Most economists will tell you that lower taxes cause people to work harder because they keep more of what they produce.

Higher taxes reduce the incentive to work, which should slow GDP growth, but the data weren't cooperating. I tabulated all the years in which the top marginal tax bracket was greater than 80 percent. In 1941 the top bracket was raised to 81 percent, in 1942 to 88 percent, to 94 percent in 1944, and then trimmed to 91 percent in 1946, where it remained until 1964, when it was reduced to 77 percent. Over that twenty-three-year period, real GDP grew from $1.27 trillion to $3.59 trillion in 2009 dollars, or a 4.6 percent compounded growth rate. Those were actually among the strongest growth rates since the United States has kept reliable statistics.

To explain a vigorous economy with high taxes, I needed a different story. When the United States was coming out of the Great Depression, many people were barely getting by. Increased taxes might have forced people to work more to keep up their standard of living. Pitching in for the war effort was considered a patriotic duty. Because this annoying evidence was a few decades in the past, no one cared about it.

Between 1981 and 1990, the top tax bracket was chopped from 70 percent to 28 percent. During that stretch, real GDP growth was 3.4 percent a year, also above average, but not as much. If you were determined to show the benefits of lower tax rates, you'd compare the period between 1981 and 1990 against the previous nine years, which had been abysmal, but that might not be a fair comparison. Oil prices had jumped between 1972 and 1981, and fallen back in the Reagan years. Interest rates had spiked to unprecedented levels by 1981 and then reverted back. In the earlier period, the unpopular Vietnam war had wound down, and Richard Nixon became the only American president ever to resign from office.

The Reagan tax cuts were intended to be a straightforward case, and I wondered whether it was possible to use economics to invest intelligently when causation is so hard to trace. In economics, all else is *never* equal. You can't look at one factor in isolation. There are depressions, wars, inspiring leaders, oil price surges, and crashes. Innovations are discovered in clusters, not neatly scheduled at appointed times. Every economic action has indirect effects and antecedents that you don't immediately see. Often it's nearly impossible to figure out even the direct effects. Statistics move together, like tax rates and GDP growth between

1941 and 1964, but that doesn't tell you what caused what; correlation doesn't prove causation.

Trading on Economics

At Drexel, the obvious way to show that my judgments had a market value was to trade.

Investors and traders aim to strike a delicate balance—accepting new information but not getting lost in redundancy, and being neither over- nor underconfident in the truth of their facts and logic. Then, I could be fleetingly brash about things of which I knew little, reflecting youthful bravado more than anything else, leaving me to blow with the winds as news reports arrived. In the end, my risk posture was dictated by cir- cumstances. While working at Drexel, I was finishing my second year of business school. My tiny bank balance was more than offset by tuition bills, not to mention large student loans, so I had to start small, with one futures contract.

By putting down a small deposit of perhaps $1,500, I was able to "con- trol" a $1 million Treasury bill contract or a $100,000 Treasury bond contract; the balance was implicitly borrowed. Dozens of other types of futures traded, but I couldn't apply my knowledge as a research econo- mist to them. If the value of the Treasury bond changed by a point—that is 1 percent of par—the contract would gain or lose $1,000. Every day, based on price movements, winnings or losses are settled in cash. If you are offside, you can lose your initial margin in a day or two. If you are right, your money multiplies quickly.

Every day, I could feel the economy getting stronger. In January 1983, the unemployment rate had been 11.4 percent. By May, it had plunged to 9.8 percent, and by December, 8.0 percent. I was absolutely rooting for a buoyant employment picture, which would also bolster stocks. But usually when the economy is galloping, interest rates rise as bondholders fret about inflation. A big part of Drexel's futures business came from hedgers who were trying to protect against rising interest rates. A jump in rates, or even just worries, would bring in more hedging business. Every- thing I wished for fit together as a worldview.

I was convinced that a rebounding economy meant interest rates definitely had to go back up, so that's how I bet in the futures market. For about three months, everything worked magnificently. Soon I had made enough to add another contract and another and so on. Sometimes I would do pairs of contracts, such as long Treasury bills and short certificates of deposit. The margin requirement for these "spreads" was less than for either contract individually.

For those three months, I was sure I had the magic touch. I decided to speculate with conviction. I pyramided my winning positions as they moved in my favor. Like alcohol, financial leverage can induce overoptimism and overconfidence. Once I had accumulated twenty-five contracts, and realized that every flicker might make me $625 richer or poorer, the screens hypnotized me. Just three ticks in my favor would throw off more than enough cash to add another contract. The profits gushed in so much more quickly than with stocks. Over a dozen weeks, I had collected more than $40,000, which exceeded my annual pay. I fancied launching a brilliant career as a trader.

In under a month, it all went splat. The economy kept growing vigorously, but inflation inexplicably slowed and interest rates tumbled more rapidly than they had risen. Other than the fact that I had lost money, I had no way to tell whether I was right or wrong, or to pinpoint the source of my mistakes. Some of the statistics had to be flukes. Maybe I hadn't focused enough on the right economic statistics. Maybe I had simply missed something. My personal account, final exams, the Chartered Financial Analyst test, and my job were all wrangling for my attention.

My forty grand in winnings vanished faster than they had appeared. The margin clerk was visibly alarmed to note my cash balance of zero and that my positions had a hypothetical value of hundreds of times my annual income. I told him that was all I had, keeping silent about my student loans and bills. He sold out my account.

Stocks Anticipate

The margin call also blew apart my efforts to develop a stock market timing system. I had dabbled in stock index futures; but having lost all my play money and more, I had to stop. My goal was to connect economic statistics with interest rates, then link interest rates with stock indexes, then maybe stock indexes with specific stocks. I had figured out how some economic statistics tied in with other data, but simply could not connect economic data, interest rates, the stock market, and ultimately, trading profits.

Most investors assume that fluctuations in the economy tell you what the stock market will do, but they have it backwards. The stock market tells you what the economy will do. The Conference Board compiles an index of leading indicators that is meant to turn up or down before the broad economy. Of the ten leading indicators in the index, the most consistently effective one is the S&P 500 stock index. Investors look ahead a bit further than purchasing managers, for example. Arguably, slumping stock markets depress animal spirits and *cause* recessions.

Because economic statistics affect interest rates, many investors try to predict stocks by way of interest rates. Sometimes stock and bond prices move up or down together, and sometimes they go in opposite directions. When interest rates are rising and bond prices are falling, the economy and profits are usually advancing. Which matters more, interest rates or profits? It all depends.

Investors who focus on *levels* of interest rates will reach different conclusions from those who watch the *changes* in rates. Most investors assume a drop in interest rates will lift the economy and profits, and justify higher price/earnings ratios (P/Es). All of that is positive for stock prices. But it turns out that when inflation-adjusted interest rates are very low, returns on other financial assets are quite poor as well.

In the long run, stock prices reflect earnings, so many market-timers watch corporate profits. Again, some watch the levels of profits over time; others watch the rate of change. Most market-timers turn bullish when earnings seem set to jump. Usually, they pay no attention to the intrinsic value of those profit streams.

There is a market-timing signal in forecasts of corporate profit growth, but it's not what you might think. Everyone is trying to look ahead, and your bet will pay off only if it is correct and different from what others anticipate. When it's totally obvious that profits will be sluggish or fall, the stock market has already dropped, and it's a great time to buy.

The opposite is also true. For the four decades through 2015, in years when S&P 500 earnings growth has been fastest, P/Es have on average contracted, often so sharply that total returns were negative. When S&P 500 profits fell, on average P/Es expanded so much that stock prices increased.

To Know Yourself, Study Others' Mistakes

In the decades since my trading debacle, I've seen many investors blow up their portfolios using top-down investing, basically in two related ways. They (1) invest with no notion of fair value and (2) fail to assimilate new information. Foreign currencies, commodities, and many other instruments that macro traders use don't have an intrinsic value. Instead currencies, for instance, have a fair value implied by purchasing power parity. Without any concept of intrinsic value, it's impossible to gauge whether the market has already picked up on your insight. To diagnose where a trade tripped up, you either need to follow all of the links between cause and effect (which is doubtful for macro trades), or you need some basis for calculating a fair value.

Investors constantly search for overlooked insights that, if widely understood, would prompt a large market price movement, but assessing what's in the public domain can be done only obliquely. For simple situations, investors can trace the causal links and identify which element the market hasn't grasped, which is rarely possible with complex big-picture issues. The notion of fair or intrinsic value doesn't tell you *which* idea is mistaken, just that the price might be wrong. A visible gap between market price and your calculation of intrinsic value indicates that either you or the markets must be misguided.

Intrinsic value also serves as a way to determine whether an investment idea was flawed, and as a guide to action. When losing money is the only clue that something's amiss, you are in deep trouble. Momentum investors buy stocks that have gone up and sell those that have gone down. I think this implies they would buy a rising stock at $40, sell it as it dips to $35, and then buy it again when it pops back to $41. If I believed a stock was worth $50 and purchased it for $40, I would be even more enthusiastic when the price slipped to $35, provided that the value had not changed. If the news that prompted the decline reduced my estimate of fair value to $30, I would sell and accept my loss.

In religion, politics, and love, true believers are meant to remain steadfast, regardless of the evidence. Investors aim for the rationality of natural scientists, but can never achieve it because businesses and economies are structures of human beings. As issues in economics become vast and multifaceted, they tend to shade into political and philosophical beliefs. For example, when a wealthy creditor nation cannot collect repayment from a destitute nation, people make moral and political judgments unlike those made when a business fails. When I think about social systems in ways that touch on personal values, it is hard to avoid groupthink. In cases like that, I don't trust myself to invest strictly based on what I expect to happen rather than what I want to happen or think is right.

The garden variety versions of failures to consider intrinsic value and take in new information are permanent bears (who always expect stocks to tank) and goldbugs. This isn't to say that bear markets don't occur or that gold can't be a useful store of value. Value investors are likewise intent on preserving capital, but we worry about the opportunity cost of holding assets that produce little income (like cash) or no income (like gold). Permabears and goldbugs often tell sagas of impending disaster, with accelerating inflation usually following from high and rising consumer and government debt. Every data point is reinterpreted to support their cause. It's intelligent to worry, but that doesn't mean the most worrisome analysis is the most intelligent.

I have some sympathy with the permabears, as the average P/E of the S&P 500 in the quarter-century between 1992 and 2016 has been higher than in the quarter-century before it, or just about any quarter-century since the index was created. Some argue that higher multiples are justified by globalization, increasing monopoly power, and new technologies. Those who believe market valuation metrics are nonetheless mean reverting have appeared to be permabears. A distinction might be found in their actions during bear markets like 2009, when market multiples tumbled far below even the averages of longer histories. If they bought stocks then, they are not permabears.

Gold may be a store of value, but how much value isn't clear. Since gold earns no income, it has no intrinsic value, but over time it does seem to have an average value measured by a basket of consumer goods, with a huge variance. Yet in 2001, gold traded at $270 an ounce and in 2011 at $1,900. Even making a generous adjustment for consumer price inflation, in 2011 the real price of gold was five times what it had been a decade earlier. The popularity of tales of hyperinflationary disasters in Weimar Germany and Zimbabwe peaked coincidently. In a weird parallel to inflationary fears, large quantities of securitized paper gold were issued. Investors with a sense of value and the ability to change their mind might have reduced their gold holdings at that time.

Keynes: The Great Economist as Investor

When I learned that John Maynard Keynes was not only the founder of macroeconomics but also an outstanding investor, I hoped that he might provide a role model for applying economics to investing. Keynes's approach evolved over time and brought varying degrees of success. Keynes began his career as a speculator by trading in currencies, generally buying U.S. dollars and selling short European currencies like the German mark. In 1919, Keynes wrote a book arguing that Germany would be unable to pay reparations for World War I, and that forcing it to do so would cripple its economy. That was exactly what happened, *eventually*.

With its economy a mess and struggling to pay reparations, Germany went into hyperinflation and the paper mark completely collapsed in 1923. Keynes would have reaped spectacular gains if he had stayed short the mark until then, but he had borrowed money to do this trade. In May 1920, the mark's descent was interrupted by an abrupt rally, which wiped Keynes out and left him in debt to friends.

When he again had (other people's) money to play with, Keynes returned to commodities trading. In this endeavor, he had what I would call unfair advantages: access to historical price data for commodities at a time when this information wasn't widely available, and close connections with government policy makers. But his overall results from commodity trading were very mixed, particularly if you include some devastating losses at the start of the Great Depression.

In addition to his personal account, Keynes began to manage the Chest endowment funds for King's College at the University of Cambridge. For several years at the start, he used economic and monetary analysis to decide when to switch between stocks, bonds, and cash. In current jargon, Keynes was a top-down asset allocator and sector rotator using a momentum style. Cumulatively, his results in the 1920s lagged behind the British market (figure 7.1).

In his investment report to King's College, Keynes wrote, "We have not proved able to take much advantage of a general systematic movement out of and into ordinary shares as a whole at different phases of the trade cycle." He also observed, "Credit cycling means in practice selling market leaders on a falling market and buying them on a rising one and, allowing for expenses and loss of interest, it needs phenomenal skill to make much out of it." If the greatest macroeconomist ever, with special access to information and policy makers, couldn't trade successfully on credit and business cycles, I don't know who could.

The 1929 crash and Great Depression caught Keynes by surprise, both as an economist and as an investor. In "The Great Slump of 1930," he wrote, "We have involved ourselves in a colossal muddle, having blundered in the control of a delicate machine, the workings of which we do not understand." Keynes personally lost about four-fifths of his net

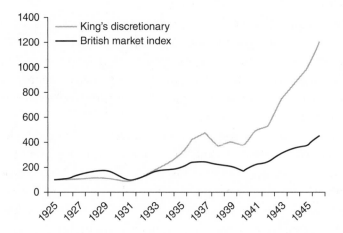

FIGURE 7.1 Keynes versus index, 1926–1946.

worth from top to bottom, partly because he never stopped using borrowed money. The King's College portfolio held up better. In this portfolio, credit cycling had helped because Keynes sold shares into a falling market that kept plunging.

Keynes recognized that his approach wasn't working and changed it. Instead of using big-picture economics, Keynes increasingly focused on a small number of companies that he knew very well. Rather than chasing momentum, he bought undervalued stocks with generous dividends. On average, the stocks he purchased had a dividend yield of 6 percent. This yield was far above that of the average British stock or bond, and, where Keynes had borrowed funds to invest, as he usually did, it more than covered the interest expense. Most were small and midsize companies in dull or out-of-favor industries, such as mining and autos in the midst of the Great Depression. Despite his rough start, Keynes beat the market averages by 6 percent a year over more than two decades.

Where Does the Efficient Market Hypothesis Apply?

Although Keynes and I both ended up favoring undervalued, mostly smaller companies, I think Keynes held a different view of our ability to predict the future. Both of us started with hopes of using economic predictions to trade markets but failed to do it well enough to make and keep serious money. Keynes wrote of the precariousness of our knowledge of the future earnings yield of any specific stock, a concern that I would extend to the future of any complex economic system.

Earlier in this book, I discussed the efficient market theory, which posits that market prices are essentially fair and that no one should expect to consistently beat the market. That would follow if all information were publicly available to everyone, and on average correctly interpreted. For statistics and trends that are universally important enough to be reported on TV or the Internet and draw audiences of millions, this seems a fair description of reality.

In its strong form, the efficient market hypothesis (EMH) states that even private or insider information will be reflected in market prices. This seems incorrect to me, as I still see news reports of large profits made with inside information on stocks. But, other than the movie *Trading Places*, I'm hard pressed to think of a major (real) example of insider trading on economic data. By definition, economic data involve large markets, so the potential profits should be massive. The lack of insider trading scandals hints that for economic data, the strong form of the EMH may apply. Most information about the big picture is widely known, or at least is reflected in the prices.

Thinking Small

You can't make money in the short term from anything millions of viewers have seen on TV or the Internet. To use big-picture economics successfully, you must carefully check whether one thing really does lead to another, based on historical examples, and be alert to the possibility that you are mistaken. You have to check whether the models you learned in school work or not, and under what circumstances. The result is more of a mosaic than a data point, which does nothing to simplify things, because there are so many news reports and so many connections. Every piece of information isn't equally important; most are redundant.

So instead, I try to think small. There are fewer news reports on a specific company than on the economy as a whole. Analysis of stocks is less a matter of careful interpretation than analysis of the economy. It's not inside information; it's simply that most people aren't paying attention, especially if the company is small. Everyone makes mistakes in figuring out what the future will bring. If the connections are clearer and more direct, your forecasts are more likely to be accurate. Unlike more cosmic subjects, it is easier to know what you don't know with a specific stock.

Any investor, big-picture or not, needs some concept of fair value to serve as his or her guide star. The idea of fair value not only indicates which trades are most attractive but also helps calibrate the weight of new information and aids in deciding whether to add to a position or reverse course. Arguably George Soros's theory of reflexivity explains why the British pound became grossly overvalued relative to purchasing power parity, and then stopped becoming more so. Beyond that point, Soros's most powerful tool was the notion of fair value.

Both macro investors and stock-pickers must fearlessly seek the truth, but for me smaller errors are easier to admit. Once I've committed to a theory that explains big, important things, I rarely change my mind. It's more unsettling to admit that I don't comprehend the world around me than a small situation of narrow interest. While I make fun of investors who incessantly think the stock market is about to implode or that gold is the only safe asset, I also have my own settled beliefs. An idea about a specific stock is just one among many, and I know all along that a certain fraction of them will be duds. A smaller mistake is generally easier to repair. Thinking small not only reduces the severity and frequency of errors, but it also puts you in a better frame of mind to expect them and fix them.

8

Bulls in the China Shop

In a country well governed, poverty is something to be ashamed of. In a
country badly governed, wealth is something to be ashamed of.

—CONFUCIUS

WHEN I VENTURE ABROAD, some of the things I don't know are more obvious
than others, like language. Yes, I'm biased toward countries where English is
a language of business. But legal and social institutions also vary. "Property"
does not mean the same thing and is not equally protected everywhere, especially if you are a foreigner. Courts in some nations follow the rule of law;
others don't. Tax rates (and the things taxed) have not been harmonized
globally. Inflation rates vary. Accounting numbers are metaphors whose
meaning varies by context and locality. The social status of businesspeople
varies; it is tied in some nations to employee count, in others to profitability. All of these factors affect how corporate executives behave. Intuitions
derived from American experience about the dynamics of profitability,
growth, certainty, and even corporate survival may be totally off base.

The basic rationale for international investing is that it offers a bigger
pond to fish in. Canada and the United Kingdom together have more
listed stocks than the United States. So do Bermuda, Australia, Hong
Kong, and Singapore, not to mention the rest of the English-speaking
world. You do get greater diversification by investing overseas, but as
businesses have globalized, some of these benefits have been reduced.

International investing also adds a series of risks, especially in the
developing world, where the rights of small foreign investors are often
poorly protected. Never assume that the conditions that prevail in your

home country exist around the world. With foreign institutions and culture, you want to be sure the answer to "Do I understand it?" is "Yes." Unless you take the time to understand the differences, investing beyond your comfort zone is perilous.

In developed nations that were part of the British Empire, most businesspeople speak English. Company financial accounts and research reports can be technical enough in English without adding the subtleties of translation. In many nations, especially in northern Europe, English is a language of business. Some companies, especially larger multinationals, publish press releases in multiple languages. While computer translations of press releases are roughly correct, sometimes there are major glitches. Moreover, the same words in different languages often have very different connotations. The leading brand of bread in Mexico and Spain is Bimbo. That's BEEM-bo, you bimbo. I had never thought of Sara Lee as a Bimbo, but it's one of Bimbo's brands.

Foreign investments will be priced in a foreign currency, which can add risk. Some currencies are linked to the U.S. dollar as a matter of government policy, usually because there's a lot of trade with the United States. The Bermudian dollar is always worth a U.S. dollar, and the two currencies can be used interchangeably in Bermuda. The Hong Kong dollar is roughly pegged to the U.S. dollar as well. The British pound tends to stay in wider bands relative to both the euro and the U.S. dollar. Currency movements also reflect inflation in the country. Given modest trade with the United States and very high inflation, the Zimbabwe dollar plunged from parity with the U.S. dollar in 1983 to 300 trillion to the dollar in 2009 before being phased out entirely. Some countries block or limit movements of money out of the country.

Some investors believe that democracy and rule of law do not matter to investors, as many economies are growing rapidly without these frameworks. I disagree. If I am going to send capital to a place far away, I want to know in advance what the laws are and how they will be enforced. As a foreigner, I prefer the rules to be as general, equal, and certain as possible. Even in countries with rule of law, acquaintances and locals get better treatment.

Property means different things at different times and in different places. The idea of governments protecting property rights goes back to the thirteenth century and the *Magna Carta*. The Enclosure Acts in England created individual property rights on farmland that had been held as commons. In the United States before the Civil War, two-fifths of the population of the southern States was considered property. Conversely, intellectual property hardly existed in 1860 but has been increasingly protected in the United States. Copyrights originally ran for fourteen years plus a renewal, but now may extend to 120 years. Every major government owns some land and businesses collectively. In communist countries, the government owns most of the economy.

For most of the twentieth century, the British government took an increasingly large role in its economy. A number of companies and industries were nationalized, including telephone, electricity, gas, and water utilities. Basic industries like coal and steel were also taken over, as were transport industries like bus and rail. The government also owned Rolls-Royce (the aircraft engine producer), British Leyland (producer of Jaguar and other automobiles), Amersham (life sciences), and the British Broadcasting Corporation. The top tax bracket in the UK peaked during World War II at 99.25 percent and was 95 percent in 1966 when the Beatles released their song "Taxman."

In the 1980s, British Prime Minister Margaret Thatcher set in motion a massive program of privatizing industries that had been owned by the government, including most of the companies listed above. As Fidelity's natural gas utility analyst, I followed British Gas after it had been privatized in 1986. It did well, and Thatcher's regulatory framework seemed more attractive than the American rules. As with American utilities, the regulator had a rate of return in mind, but it was stated in inflation-adjusted terms. During the 1970s, American utilities had been devastated because their tariffs had not kept up with inflation.

When the water industry was privatized, the shares were packaged and priced to move. There were ten water and sewage companies, initially sold as a bundle. You had to pay only for part of the package up front and the rest in a later installment. The dividend yields were attractive, and I presumed would rise with inflation. The British government had injected a stack of cash, the "green dowry," to prefund enormous capital investments that were mandated to meet environmental and water quality standards. Best of all, the stocks were all offered at single-digit price/

earnings ratios (P/Es). The bargain prices reflected investor fears that water quality laws would be tightened further, forcing even more spending. Water privatization was politically unpopular, and some speculated that the regulator would favor its critics.

Because water mains last for decades, they could be run at the lowest cost by skimping on maintenance (especially of sewers) and the environment. The regulator thought that the waterworks could be run more efficiently each year, which should curb the increases in the water bill. Some regions were more rural or had more coastline, like South West Water, and so needed to spend more on water quality and cleanup. For shareholders, the allowed return on capital was likely to be close to historical real returns on British stocks. Water seemed like a less risky business than average, and it had inflation protection. I initially invested in the bundle of all ten companies, and then shifted toward a few with lower P/Es and the strongest balance sheets.

By 1997, seven years later, most of the water stocks were not far from tripling their fully paid price at privatization. That's a spectacular result, but it turns out that the S&P 500 index of American stocks and the FTSE 100 index of British stocks were up roughly the same amount. While the water companies were good stocks, they weren't great bull market stocks. If I beat the market over that period, it was mostly because the dividend yield on the water stocks was much higher than on the average stock. There was also some benefit from paying for the shares on the installment plan. I had obtained favorable performance with relatively low risk.

I had worried that Britain might be a lackluster place to invest, but I now believe that English-speaking countries are some of the best places to start investing abroad. GDP per capita grew more slowly over the last century in the UK than in many other nations. Usually investors flock to the countries where the most vigorous growth is anticipated. One of the surprises of international investing is that the countries with rapid growth in GDP per capita are not the ones with the best real returns to stockholders. Japan and Italy had among the highest growth in per capita GDP over a century, but stock returns in Japan were only average and in Italy were comparatively low. Wars had catastrophic effects on both of these nations and their stock markets.

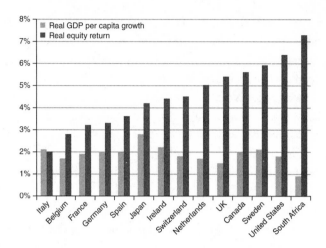

FIGURE 8.1 Real equity return and real GDP per capita growth, 1900–2015.

Throughout the century, Australia, Sweden, South Africa, the United States, Canada, and the UK were the countries with the best stock returns (figure 8.1). GDP per capita did not grow particularly fast in these countries, but several did have above-average population growth. Immigrants and capital are both attracted to countries with rule of law. Where there's rule of law, there's also more trust in business relationships. English-speaking countries also tend to require more complete disclosure to investors, which makes it easier to choose specific stocks. Where the language and culture are more familiar to you, you have a better handle on what you do not know. At a horizon of ten years, the better decision rule for choosing among countries with rule of law has been to favor markets with lower P/Es rather than those with rapid recent economic growth.

Turning Japanese

Japan is a safe, democratic, capitalist country with rule of law and respect for property rights. Socialism has never been popular there. The conservative Liberal Democratic Party has been in power since 1955 with only brief interruptions. Japan has nationalized fewer companies than the United States. By all reports, fraud and corruption are rare in Japan outside of the *yakuza*-infested construction industry.

In 2011, Japan was a fantastic place for an investor to look for value. I was delighted to find shares of many well-managed, well-financed companies selling for less than book value and at single-digit P/Es. I scheduled a trip to meet as many companies as I could in a week. With many stocks to choose from and low prices, I figured the downside was tame and the upside substantial. I was there during the 9.0 magnitude Tohoku earthquake, which may have contributed to the somber mood.

I had a very productive week. Between a Japanese small company conference and company visits at the Fidelity offices, I met executives of about two dozen prospective investments. Overall, the companies I met were dynamic and entrepreneurial. Some executives had founded their companies and owned big blocks of stock, which isn't the norm in Japan. You don't need a translator to see when managers are enthusiastic about their business.

In the United States, every executive has been instructed that his or her top goal is increasing shareholder value. When I bring up this idea in Japan, most businessmen (and in Japan, they are men) have no clue what I'm talking about. Perhaps it's because employing armies of people and having a dominant market share bring more prestige in Japan than high profits. Some argue that the Japanese are taking a longer view than American corporations. Eventually, having a strong market share should lead to profits. On average, though, Japanese companies earn lower returns on equity than other businesses around the globe. Social ties and responsibilities are conceived differently in Japan.

"The nail that sticks out gets hammered down"; so goes the Japanese proverb. If making too much money would make them stick out, they won't do it. CEOs in Japan are paid much smaller multiples of the average employee's pay than CEOs in America. Employees probably do feel greater loyalty to their company when everyone is more nearly in the same boat. This might explain why politics is less polarized in Japan. But today the "salaryman" system of lifetime employment really exists only at larger companies. Many companies try to prevent being hammered down by holding large cash balances and avoiding debt.

In the 1980s, Tokyo was the world's stock market darling. The Nikkei index peaked in December 1989 at a daily close of 38,916, which put its P/E near seventy. Some said that asset values mattered more than corporate earnings, and companies had lots of assets. But real estate assets were in an even bigger bubble than stocks. Trophy properties in Tokyo's Ginza district sold for as much as $1 million a square meter. For an average size home in the United States, that would equate to a price of about $200 million. For a period, hundred-year mortgages were used to finance these properties. Cynics said that earnings were inflated by *zaitech*, which usually meant borrowing money to finance speculative trading. Two decades later, the Nikkei languished around 10,000, down about three-quarters from its peak, which it has never revisited.

Looking around Tokyo, you would never suspect that its stock market has been dismal for a quarter of a century. It feels like a country with a very high standard of living. GDP per capita has grown as fast in Japan as in the United States, and unemployment is lower. In the center of Tokyo, the area around the Imperial Palace feels calm, dignified, and safe.

As an investor, I want profits that will keep sticking out and not be pounded down quickly. The retail industry is where I've most often found the un-Japanese desire to stand out, and these have indeed been standout investments for me. Cosmos Pharmaceutical is a discount drugstore chain on Kyushu, a smaller island on the southwest corner of Japan, far away from Tokyo. Cosmos offered very sharp prices to consumers by keeping a tight rein on operating costs. Its selling, general, and administrative (SG&A) expense was just 14 percent of sales, an outstanding number. Walmart, which also pinches pennies, spends 19 percent of sales on SG&A.

Cosmos was founded in 1983 by its CEO, Masateru Uno, and has grown rapidly. Perhaps because Cosmos is in a less populated region of Japan, good store locations can be secured more quickly and at a lower cost. Drugstores earn better profit margins on private label products than on branded products; Cosmos sells a lot of private label. Cosmos turns its inventory over faster than the leading American drugstores, CVS and Walgreens. The average life expectancy is four years longer in Japan than in the United States, so the population is aging. This would seem to set up drugstores for strong growth, but the stock was trading at only ten times earnings in 2011. Over the next five years, the stock soared sixfold, as growth continued and the P/E expanded.

China

For the super-rich, Hong Kong is a libertarian paradise. It's easy to do business in Hong Kong, with free trade, little regulation, and courts that protect property and enforce contracts. If you invest internationally, these institutional factors often turn out to be more critical to investment returns than GDP growth. China ranks number 139 on the Heritage Foundation Index of Economic Freedom, so people go to Hong Kong (and Macau) to do things they cannot do in China. The disparity in economic freedom is historically rooted. For centuries, China confined foreign trade to designated cities. The British East India Company illegally imported opium, creating social devastation and triggering the Opium War of 1839–1842. This reinforced China's suspicion of free trade and foreigners in general.

My first visit to China in 1993 was to factories and offices of companies listed in Hong Kong. The Chinese stock markets had opened only a few years earlier, and *gweilos* (foreign white devils) would not be allowed to trade on them until 2014. Apparently, many state companies were not eager to talk with foreigners. This was my first visit to a developing nation, so I wasn't sure what to expect.

Social conditions bear directly on the dynamics of profitability and growth in China. Unlike in America, labor is cheap, so even at modern electronics plants, squadrons of live humans visually inspected circuit boards for minute defects. Many companies provide spartan employee dorms and board, which affects their cost structure. Migrant workers need to obtain a local *hukou* (residency permit) to obtain social services such as health care, education, and welfare, which may affect labor supply or chain workers to an employer. Environmental and product safety regulations are enforced sporadically, which might minimize costs. Everything depends on government officials. Corruption in America means the rich buy politicians; in China, officials in the Communist Party become rich.

People have varying appetites for the unknown. I had eaten adventurously and learned a lot in China. But I felt as though my eyes had been opened about how little I knew about Chinese culture and institutions. Warren Buffett is wildly successful largely because he sticks to things he knows and understands thoroughly. Despite one of my most memorable trips ever, I bought only a few stocks in Hong Kong, and those were small positions. Among them, Yue Yuen, which manufactures shoes for Nike, Adidas, and others, had grown briskly while paying a large dividend yield. I still needed to learn more, especially about the details of individual companies.

Foreigners are not allowed to own certain Chinese technology or communications firms. Although you can invest in a whizzy Chinese Internet stock like Alibaba, Baidu, or Ctrip, what you own is a variable interest entity. All of the licenses and permits to operate in sensitive industries are legally held by a Chinese company. Foreigners buy shares in a holding company, which can be domiciled outside of China and receive fees and royalties from the Chinese company but doesn't own it. Exactly what that means is up to the Communist Party.

Can't See the Forest for the Trees

Around 2000, a brokerage analyst informed me that China was one of the fastest-growing markets for Canadian forest products and that there was a Chinese tree plantation company listed in Toronto. It was named Sino-Forest, had grown rapidly, and the stock was around $1 a share, which equated to about half of book value and three times earnings. Sino had some debt, including some convertible debt, and some warrants, but adjusting for them didn't change my view. The stock stagnated for three years; then six months into 2003, it abruptly doubled. Sino-Forest took the opportunity to raise money by issuing new shares.

When a company issues new shares at a low multiple of earnings and asset value, I always wonder why. Sometimes executives don't realize how dilutive this is for existing shareholders. When I met Sino-Forest management, they didn't seem ignorant of shareholder value. Banks can force distressed companies to raise equity capital, but this didn't seem to be the case. Management contended that they were issuing new shares at a disadvantageous price because they had spectacular opportunities to use the capital.

I wasn't completely sure what Sino's business was. Sino bought the rights to harvest timber, I assumed, from the government, but it also sold cutting rights—to whom, I never knew. Sino claimed to use marketing agents that it could not disclose, who sold to unknown customers.

And what, exactly, did Sino-Forest own? In China, no one owns land; the government owns it all. Chairman Mao completely nationalized private property in 1956. This was a repeated pattern in Chinese history; during the Ming Dynasty, emperors expropriated landed estates and then rented them out. Even in Hong Kong, the only freehold land is St. John's Cathedral, an Anglican church. Property owners in China own leaseholds or rights of usage or rights of development that last from thirty to seventy years. Especially outside of Beijing and Shanghai, there is no uniform system for registering property, so I was never able to verify Sino-Forest's property. Sino-Forest insisted that the lease agreements and names of counterparties were confidential.

Despite my concerns, Sino-Forest stock was a rocket ship. Between 2002 and 2007, Sino-Forest's earnings per share more than doubled even as the number of shares increased dramatically. The stock had surged to $18, giving it a P/E of twenty. Investors had bought into the story that China would gobble up all of the world's natural resources.

But I couldn't let go of nagging doubts about property rights in China. One Chinese analyst asked, "If China is such a land of opportunity, why is everyone moving family and capital out?" I prayed Sino's business didn't depend too much on political favor. Sino-Forest's cofounder and other senior executives bailed out of some of their shares. I followed their example and sold out my position. Over the next four years, Sino-Forest reported that the hectares of forest it managed more than doubled, as did revenues and earnings. The stock slumped during the global financial crisis and then recovered.

In 2011, a Canadian research firm called Muddy Waters published a report asserting that Sino-Forest had falsified its financial statements. Unlike most American frauds, which embellish reality, Sino-Forest had made up almost everything. The Muddy Waters report alleged that

Sino-Forest used "authorized intermediaries" to buy and sell forest products and pay taxes and expenses so there would be less of an audit trail. There were also transactions that might involve self-dealing by officers, a feature that you often find in developing-world frauds.

The Muddy Waters research exposed way too many details that I hadn't known. Sino-Forest put up no money to buy logs or make wood chips and didn't get cash from the buyers of wood chips; everything happened through the intermediaries. In 2010, Sino-Forest claimed to have harvested more than six times its legal quota in Yunnan, a remote province in southwest China with poor roads that is 92 percent mountainous.

For me, the biggest revelation was that Chinese companies must file financial statements with the State Administration for Industry & Commerce (SAIC) and that Muddy Waters had been able to access the SAIC reports. The numbers shown on the SAIC forms were utterly different from the figures reported to investors. I hadn't known that SAIC forms were available to the public for cross-checking. Briefly, I requested SAIC forms on every Chinese company with a scent of fraud. Later, it became impossible to get these forms as the Communist Party closed ranks to protect its own.

In 2012, Sino-Forest filed for bankruptcy in Canada.

Rule of Law

Before you invest internationally, you should consider your own comfort zone and appetite for learning. For most investors, the developed countries of the former British Empire are the best places to start—and stop. In these countries, the rule of law applies. The language, legal systems, business customs, and accounting standards are similar enough that, given a set of facts, the investment conclusion is the same as it would be in the United States. Investors who are willing to study foreign cultures should still stick to countries with rule of law unless they have extensive research support. They also need to understand that in many parts of the world, social position is not always linked to the profitability of an enterprise and matters more to business decisions than profits.

PART III
Honest, Capable Fiduciaries

9

Dare to Be Great! Or, Distinctive Character

Never do things others can do and will do if there are things
others cannot do or will not do.

—AMELIA EARHART

THE VALUE OF A BUSINESS DEPENDS ON the quality of its management, and
good managers are skillful and honest. If they are not skillful, they'll
squander your capital. If they lack integrity, they'll steal it. So how do
you test for skill? At the risk of ignoring critical skills like leadership,
I hone in on two markers: distinctive capability and capital allocation.

In this chapter, I assert that companies are not well run if they are
not constantly striving to be ever more uniquely valuable to customers.
Unless customers would miss a company if it went away, it eventually will. Companies need products distinctive enough to justify high-
profit margins, plus a barrier to entry (or "moat") to protect those
high profits. Without distinctiveness, businesses have fewer opportunities to deploy capital profitably. As a value investor, I'm looking
for companies that are increasing the amount by which their intrinsic
value exceeds their accounting values. This difference is called *economic goodwill*.

In chapter 10, I'll show how I look for companies that are great stewards of capital. Relative to the capital invested, they make high profits. If
they acquire businesses, they find like-minded people and don't overpay.
When they are short of great uses for capital, they return it by paying
dividends or buying back shares.

Distinctive Character

You might wonder why I focus on character rather than business strategy or positioning. In brief, character doesn't change and positioning does. Everything that has brought a company to the present moment has shaped its character. A company has to be open to new possibilities but will be more suited to some opportunities than others. Whenever a company attempts a strategy that defies its history, I generally expect the past to catch up with it, as when J. C. Penney cut back on specials and coupons in hopes of moving upmarket. Managements that accept their limitations are more likely to find ways to make them less of a handicap—and thereby succeed. From an analyst's standpoint, this method is not only prudent but convenient. A company's character needs to be assessed only once, whereas tracking a company's strategy and tactics demands constant updates. Most companies lack a strong character. This does not mean that they will be poor investments—only that they are less apt to be exceptional.

When I set out to understand a company's character, I pretend that I'm a potential customer. I check out the marketing website or sales flyers or visit a store. Any forum will do, as long as the business is trying to convince prospects that it offers better merchandise, or at least a cheaper price. Occasionally, annual reports and basic research reports from brokerages help with this task, but I ignore everything about quarterly reporting during my examination of a company's character. To me, Apple seems smart, elegant, and occasionally quirky but otherwise easy to get along with. GEICO is honest, thrifty, and good-natured. Many companies have a bland character. If after an hour of study you are still baffled, don't sweat it. Move on to the company's strategy.

The secret of success in business and investing is to do something useful that no one else is doing. The job of skilled managers is to protect and extend that distinctiveness. Once others imitate it, the bloom is off the rose. Some businesses have unique and innovative products, other companies are organized distinctively, and still others have brands that resonate with customers. Competitors will copy what they can, so what was once special will become mundane. Customer tastes will change, so businesses must constantly evolve to remain distinctive. While I think there is great value to studying the best manufacturing or financial practices of competitors, the point of strategy is to do well something those competitors are *not* doing or are doing badly. Character provides clues about what that uniqueness might be.

Strategy: Do What Others Can't

According to strategy guru Michael Porter of the Harvard Business School, successful business strategies are at the opposite poles of each of two choices: (1) aim to dominate the entire industry or, alternately, target only the few segments in which it can excel; (2) choose between winning by marketing superior products or, alternately, by offering bargain prices. Companies run into trouble when they are not clear about whether they are serving the whole market or just focusing on specific niches. Also, quality products and low prices can't be equally important objectives, or a company will be stuck in the middle. If you can't discern whether the goals are market domination or focus, superb products or bargain prices, odds are that the strategy won't work, Porter says. A fuzzy strategy also suggests that a company has not given much thought to its circle of competence.

A strategy must be tailored to a business's character and limitations or the result will be a sloppy fit. Even robust enterprises have limitations; the market leader can't grow much faster than the industry. Many of my investments are in small companies with finite resources. There's no way they could offer all of the best products in every single segment and geography. Nor could they be the lowest-cost producer of everything that an industry offers. Instead, they must pick their spots. They focus on a regional market area or find a niche. Cement, for example, is expensive to ship, so the competitors that matter are usually local. Lululemon Athletica sells only yoga-themed clothes, serving a not-so-small market that major apparel companies had previously neglected.

In commodity-like businesses, the products are all pretty much identical, so the only way to compete is with low prices. Some industries have major economies of scale, which implies that the biggest companies will have the lowest costs. Managing the supply chain, which includes squeezing suppliers, is generally a large-company game as well. But there are ways for small companies to keep costs down, like cutting out elements of a product that customers don't value highly. Customers are generally more loyal to companies with superior products than to those with low prices, so quality is the better way to go if a company has a choice. Staying a step ahead of competitors creates an endless rat race, though, especially in rapidly evolving industries.

If successful strategies aim at either the total industry or specific segments, and at either quality or price, there are four possible combinations of strategy. Let's consider each of them, starting with a **superior product for the whole industry**. The most exciting way for a business to be distinctive is to create an innovation that is totally new to the world. In the 2004 initial public offering prospectus for an Internet company, I read, "We believed we could provide a great service to the world—instantly delivering relevant information on any topic." Few companies would make such a bold statement, and even fewer should. The company was, of course, Google.

Google didn't invent the search engine; its innovation was the power of its algorithms. Any company that talks about service to the world will not be content with niches; it is shooting for global domination. Google is the best search engine because it treats some categories of search as specialties—scholarly, patents, maps, and images to name a few. I suspect the algorithms behind these specialties have overlapping pieces. Most technically driven businesses protect their position with patents, so the number and quality of patents can indicate the strength of their position. Google had only thirty-eight patents by the end of 2006, but in 2016, for example, Google filed 2,835 additional patents. Patents might no longer even be necessary, given Google's brand and constant innovation. The Google name—like Xerox and Clorox—has become synonymous with its category. (In 2015, Google created a holding company, Alphabet Inc., for Google and its moonshot ventures.)

Walmart is an example of a company with a well-executed strategy of selling to a **very broad market at low prices**. Currently, it has more than 11,000 stores in more than two dozen countries. Other than entire houses, cars, and gasoline, Walmart carries just about every product that a moderate-income family would buy. Until the 1980s, though, you might have called Walmart a niche player. It didn't introduce groceries until 1988, and nearly all of its stores were in the southern United States. Measured by return on equity, profits peaked in the 1980s, but in dollars, profits reached new highs almost every year until 2013. Over time, Walmart's character hasn't changed; it is still frugal, efficient, dependable, and family-oriented. What competitors see, and shoppers don't, is that Walmart has always been an eager learner. It gathers data on everything and studies all the brightest ideas in retailing.

Walmart is constantly on a treadmill; low prices are only a winning business strategy when expenses are even lower. Like its initial customers, Walmart was frugal because it had to be. As an undifferentiated general store, it's tough to make money from people who don't have much. Vendors go to Walmart's headquarters in Bentonville, Arkansas, knowing they will be squeezed. On the other hand, suppliers benefit from volumes that can be enormous and from Walmart's suggestions for cost reductions. To get rock-bottom costs, manufacturers standardize on products without frills or whimsy. With bar coding and just-in-time purchasing, Walmart keeps inventories at appropriate levels, as do vendors. As Walmart expands, administrative costs get spread over a larger volume of sales. Walmart rarely locates stores in high-rent districts; most of its employees are nonunion.

GEICO is an example of **competing on price by focusing on a niche** of customers who don't need or want certain services. It was founded as Government Employees Insurance Company because it initially provided coverage *only* to government employees, who were statistically safer drivers than average. Most car insurance is sold through sales agents, and sales agents are costly, but they help insurance companies assign risk categories to customers and they provide advice, especially when an accident occurs. GEICO didn't have a large agency sales force and, being of thrifty character, wasn't eager to pay up to recruit sales personnel. Instead, GEICO management organized themselves differently; they sold insurance directly to policyholders.

By eliminating sales agents, GEICO cut out a service that, for safe drivers, costs more than it's worth. If you really don't know which insurance coverage is appropriate, or you anticipate that you will be in an accident, an agent could be helpful. But if you know what you want and never file any claims, you have no need for a relationship with your auto insurance agent. Not everyone is an above-average driver, so this niche isn't for everyone. For its part, GEICO doesn't want to cover you if you don't fit a low-risk profile. Good drivers have accidents too, and GEICO doesn't skimp on claims service. No one wants to look tacky while bargain hunting, so GEICO uses humor in its advertising to get us to admit that, yes, we'd like to save money.

Energetically Fizzy

For small companies, my favorite strategies combine **superior products with niche markets.** By definition, niche markets are not mainstream, so you need to keep your eyes open to spot niches. Luck helps, too. Shortly after the Internet bubble burst, I attended a technology stock conference. The share prices of many of the presenting tech companies were still tumbling back to earth. Thirsty and drooping a bit, I was delighted to see an investor booth and free beverage bar for a company called Hansen Naturals. The fruit drinks they served were all natural with no artificial flavors or colors or sodium, similar to Snapple.

Other than maybe its distribution system, though, Hansen didn't want to knock off Snapple; it catered to edgier, more adventurous Californian tastes. Hansen had started by selling fresh natural juices to Hollywood film studios. Later it added zing with spices and other natural ingredients. New Age teas and sodas fit in with Hansen's heritage, but Snapple had a powerful brand and better distribution. Instead, Hansen focused on "functional" drinks—drinks sold on their benefits, such as energy, vitamins, or antioxidants, rather than flavors. Not that Hansen could ignore taste, especially for its original juice beverages. At the time, this focus was so distinctive that it seemed to be out in left field.

Hansen's Monster energy drink tasted even better than Red Bull, the leading alternative, which had been introduced in the United States in 1997. Most people wouldn't want a beverage with the bracing tastes of ginseng, guarana, and taurine, but I would have when I was a student. I figured there might be an unserved market of engineers, party animals, truckers, night shift employees, and extreme sports players. But how big was the market really? Whenever basic ingredients like water, caffeine, and sugar are sold by the serving, the key to success is branding and marketing. But the Hansen brand was all about pure, natural, relaxing, and refreshing, which didn't fit with the energy drink. Ginseng and gua-rana are plants, so Monster was arguably more natural than Gatorade, but the idea of an energizing concoction seemed incompatible with the "natural" identity that Hansen had created. Monster had to create its image from scratch. The jagged neon green logo M on a black back-ground stands out on store shelves.

Hansen was a tiny company, but its sales had grown rapidly, it didn't have much debt, and its stock traded at ten times earnings. I bought some shares for around $4. Since then the shares have split many times; each share has become forty-eight shares so the current shares have a cost basis of 8 cents. Unexpectedly, sales and earnings went exponential. Fast-forward sixteen years: Sales of the Monster energy drink exploded, overshadowing the original fruit drinks so completely that the company was renamed Monster. Coca-Cola acquired a minority interest in Mon-ster and agreed to distribute its products. The stock price had multiplied more than 600-fold, touching a price of $54.

When I consider selling Monster from the fund, I search for a replace-ment company that is doing more to offer something customers find dis-tinctively valuable. Everything has a price, but among my most rewarding stocks, almost all had a unique character and positioning. Some Monster drinkers are zealous fans, which you don't often find with commodity-like businesses. Even as colas slip, sales of energy drinks are continuing to grow rapidly. When you do find a company that is truly one-of-a-kind, even in a small niche, it is a mistake to casually swap out of it for some-thing run-of-the-mill.

One of the ways I know that a management team is talented is that it develops a business with a distinctive character and unique capabilities. The best managers are product enthusiasts who bring to market products that they would personally buy but can't find elsewhere. Although larger companies can be category-killers, most companies can be markedly superior only by focusing on a narrow niche and building on that. It's never easy to maintain first-rate offerings or keep costs at rock bottom, but I give better odds to the quality strategy as long as the managers are product people. The exception is where costs can be slashed by cutting out an element that customers do not value.

Bang for the Buck

Part of the $10 million I spent on gambling, part on booze, and part
on women. The rest I spent foolishly.

—GEORGE RAFT

Capital Allocation

THOUGH YOU MAY BE THE LEGAL OWNER of a security, many of the
decisions that determine its value are made by others, so it's essential to choose good stewards for your assets. Your agents and managers, however able, are human beings, with a tendency to favor their
own interests if there is a dispute, so it's critical to find ones with
a demonstrated fiduciary mind-set. In extreme cases, normal self-
interest can veer off into criminality. Often your stewards attained
their position not by being capable stewards, but through ambition
and other accomplishments. CEOs often got to the top by force of
will and by being fantastic salesmen, plant managers, engineers, or
accountants.

Lacking both the time and the inclination to send out interviewers
or gumshoes to properly assess stewardship skills, I prefer to focus on
capital allocation. Really, I'm more of an armchair detective. I look for
something more numerical that I can get from readily available sources.
Capital allocation is a clunky term, but a useful concept meaning: follow
the money. Is it going to the right places? Have the managers directed
the capital at their disposal to the highest and best use possible given the
situation?

There are two related statistical ways to measure success—rate of return and present value—but both involve somewhat tenuous forecasts of the future. The first method compares the projected rate of return on capital improvements with a hurdle rate. Usually, this hurdle rate is tied to the "cost of equity," or the lowest rate of return that long-term shareholders would find acceptable. If investors require a return of no less than 8 percent, the company should reject capital projects that return any less. Assuming that a company with an 8 percent cost of equity invested in something that would return 13 percent over the next year, it would have invested one dollar to create roughly $1.05 ($1.13/1.08$) of present value. The goal is to add the largest possible amount of value.

When I tried to study capital allocation in two of my first industry assignments at Fidelity—coal and tobacco, I was stumped. What I was missing was the idea of off-balance sheet liabilities and *economic* goodwill. The historical accounting numbers didn't capture the value of capital and liabilities in these industries. For example, companies in both industries were defendants in lawsuits related to black lung disease and lung cancer. It was foreseeable that as verdicts for damages were rendered, companies would grudgingly settle claims, using capital in ways that offered no prospect of return. Cigarette companies at least had a positive offset to these anticipated liabilities in the form of powerful brand names. One subtlety was that the Surgeon General's warning issued in 1964 acted as a partial legal shield thereafter. Cigarette companies' exposure was proportionate to their *market share in 1964*. This favored Philip Morris, which had grown dramatically since then.

The other challenge was in determining the value of intangible assets such as brands. Marlboro and other powerful brands were on the books at nominal amounts but had tremendous customer loyalty, suggesting huge economic goodwill. Philip Morris and RJR Nabisco had acquired food companies with leading brands like Maxwell House and Oreo, and here the intangible acquisition cost was shown in their accounts as trademarks or goodwill. It was an accident of history that Philip Morris and RJR paid billions for their food brands and not so much for their cigarette brands. The historical cost has little to do with current value. One approach to valuing these brands is to use market prices rather than historical accounting cost. But the ratio of profits to the stock market value of a company is its earnings yield, or the inverse of the price/earnings ratio. This, while useful as an investing guide, says nothing about the quality of management's decisions.

I decided to forge ahead and use the accounting numbers despite their defects. The ratio of a company's earnings to its stockholder equity is called its return on equity (ROE). A high ROE suggests that a company is maximizing the profit per dollar of capital that shareholders put into the company. At the time, 12 percent was considered an average ROE. Almost the entire tobacco industry seemed to be head and shoulders better. U.S. Tobacco, which makes moist snuff, had an ROE approaching 50 percent, Philip Morris nearly 30 percent, and so on. RJR Nabisco, British American Tobacco (BAT), and American Brands all earned ROEs topping 20 percent.

In retrospect, the relative rankings of ROEs of companies in the late 1980s were a powerful indicator of their future returns. I also wanted to know the *reasons* for the high ROEs. U.S. Tobacco and Philip Morris had the highest returns and the most distinctive brands. U.S. Tobacco's Copenhagen and Philip Morris's Marlboro were (and are) by far the top brands in moist snuff and cigarettes. A more forward-looking assessment of capital allocation could be gleaned by studying specific uses of cash.

Expanding the Business or Building Value?

For potential growth projects, everything is considered on an incremental basis. The increases in sales and profits are compared with the added capital required. For tobacco companies, the profit on increased sales from an existing plant is surreal. In 2016, the cost of goods sold for Altria (parent of Philip Morris USA and U.S. Tobacco) was 30 percent of sales. Tobacco leaf, paper, filter, and packaging were less than half of the cost of goods, with legal settlements accounting for the majority. Marketing, research, administration, and corporate took another 10 percent of sales. Even after excise taxes of 25 percent of sales, an operating profit margin of 34 percent remained. (The operating profit margin for the S&P500 was about 12 percent in 2016.) If a company has spare capacity and can make and sell more products, it can spread its fixed costs. The incremental rate of profit will be even higher than the already spectacular average.

Even though returns on fixed assets are out of this world in the tobacco business, that math doesn't apply to building new capacity. Cigarettes are made in very few factories. Producing more in one plant often means making fewer in another. If new capacity could be used as fully as the existing facilities, the profit margin on those sales might look like the overall average of 34 percent. Few businesses have margins that wide; better still, cigarettes take little capital to produce. Altria logged $25.7 billion in sales in 2014 using property, plant, and equipment with a depreciated cost of just under $2 billion. Yearly operating profits were more than 400 percent of the value of its physical plant. Obviously, that return soars above any normal hurdle rate, which might be closer to 10 percent. Distinctive businesses can grow at only a certain rate and keep their character and profitability.

Around the world, cigarette consumption has fallen in wealthier countries (figure 10.1). By contrast, in the poorer places, rising incomes brought more smoking. In those countries, investments to expand production paid off handsomely, even though selling prices were lower. For historical antitrust reasons, the companies that owned brands in the

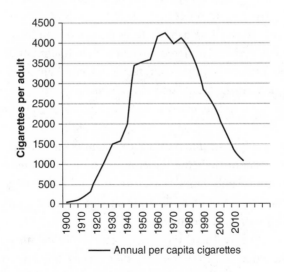

— Annual per capita cigarettes

FIGURE 10.1 U.S. cigarette consumption, 1900–2014.

United States often did not control them overseas—Marlboro being the prime exception. Marlboro is *the* truly global brand. In many cases, tobacco has been a national business. For tax and regulatory reasons, cigarettes are mostly made in the countries where they are sold.

In the late 1980s, as foreign markets opened up, RJR Nabisco vigorously expanded its export sales off a low base, opening a gigantic, highly efficient new plant. In many manufacturing industries, overinvestment can lead to disaster, but the Tobaccoville plant consumed only a modest chunk of RJR's cash flow.

For cigarette companies, marketing spending was larger than capital spending, and it was critical to know whether money spent on marketing actually kept customers and brought in new ones. Advertising spending can be an investment in building brands (and economic goodwill) or just cash out the door. Managements themselves often can't know. Unless future sales are under contract, accountants expense the whole cost. Apple, Nestlé, Louis Vuitton, and Walt Disney spend and charge off billions in marketing costs each year. Generally, their brands become more valuable over time, increasing economic goodwill. RJR was in a tough spot, supporting many smaller brands while Philip Morris had a blockbuster in Marlboro.

For Philip Morris, spending marketing dollars on a single powerhouse brand carried more potential benefits than RJR's spending on a multitude of brands. RJR splashed out hundreds of millions on sports marketing, keeping thirty athletes on retainer. It bought billboards in stadiums so that they would be seen during televised games. Packaging was restyled. Joe Camel, a new cartoon brand mascot, drew the attention of youthful smokers and regulators. RJR maintained a stable share in a shrinking market.

In all businesses, profits and losses today stem from a collage of decisions, big and trivial, made in the sometimes distant past, often by people who are no longer around. Dumb luck can be as influential as good judgment. Ross Johnson, CEO of RJR, quipped, "Some genius invented the Oreo. We're just living off the inheritance."

Similarly, before it featured the rugged cowboy in its ads, Marlboro had been launched as a ladies' cigarette that was as "mild as May." The red filter tip, meant to hide lipstick stains, was later switched to a manly cork brown. Decades after the rebranding, Philip Morris was still reaping the benefits of an iconic package and mascot. Over a quarter of a century, the company catapulted from an also-ran to the market leader.

Price discounting suggests that either prices are too high or product features don't matter much. Around 1984, RJR repositioned Doral as a branded discount cigarette. At sharply reduced prices, the margins on cheap smokes were lower but still attractive. By 1992, RJR's fastest growing segments were Doral and its generic cigarettes. To gain market share, RJR dropped wholesale prices of discount cigarettes by 20 percent. It worked; the next year, 42 percent of RJR's volume was discounted. Marlboro sales eroded, so Philip Morris slashed prices as well. My suspicion is that, having weaker brands, RJR let its marketing strategy be led by its superior manufacturing capacity.

In the 1990s, R. J. Reynolds made a controversial investment in a smokeless cigarette called Premier. Research and development for Premier cost at least $300 million, and the all-in costs may have topped $800 million. Smokers become habituated to tobacco by the nicotine, but the real health risks come from inhaling burning tar. The Premier cigarette heated tobacco and delivered nicotine vapors to smokers. Around launch time, RJR sent me a carton of Premier cigarettes. Not being a smoker myself, I turned to Beth, a portfolio manager who both smoked and invested in tobacco stocks. She pulled out her lighter and after half a dozen attempts was able to inhale a few puffs.

"Jesus!" she bellowed, "It takes a fucking blowtorch to light this thing and then it tastes like shit."

Apparently, many others agreed. RJR advised consumers that they would need to smoke at least a couple of packs to get the hang of Premier, but Beth didn't stick around for that. About a year later, RJR folded Premier, although the vapor idea was later revived as Eclipse. At the time, I thought that the whole fiasco was a colossal boondoggle. With hindsight, perhaps RJR should have pushed Premier harder. Jump ahead to the new millennium when better e-cigarettes and vaping technology have entered the market. RJR launched Vuse e-cigarettes, which finally did get a favorable reception.

RJR generated far more cash than it invested. Unless a business is growing exponentially, I expect it to be financially self-sufficient with internally generated funds (including retained profits) more than enough to cover all of its growth. To check this, I look to the statement of cash flows in a company's financial report. Cash flows from operations are the sum of net income, depreciation, amortization, changes in working capital, and other items. Then I sum up all the categories of capital spending needed to maintain and expand the business. These include purchases of property, plant, and equipment and investment in software, but not purchases of investments or other businesses.

My definition of "free cash flow" is "cash flows from operating activities" minus all of the cash paid out for the investing activities listed above. Then and now, tobacco firms reinvested tiny fractions of their cash flows in the business. In 2014, Altria had $4.663 billion of cash from operations. Capital spending was $163 million, a bit under depreciation. This left $4.5 billion of free cash flow. Free cash flow is available to buy businesses and investments, pay off debt, or return to shareholders through dividends or share buybacks. We'll soon come back to those alternatives.

Most companies that run negative free cash flow are trying to grow faster than their ROE will allow. If a corporation doesn't issue or buy back stock or pay dividends, its equity will grow at the same rate as its ROE. Despite recent ROEs of more than 100 percent, Altria is not trying to grow 100 percent a year. There are congenital optimists who habitually outspend cash flow in industries such as independent oil and gas, home building, and airlines.

To tell whether negative free cash flow is worrisome or not, I check a company's ratio of profits to capital invested—that is, its return on capital employed (ROCE). This is defined as operating profits as a percent of total capital, including both debt and equity. I'm much more impressed by an ROE of 13 percent based on a 13 percent ROCE with no debt than by the same ROE built on a 7 percent ROCE and a lot of debt. In a downturn, the profits of the levered company usually fall harder. A low or falling ROCE might signal that management is taking on some mediocre projects. When low or falling returns persist for years, I'm especially wary of negative free cash flow and rising debt.

Acquisitions and Spin-Offs: Bigger or Better?

Most studies say something like two-thirds of acquisitions miss the financial targets used to justify their purchase price. Acquisitions rarely happen without the buyer paying a control premium. To earn back the premium, a buyer must do something with a company that wasn't already being done. Profits have to be improved somehow. That could happen by increasing sales or cutting costs or at least avoiding taxes.

Some deals are about financial engineering and rely on borrowing money cheaply or the willingness of the buyer to accept a lower rate of return. Often the shares of the acquiring company slip after the deal is announced. In general, the mergers and acquisitions that have the best odds involve low valuation multiples and premiums and combine similar businesses.

The specter of antitrust litigation prevented takeovers in the tobacco industry until the mid-1990s; then there was a deluge. In 1994, American Brands sold its American Tobacco Company to BAT's Brown & Williamson division and changed its name to Fortune Brands. In 2003, BAT's Brown & Williamson was merged into Reynolds American, giving BAT a 42 percent stake in the combined company. RJR sold its international operations to Japan Tobacco and bought Conwood, a moist snuff producer. U.S. Tobacco was purchased by Altria in 2009. In 2014, Reynolds agreed to acquire Lorillard. As far as I know, none of these deals has disappointed. They were done at reasonable prices and were of businesses the managers understood well enough to know where to find cost savings.

RJR Nabisco returned to the public market in 1991, two years after its mostly debt-financed buyout by Kohlberg Kravis Roberts (KKR). RJR set about selling bits and pieces of businesses and carved out Nabisco as a separate food company. In 1995, 19 percent of Nabisco was sold in a public offering. Before the buyout, RJR's powerful brands gave it a large amount of economic goodwill, but after the buyout, their value was fully (maybe overly) reflected on its balance sheet as intangible assets of more than $20 billion. Both RJR Nabisco and Nabisco limped through the 1990s with single-digit ROEs in most years.

Acquirers must do something different with a business to justify paying a takeover premium, so it's not surprising that results were generally best in somewhat-related businesses. Packaged food and cigarettes are mass-market perishable consumer goods made with agricultural inputs. RJR's tobacco executives probably understood Nabisco's marketing and distribution strategies far better than they understood anything about shipping or oil. Likewise, Philip Morris was happier with General Foods and Kraft than with Mission Viejo, the home builder.

When a buyout is announced, historical operating profits and the price are usually disclosed as well, so an analyst can estimate a ROCE. It will, of course, be a low estimate as it doesn't reflect the profit improvements yet to come. The RJR Nabisco leveraged buyout had a $31 billion enterprise value—cash price plus debt assumed—and $2.8 billion in operating profit, for a ROCE of 9 percent. Even if nothing changed, it looked like an OK—but not amazing—deal.

Tobacco companies have reversed almost all of their diversification, indicating that either times have changed or it was a mistake all along. In 2000, RJR sold Nabisco to Philip Morris, leaving only tobacco operations. (Later it renamed itself Reynolds American.) In 2007, Philip Morris spun off Kraft, including Nabisco. The next year, Philip Morris split into Altria and Philip Morris International. During the period when Reynolds was a pure play and Philip Morris was diversified with Kraft Foods, Reynolds' stock more than quadrupled, while Philip Morris's stock more than tripled. Both were far in front of the stock market, but the pure tobacco company did better. RJR had resumed buying back stock and outdid Philip Morris, but this was partly a side effect of the Nabisco transaction, because Philip Morris had less cash to buy back its shares, having paid $9.8 billion to RJR to acquire Nabisco.

Philip Morris spun off Kraft in 2007 (and later Kraft spun out Mondelez). The stocks of the food company spin-offs have beaten the market, but so have the cigarette stocks. If there were benefits to the combinations, no one seems to have missed them. And these were the biggest, best deals. I don't think anyone really expected great things from the plant nursery, ballpoint pens, mortgage banker, or shipping line. For most executives, it's an unnatural act to reduce their prestige and span of control by spinning off and selling businesses. When it becomes clear to them that it is the best course of action, shareholders have often been asking for it for years.

Dividends

Businesses create wealth by making profits. Usually dividends reflect those profits, but paying a dividend doesn't itself create wealth—it just distributes the wealth that was created. In the twentieth century, most companies paid out half or more of their earnings in dividends. Currently, most companies issue dividends of less than half their profits. There are several reasons for this, including tax policy, the institutionalization of investing, and the rising popularity of stock options. Dividends are taxed as received, whereas the tax on the capital gain resulting from share buybacks is deferred until the investor sells. Most employee stock option plans do not adjust for dividends, so executives act as if the goal is the highest possible stock price rather than the greatest total return.

Companies that pay out a large proportion of their profits as dividends transmit two sometimes contradictory signals. First, a high payout ratio hints that a company has demanding standards for returns on expansion projects. Since the company can't find highly profitable growth projects, it is returning the cash to shareholders, who can use it better. A company with an unremarkable return on equity that isn't returning cash to shareholders may be putting money into projects with mediocre returns. It's especially worrisome if assets are growing robustly but profits are not.

Second, the payout ratio tells you whether the company sees a lot of profitable expansion opportunities. Small companies that are trying to grow explosively usually don't pay dividends. Some companies are more optimistic and confident about their prospects than others. Berkshire Hathaway has not paid a dividend since Warren Buffett arrived; share repurchases have been rare as well. This profile proclaims supreme confidence in Berkshire's ability to allocate capital better than its investors. For most CEOs other than Buffett, I would infer hubris or low standards for returns. Tobacco companies have the opposite approach. They pay out roughly three-quarters of profits as dividends and top that off with share repurchases.

Statisticians say that stocks with healthy dividends slightly outperform the market averages, especially on a risk-adjusted basis. On average, high-yielding stocks have lower price/earnings ratios and skew toward relatively stable industries. Stripping out these factors, gener-ous dividends alone don't seem to help performance. So, if you need or like income, I'd say go for it. Invest in a company that pays high divi-dends. Just be sure that you are favoring stocks with low P/Es in stable industries. For good measure, look for earnings in excess of dividends, ample free cash flow, and stable proportions of debt and equity. Also look for companies in which the number of shares outstanding isn't rising rapidly.

To put a finer point on income stocks to skip, reverse those criteria. I wouldn't buy a stock for its dividend if the payout wasn't well covered by earnings and free cash flow. Real estate investment trusts, master lim-ited partnerships, and royalty trusts often trade on their yield rather than their asset value. In some of those cases, analysts disagree about the eco-nomic meaning of depreciation and depletion—in particular, whether those items are akin to earnings or not. Without looking at the specific situation, I couldn't judge whether the per share asset base was shrinking over time or whether generally accepted accounting principles account-ing was too conservative. If I see a high-yielder with swiftly rising share counts and debt levels, I assume the worst.

Share Buybacks

The winners and losers from buying back shares depend on the price the company pays for them. Like dividends, share buybacks distribute wealth; they don't create it. Unlike dividends, however, share buybacks can *redistribute* wealth among shareholders. If shares are repurchased at intrinsic value, the transaction is fair to all. But when shares are repur-chased at a premium over intrinsic value, value is taken away from loyal shareholders and given to those who depart. When shares are repur-chased at a discount from intrinsic value, selling shareholders lose and the remaining shareholders gain. Different people will arrive at different estimates of intrinsic value, so it's not always clear whether a buyback occurred at a favorable price or not. Without an estimate, though, one can't judge whether management is adding to per share value by buying back stock.

To understand the transfer of wealth, consider a corporation with 100 shares, whose only asset consists of $10,000 in cash with no ongoing business. The intrinsic value of each share is equal to the proportional share of the cash, or $100. Suppose that forty shares were repurchased for $160 a share, for a total of $6,400. The company would then have $3,600 in cash and sixty shares outstanding, or $60 per share. Selling shareholders would be ahead by $60 a share, while loyal shareholders would lose $40 per share in intrinsic value. Conversely, when a company buys back shares at a discount to intrinsic value, the loyal shareholders gain a proportionate share of that discount.

Buybacks are most popular when companies are feeling flush, and those are often the moments when buybacks are least beneficial. As the market was topping out in the third quarter of 2007, S&P 500 companies bought back $171 billion of stock. A year and a half later, the S&P crashed to half its former value, and in the first quarter of 2009, only $31 billion of stock was repurchased. This is disappointing not just because the timing of the buybacks was inopportune, but also because buybacks signal confidence in the company's value and outlook. Cheer is most appreciated when despair is all around. When I study some buybacks that turned out badly, I find that very few companies took the action because of a discount to intrinsic value.

Technology companies especially try to offset the dilution from hefty employee stock option grants. As share prices rise and options become more in the money, accountants consider a rising fraction of the shares under option to be outstanding. To keep a constant share count, shares will be bought back most urgently at the peak. Many companies have issued shares under option at lower prices and later repurchased them at higher prices. Return to our previous example of a company with 100 shares and $10,000 in cash. Suppose that it issued options on fifty shares to employees with a strike price of $100. Based on an option pricing formula, the value of the options might be calculated as $10 each or $500 in total. This amount would be reflected in the profit and loss, although shareholders would be urged to ignore it as a noncash charge. Suppose the stock then leaped to $160, all of the options were exercised, and the fifty new shares were repurchased. The company would collect $5,000 from the options exercise and shell out $8,000 to buy them back, leaving its cash balance at $7,000. Although the share count is steady, shareholders are out $3,000, or $30 per share.

Another reason why buybacks peak along with the stock market might be that a company's profits are topping out then. Perhaps cash *should* be returned to shareholders. But there's no law that requires this to be done immediately. In prosperous times, estimates of intrinsic value will be higher. Perceptions of the best balance of debt and equity will be less conservative. This may encourage companies to make an ill-timed decision to move to a more "efficient" balance sheet. That means taking on debt to buy back stock. If it is late in the economic cycle, and profit growth is slowing, per share earnings growth can be sustained by borrowing money to repurchase stock.

All of the tobacco companies consistently repurchase stock and have usually added value in doing so. The exception was RJR during the 1990s. Restrained by a large debt burden, it not only didn't buy back stock, but it also had to issue equity. I was glad that by this time I was no longer the tobacco analyst. RJR stock had fallen from its initial launch price, went sideways for years, popped, and slumped, leaving it lower at the end of the decade. Between 1990 and its peak in 1998, Philip Morris shares quadrupled in price, putting it miles ahead of the index and RJR, with the help of large stock buybacks. As RJR's finances strengthened, and after it sold Nabisco, it stepped up share repurchases and, as noted earlier, outperformed Philip Morris in the new millennium.

Stable, High Returns

Philip Morris and Reynolds were both above average in creating distinctive businesses and in allocating capital, but between them, Philip Morris was superior. In the 1970s, the total return on R. J. Reynolds was better than the overall market, but Philip Morris was far ahead. The same was true in the 1980s, if you take out the run-up to RJR's buyout in 1988. KKR's investors did not make money on the RJR deal, so again Philip Morris was in the lead. The pattern continued through the 1990s, but reversed in the new millennium.

One indicator of superior capital allocation is high and stable ROCE. Philip Morris's returns were higher and more stable over several decades. In some industries, an outsider can use rules of thumb to estimate incremental returns on growth projects and advertising, but not in tobacco. My sense is that Philip Morris did a more effective job. Mergers and acquisitions can be very good or very bad but, on average, disappoint. The odds are best for combinations of related businesses done at reasonable prices. Philip Morris had more success with its acquisitions than Reynolds, which may be why it continued to diversify even as Reynolds was going back to basics. Spin-offs go against the normal empire-building tendency, and as a result are often fantastic opportunities for investors.

If a company lacks opportunities to use capital at higher returns than an investor can find in the stock market, it should return the capital to shareholders through share buybacks or dividends. Through the 1990s, Reynolds's stingy capital return policy was a major factor in its underperformance. Because of declining volumes, litigation, and taxation, P/E multiples on tobacco stocks have generally been lower than for the S&P 500. All of those factors would have to go into the valuation of tobacco stocks, but I would submit that most of their share repurchases have been at least neutral to the remaining shareholders, and often quite positive.

Do the Bad Guys Wear Black Hats?

MARK BAUM: But that's not stupidity. That's fraud!
JARED VENNETT: Tell me the difference between stupid and illegal
and I'll have my wife's brother arrested.

—*THE BIG SHORT* (MOVIE, 2015)

IN CLASSIC WESTERN MOVIES, you can always tell who the bad guys are because they wear black hats. Darth Vader's black helmet warns that he is evil. But in the Harry Potter stories, black work hats identify sorcerers both good and evil. Magicians and financial shysters both create illusions that depend on their audience's suspension of disbelief in their supernatural abilities. On closer inspection, magic tricks and fraud turn out to consist not of miraculous events but of misdirecting the eye away from one action and toward another. That said, fraud is a detective story in which, despite examining the evidence carefully, innocent bystanders are often suspects.

Bad guys do share some common identifying markers, but, inconveniently, blameless people display them as well. Statistically, when the error rate on a test is greater than the frequency in a population, noise overwhelms the signal. The tests for fraud are quite noisy. For example, if there's one rogue in five hundred and the test has a 2 percent error rate, 9.98 (499 × .02) false positives show up along with (usually) the one bad guy. Because the tests are somewhat unreliable, I eliminate only the prospects that I think would be disappointing investments for other reasons. For example, companies that constantly require outside financing might be at greater risk for fraud, but I avoid them because of the dilution from financing.

Unless you've never fibbed out of kindness or guilt, you also know that there are shades of dishonesty. In my years of investing, I've seen a couple of blowups, which led me to think further about character. Means, motive, and opportunity are the traditional clues used to detect criminals, but in financial cases, the fraud triangle applies: pressure, opportunity, and rationalization.

Highly Overconfident

Of the sample set of hundreds of analysts and portfolio managers I have worked with at Fidelity, just one went on to become a newsworthy financial scoundrel (after he left the firm): Florian Homm. Homm left Fidelity Boston more than a quarter-century ago, and his alleged misdeeds occurred nearly two decades later. Homm's office was next to mine, so we became well acquainted. At the time, I pegged Homm as a brilliant, erratic, European playboy, not a swindler. Everything that follows is a matter of public record, mostly in Homm's autobiography, *Rogue Financier.* Homm was larger than life, nearly superhuman: 6'7", well built, graduate of Harvard and Harvard Business School, uberwealthy family, played in the German national basketball league, brash, and personable. On his very first day, he was assigned to manage a fund. (I waited three years to manage money.) I don't think any of those characteristics should be used to spot trouble.

Still, I wasn't totally shocked that Homm got into mischief later. Cocky, talented characters like him are given more leeway to behave badly. Florian was hyperactive and craved thrills, which might have made him more likely to take those chances. Moreover, the rules aren't always applied to charismatic rogues. More generally, the appeal and the peril of charismatic leaders is that they get people to do things that they otherwise wouldn't.

Greed was the obvious motive for Homm's alleged crime, but there's more to it than that. Badly designed incentives—including too much of a good thing—create pressure that leads to bad behavior. When he worked at Fidelity, Homm managed a smallish fund that might have carried a fee of 0.55 percent of assets. His pay was likely a fraction of the fee, and not directly based on the fee. Financial incentives to misbehave came years later in 2004 when he cofounded Absolute Capital Management, a hedge fund management firm, which at its peak handled more than $3 billion in assets. Hedge funds customarily charge 2 percent of assets, which would equate to $60 million a year. On top of that, they collect 20 percent of the profits, which, in a bullish year, would be an even grander sum. Absolute Capital's fund performance was at the top of the charts in the European financial press. The management company was initially offered to the public in London, and Homm remained a key shareholder. By 2007, Homm was listed as one of the 300 richest individuals in Germany, worth 400 million euros.

Usually, when founders and senior executives are major shareholders of their companies, as in Homm's case, interests are aligned. I worry more about executives who collect massive option grants but don't hold as many shares. At Enron, CEO Ken Lay and other officers had many more option shares than directly owned shares. Stocks can go up or down, but options have only upside. When executives don't share in the downside, they take bets with huge upside and downside, and hope. However, Homm's interests lined up with those of his management company, not his fund holders. For fiduciaries, they should be related, with fund holders first.

Pride in an exceptional track record sounds like a fluffy motivation compared with greed, but in Homm's case I suspect that the pressure to keep it up was powerful. Homm was a *phenomenon*, not just some top-performing hedge fund manager. He was labeled the "Antichrist of finance" because his bear raid on Bremer Vulkan triggered the shipbuilder's collapse. He co-owned Artemis, Germany's largest "wellness bordello." He was a local hero for rescuing the popular (but insolvent) Borussia Dortmund soccer team.

Rackets can run for years, even decades, before they are recognized as such; then they often unwind quickly and dramatically, as Homm's did in 2007. The U.S. Securities and Exchange Commission alleged that funds managed by Homm at Absolute Capital had been running a pump-and-dump scheme. His funds would buy huge blocks of lightly traded penny stocks, sometimes as private placements, often executed by Hunter World Markets, a brokerage half-owned by Homm. Then Homm would ramp the share price with semi-fictional trades, or simply mark the price up. In an exuberant bull market like that of 2006 and 2007, the pump part was easy. As long as a fund is receiving inflows, the dump part doesn't seem urgent. Managers can use the new cash to further pump up the stock price. Or they can let the inflows reduce the portion of the fund held in the inflated stocks.

Stock markets turned wobbly in September 2007, and Homm's funds had several brutal weeks. Florian donated personal shares of Absolute Capital Management worth 33 million euros to his funds to prop up their value. Then, abruptly, Homm quit, and it was revealed that his funds held $530 million in penny stocks where Absolute accounted for almost all of the trading activity. Absolute Capital immediately halted redemptions of Homm's funds. After absconding to Bogotá, getting shot in Venezuela, and playing cat and mouse for years, Homm was arrested at the Uffizi Gallery in Florence, Italy. Perhaps it was karma, but some of Homm's alleged loot ended up invested in the Madoff funds.

Madoff with the Money

Around 2000, I met with Harry Markopolos, a Boston money manager, who had tried to reverse engineer the returns of a much-touted strategy run by Bernard Madoff. Even in sloppy markets, the Madoff funds were rumored to be perennially profitable, and I was interested in copying his investment strategy (which I assumed to be legitimate) to improve my fund's performance. Markopolos wanted to show me that Madoff was a hoaxer. I gleaned no investment insights because nothing in Madoff's ostensible strategy made sense; Markopolos was right. He had tried and failed to correlate Madoff's returns with all manner of strategies and specific stocks.

Everything about Madoff's funds, including the exact numbers, was shrouded in secrecy. Investors had to be invited to gain admission to the Madoff club and then invested only indirectly, through a "feeder fund" or fund-of-funds. This distance from his clients meant that clients didn't know what they owned; it also may have allowed Madoff to keep his emotional distance from them. Most clients had no access to reports about their accounts. Madoff cleared his own trades and effectively had no external custodian.

Eventually, Madoff's operation proved to be the world's largest Ponzi scheme, costing investors billions. Madoff was well-known in the industry—chairman of the board of the National Association of Securities Dealers (NASD), a self-regulatory body that has since been succeeded by the Financial Industry Regulatory Authority. He had helped transform the "pink sheets" market makers into the NASDAQ electronic market. A cynic might wonder whether Madoff—now serving life in prison—felt he was above the rules. In November 2007, a year before the scandal broke, Madoff said, "In today's environment, it is virtually impossible to violate rules."

It is unclear whether Madoff's fraud began around 1990 or earlier. Madoff's testimony suggested that it stemmed from pressure to meet unattainable expectations and as a way to deny failure. One story is that he had set up complex long/short trades and was faced with a large fund withdrawal. Madoff sold the stocks on the long side, but the investment bank refused to let him out of the short side of the trades. Supposedly, the short leg produced heavy losses. Clients had become used to consistent large gains, and he felt he had to cover the losses. In this version, it all happened because Madoff wanted to keep his clients happy. Incredibly, some investors had suspicions about Madoff, but thought they could get out in time.

Enron's Pipeline Dreams

A memory of being once burned kept me from ever being enthusiastic about Enron stock. I have often flashed back to 1987, when I was a rookie in the arena of natural gas who had just flown in to meet Enron. At the hotel in Houston, I received a call from Beth Terrana, the manager of Fidelity Growth & Income Fund. She was livid that Enron had announced a $140 million trading loss, but I was clueless about the situation. Analysts didn't have the Internet or even cell phones then. I called Enron but didn't get a call back.

At the meeting, I recall being alarmed by the patchy details of the trading loss. Enron's CFO admitted that its traders had made a catastrophic bet on oil prices and had also diverted some money. He said that the damage had occurred nine months earlier, had been as bad as $1 billion,

but had been nimbly reduced. If Enron had disclosed the misappropriation earlier, the trades would have cost far more to unwind and might
have tripped debt covenants. While Enron was working out of the losing
trades, and shutting down the oil trading desk, it was an open question
whether the losses should be immediately reflected ("market") or deferred
until the final amount was known ("cost"). Just maybe, the billion-dollar
loss was never reversed and led to much bigger abuses. More likely, it
opened management's eyes to the accounting possibilities.

I met with several other officers of Enron that day. Kenneth Lay, the
CEO, was a PhD, which was unique in the energy business. Rich Kinder,
the chief operating officer, was nicknamed "Doctor Discipline" and
seemed exceptionally capable. At the gas trading desk, I inquired about
controls and position limits; they claimed risks were well balanced. The
deregulation of natural gas pricing had created exciting trading and arbi-
trage opportunities. I wondered whether these included opportunities to
shuffle costs between Enron's regulated and unregulated activities. But
really, gas trading seemed like any dealing desk, with telephones, computer screens, and confident, aggressive men. I still saw a company with
tons of debt, frequent extraordinary items, a drab return on equity, and
now a big trading loss. Enron stock dropped 30 percent in October 1987,
but since the stock market crashed that month, the scandal was forgotten
until 2001.

The origin of the fraud that ultimately bankrupted Enron remains
obscure, but it may have been in a change in accounting standards in
1992 that allowed energy traders to value positions at market rather
than cost. Enron and Arthur Andersen had lobbied for this treatment,
so you might surmise the scheme was already afoot. At the least, the
new accounting enabled the subsequent chicanery. An alternative theory
is that when Rich Kinder left Enron in 1996, and Jeff Skilling, a Harvard Business School grad and former chairman of Enron Finance and
then of Enron Gas Services, took the reins, Enron's financial and trading businesses ballooned. Enron's operating cash flow turned negative.
It also became much more promotional. Analysts and reporters started
producing worshipful stories. *Fortune* magazine called Enron "America's Most Innovative Company" and ranked it number 1 in Quality of
Management.

Promotional companies are bad news, and not just because they are more likely to be frauds. A hard sell usually indicates that some form of financing is impending. As a value investor, what really scares me away is that if investors believe the hype, a stock will be overpriced. Nearly all of the companies on lists of major accounting debacles had stocks trading at demanding multiples. Enron's price/earnings ratio (P/E) was twenty or higher for much of the 1990s and peaked at seventy times earnings. Without the trading businesses, Enron's goal of 15 percent earnings growth would have seemed laughable. Energy prices were stagnant. In the 1990s, American natural gas production grew but never returned to the peak levels reached two decades earlier. Enron's trading businesses had such tiny margins that between 1996 and 2000 its sales octupled from $13 billion to $101 billion, but reported earnings per share rose only 4 percent.

In retrospect, the suppression of contrary opinions at Enron was a clear sign of impending disaster. At the start of 1998, I got a tearful call from "Scarlett," an analyst at a competing firm. Enron had called her Director of Research, pressuring him to take her off of covering Enron and fire her. She did land another job but complained that her phones were tapped and she was being followed. Similarly, John Olson, a thoughtful natural gas analyst at Merrill Lynch, had not been an enthusiastic cheerleader for Enron. In 1998, Enron retaliated by cutting Merrill out of an investment banking deal. Olson "agreed to retire early" from Merrill. Other analysts were excluded from conference calls or barred from asking questions. Jeff Skilling famously called analyst Richard Grubman an "asshole" during one such call.

Those events cast a different light on Enron's policy of forced-ranking employees and eliminating the worst-performing 15 percent each year. If that many people had to be canned, Enron must have been abysmal at hiring the right ones. Teams do have to work together, so personnel decisions are unavoidably subjective and political, but forced-ranking would ramp it to a scary level. For the winners, Enron offered rewards previously unimaginable at a public utility, including shares of special-purpose entities, stock options, and more.

As Enron collapsed, lots of tawdry behavior was revealed. Top Enron executives, including vice chairman Cliff Baxter, dumped large amounts of shares while the retirement plans of lower-level employees were locked in and other paper fortunes vanished. Just before he was due to testify to Congress, Baxter committed suicide.

Arthur Andersen & Co. played a supporting role in Enron's misstatements and is itself a tale of incentives and opportunity for bad behavior. When I was in business school, Arthur Andersen & Co. was considered a forward-looking, principled employer that paid well, especially on the consulting side. In the early 1950s, the firm had developed a payroll processing system for General Electric and recommended a Univac computer to do the job. Thus was born the computer systems integration industry. In the following decades, Arthur Andersen's financial systems integration business was even more successful than its auditing practice.

The success of the consulting division provided both motive and opportunity for Arthur Andersen. As both auditor and consultant for Enron, Andersen was in the dubious position of evaluating its own work, with one arm affirming the value of the other. To top it off, Enron outsourced parts of its *internal* audit function to Andersen. Usually companies prepare financial statements, audit them internally, and then the outside auditor reviews them. On self-graded exams, there are lots of perfect scores.

Consulting billed out at higher hourly rates and was a much bigger market than audit. For example, between 1991 and 1997, Waste Management paid Andersen more than twice as much for consulting as it did for auditing. A director called one $3 million consulting project a "boondoggle"; it was never used. When Andersen discovered Waste Management's fabrications, the public accountants did not inform Waste Management's board of directors; instead, the auditors helped to *conceal* the improprieties.

Enron paid Andersen $27 million of consulting fees and $25 million in auditing fees in 2001, so the balance wasn't as skewed as it was with Waste Management. But Andersen believed that Enron could become a $100 million client. Those audit fees were also unusually large, probably exceeding ExxonMobil's, a company many times larger by any measure. I would guess that Enron's complex organizational structure and use of special-purpose entities made it a time-consuming auditing job. Or was it hush money?

Auditors and systems integrators work under different ethical principles. I suspect that as Andersen's consulting business became the larger profit center, the standards of consulting prevailed rather than those of auditing. Auditors and investment managers occupy a position of public trust, but they are also in business. Duty is meant to come before profits, and obligations to the public can come before those to the client. As with any enterprise, marketing is required but is asked to be low-key, because there are certain things that clients want that professionals should never promise. Andersen's CEO urged the firm's partners to market heavily and increase cross-sales, which was the right approach for the consulting side. Over time, the consulting business increasingly separated from the auditing practice, with the consulting side rebranded as Accenture.

Six Things That Make Me Nervous

1. Companies That Must Lie to Stay in Business

Distressed and highly indebted companies often don't want the truth to come out. If the extent of their troubles were revealed, the bankers might seize control. Any capital-raising would bring in less money. The company could become vulnerable to a takeover. Staff might become demoralized and start to circulate résumés. Suppliers might stop shipping goods, which could deepen the distress.

Corporate deceit can be rationalized in any number of ways: if the company had to be sold, bankers and shareholders might recover less in a distress auction—so it would be better not to tell them. It would be harder to attract talented executives who might solve the company's problems. A white lie is sometimes better for everyone.

2. Tiny Audit Firms

In financial crimes, opportunity arises from a lapse in the usual regulations, cross-checks, audits, and separation of functions. External auditors are meant to protect outside investors and lenders, but they don't have a foolproof test for fraud either. Auditors are paid by the company they are evaluating. The financials are prepared by the company, and auditors depend on its cooperation and internal controls. Nor does use of a big-name accounting firm guarantee against corporate chicanery. Ernst & Young audited Absolute Capital Management and never qualified its opinion. Enron engaged Arthur Andersen & Co., which was one of the Big Five auditors until it went under. Enron was the deathblow for Arthur Andersen, whose audits of Waste Management and WorldCom had also been severely criticized. However, it *was* a red flag that Madoff hired Friehling & Horowitz, an accounting firm with just one working accountant; the firm by its own admission had not conducted audits in fifteen years.

3. Inside Boards

Responsibility for poor or missing controls belongs to a company's board of directors. In principle, a good board of directors would be knowledgeable, think independently, and act in shareholders' interests because they own a lot of stock. Directors' shareholdings are listed in the company's proxy statement, but their expertise and independence can be inferred only from their résumés. When most of the directors are officers of the corporation and their cronies, you have an "inside board." And that means oversight isn't separated from management.

For shareholders, the worst combination for shareholders is an inside board that owns little stock. One way to gauge independence is to compare the CEO's pay package with those of CEOs at like-sized, similarly situated companies. If the CEO is taking home a great deal more than comparable CEOs, the board of directors is probably an inside board. A board that isn't watching over executive compensation may not be on top of financial controls either.

4. Glamorous Rollups

Glamorous, fast-growing industries suck in capital, which opens up possibilities for impropriety. When business is changing rapidly, it's impossible to prove that an expansion project will never pay off. Mergers and acquisitions not only allow companies to bulk up quickly; they also confuse the numbers. Think of all of the largest accounting scams at nonfinancial companies—Enron, HealthSouth, Qwest, Waste Management, Tyco, Sunbeam, and WorldCom. Every single one of them rolled up scores of companies. As we'll see in the next chapter, some of their misstatements were in plain sight. In these cases, the financial statements shown in the company's 10-K annual report were more accurate indicators than the more flattering "adjusted" figures. With fast-changing rollups like these, it's tough to keep abreast of everything that's going on.

5. Financial Firms

Financial companies are the jackpot for scam artists who want to get their hands on other people's money. Clients routinely trust banks and brokers with their assets. For each $1 billion of equity, most banks hold deposits and borrowings in excess of $10 billion. An electronic record of a loan or security corresponds to another electronic or paper document, not a physical property. Even if accountants view the physical collateral supporting a loan, they also need to know the other liens and contractual wording. Often these documents are confidential. The combination of opaqueness and other people's money may explain why many of the largest fraud cases involve financial firms.

6. Sunny Havens

Warm, sunny places like Florida attract more than their fair share of dubious promotional schemes. Wealthy retirees bring plenty of capital to invest and, being past their working years, may be less inclined to do due diligence. They are ripe targets, especially for affinity scams, which zero in on victims belonging to social or demographic groups. Madoff's use of affinity groups allowed him to maintain a low profile, reduced disclosure needs, and enhanced his mystique.

Along with its beautiful beaches and low taxes, Florida has a Homestead Act that protects even mansions worth tens of millions of dollars from seizure by creditors. The Homestead Act has a long history of sheltering assets of people with unstable finances. Florida homesteaders can even sell their property and protect the cash, as long as they intend to buy another home in Florida.

Places like the Cayman Islands, the Bahamas, Bermuda, and Cyprus are sunny isles for shady people. Like Florida, these jurisdictions have magnificent beaches, but are even more appealing for avoiding taxes and the law. They attract what I call homeless companies, or nomads. For example, a nomad might have most of its assets in China, most of its officers in Hong Kong, incorporated in the British Virgin Islands, with a foundation in the Dutch Antilles and its stock listed only in the United States.

Many companies incorporate in tax havens but are not otherwise outside of the law. Systems integrator Accenture, for example, is incorporated in Ireland, although operations are coordinated from Switzerland and a large part of its revenue comes from the United States. A homeless company will be "forum shopping," seeking the most lenient securities and accounting rules. In case of fraud, there's no legal recourse, particularly if managers had the foresight to relocate their personal domicile to a tax haven without extradition treaties.

Even if means, motive, and opportunity can be shown, the prosecution must still prove that securities fraud was willfully committed. For those of us who are not mind readers, mental states can't be proved definitively; even "beyond a reasonable doubt" is tough. Business misadventures are often intertwined with fraud and are common enough that stupidity, ignorance, or bad luck work as defenses. Because Enron's executives were tagged as "the smartest guys in the room," the jury wouldn't buy stupidity. CEO Lay argued for ignorance, implying that his subordinates did all the bad deeds. Bad luck can be a bona fide defense. Several energy trading companies blew up around that time, and fraud wasn't seen as the culprit in all of them. Dynegy, Mirant, Aquila, and several others had such disastrous results from energy trading that they exited the business. Enron could truthfully argue that it was a dicey operation and blowups were bound to happen.

Making aggressive deals isn't always illegal. Still, I exercise caution before investing with someone like Ron Perelman. In 2011, Perelman offered $25 a share to buy out the shares of M&F Worldwide that he didn't own. That equated to a P/E of four for the maker of licorice flavorings and bank check printer. The company had repurchased shares at $45, and the stock had been as high as $67. Don't ask me why the independent directors and a majority of noncontrolling shareholders signed off on $25 as a fair price. Billionaire Carl Icahn said of Perelman, "He was like a plumber you loan money to get him started in business; then he comes in, wrecks your house, then tells you he wants the house for nothing" (*New York Times*, 1998).

Disaster Can Be Avoided

If you try to avoid being hoodwinked, you will miss some perfectly good opportunities. Enron stock skyrocketed before it collapsed. The choice boils down to temperament. Some people can't stand to miss a moon-shot, no matter how sketchy. I prefer to avoid a small chance of quick, devastating losses. When a manager has a criminal record or a history of cheating investors or even just feels above the law, I stop right there. Crooks don't suddenly sprout a sense of fiduciary duty. When a piece of evidence might or might not tag a bad guy, I use it only if it hints at other investment defects. Glamorous hype stocks are more likely to be scams, but I avoid them because they are usually overpriced and prone to raising capital constantly. Intricate corporate structures make analysis difficult, even if nothing bad is going on.

To spot bad guys, look for the fraud triangle: pressure, opportunity, and rationalization. Philosopher Hannah Arendt had it right that "most evil is done by people who never make up their minds to be good or evil." Watch for when massive option grants or hefty fees compel people to try too hard. Pride can be a dominant motive when an audience believes in someone's magical powers. Charismatic promoters often suppress the boards of directors, auditors, and other naysayers that might prevent them from doing what they want. They cluster in industries and geographies where capital is abundantly available with little scrutiny or accountability. Lax accounting standards are also a draw. Don't buy anything someone is pushing hard. By avoiding the bad-guy stocks—and it's a short list—I slash the possibility of a disastrous outcome but scarcely reduce my opportunity set.

12

Shipping Bricks and Other Accounting Riddles

> The idea is to try to give all the information to help others judge the
> value of your contribution, not just the information that leads to
> judgment in one particular direction or another.
>
> —RICHARD FEYNMAN

FRAUD IS UNCOMMON, while bungling and business reverses occur daily,
but they share similar motives and accounting red flags. The most common symptoms of falsified earnings are negative free cash flow and bloat-
ing in receivables, inventory, or intangibles. When fraud is not involved,
high and rising receivables or inventories suggest that a company's sales
have fallen below plan. Some misstatements can be discovered only by
reading the footnotes, but don't torture yourself—you don't have to *solve*
the accounting riddles to avoid danger; you merely have to identify the
warning signs. The scariest red flag of all is disclosure that is extensive
yet incomprehensible.

Once any number becomes The Number, it will start to be cooked.
The Number is at the center of attention and must never disappoint.
For most publicly held companies, The Number is non-generally accepted
accounting principles (GAAP) earnings per share. In the case of highly
indebted companies, it is typically adjusted earnings before interest, taxes,
depreciation, and amortization (EBITDA). But it can be any number, even
page views for an Internet company.

A data point is just a snapshot; investors should care instead about the
moving picture. Some numbers are just sums, but most involve subtrac-
tion as well, especially the ones that traders obsess about. Net income
is the product of a long series of plusses and minuses, with occasional

division or multiplication. Along the way, many estimates and approximations, some correct, others not, get folded into the calculations. Magicians find that repeating an incantation, like "adjusted EBITDA," helps direct attention to the desired spot.

Good detectives turn their attention to something other than The Number and observe clues that others barely notice. Because accounting is a double-entry system, any suspicious entry must be matched by an offsetting number. Imaginary profits are paired with an asset whose value is overstated. Furthermore, when one of the three accounting statements (income, cash flow, and balance sheet) is falsified, traces will show up in the other two. Everything must add up arithmetically—even if the company is fraudulently misclassifying key figures. When all of the discussion is about "non-GAAP" and "adjusted data," check out the GAAP report. If the spotlight is on net income, study the inventories, receivables, and other items on the balance sheet. There are also clues that get missed because they are buried in the footnotes.

Readers of financial statements fall into three major categories: trade creditors, lenders, and owners. Each group watches for different signs of safety. Customers and trade suppliers want to know whether it is safe to do business with a company. Will their order be delivered or account paid promptly? Lenders are more concerned with solvency and liquidity. Does the company have sufficient assets and cash flow to cover all of its future obligations? Shareholders want to know what value remains for owners and whether their investment is safely backed by assets. Investors tend to care about liquidity and solvency only when these measures suggest that there may not be much left for shareholders. The three different constituencies rarely view the same facts in the same way. (Competitors definitely read statements, too.)

Deception may be aimed at any or all of the three groups. A troubled retailer might overstate its cash assets to ensure that suppliers keep shipping the most up-to-date goods. Lenders are more willing to extend credit to an enterprise reporting increased EBITDA. Often debt covenants will be violated if the debt/EBITDA ratio passes above a certain level or net worth falls below a set amount. For most executives, the mightiest incentives are tied to stock prices. Disappointing quarterly earnings can torpedo a stock's price, smashing capital-raising plans and managers' net worth. One lie can lead to another, and so the web of deceit will often spread to all three constituencies.

The Financial Accounting Standards Board (FASB) allows enterprises to choose between accounting principles that produce diverging answers. For example, in the oil industry, the *successful efforts* accounting method is considered more conservative than the *full cost* method. When an oil company drills a dry hole, under full cost accounting, it will (within limits) capitalize the cost as an asset on its balance sheet, thereby avoiding a charge to profits. Under successful efforts, the oil company would write off the cost of a dry hole as an expense and capitalize costs only when it finds oil.

Another example of choice of accounting principles is whether to classify some or all investment securities into one of two buckets: *held to maturity* (which will be carried at cost) or *available for sale* (which will be marked-to-market). Neither method is more conservative than the other, per se. In an advancing market, the market price will be above cost, so the held-to-maturity investments bucket will be understated, while in a tumbling market, marked-to-market will be more conservative. What is never conservative is reclassifying investments into whichever bucket is more flattering.

Unethical innovators are constantly devising new forms of accounting fraud, but I will focus on four standard categories: (1) recording sales too soon, (2) fabricating revenues, (3) shifting expenses to the future (or the past), and (4) failing to disclose liabilities. For the first two, the warning sign is high or rising receivable Days-Sales-Outstanding. When a sale is made, unless cash is received, a receivable is usually booked. Sometimes sales are recorded before customers have fully signed off on them or when there are important uncertainties or a future service obligation. When sales aren't made up out of whole cloth, companies fabricate revenue by misclassifying exchanges, rebates, asset sales, and other transactions that aren't properly sales.

Companies can use several tricks to shift costs to future periods. They can simply ignore costs during a period, but the benefit to hiding the bill in the drawer is short-lived; if the outside auditors don't catch them, their creditors will. WorldCom and American Italian Pasta classified current operating expenses as capital assets, which would be depreciated over many future years. Waste Management reduced its depreciation expense by assuming longer service lives for its dumpsters and garbage trucks.

When Tyco made acquisitions, it created reserves that would allow it to ignore certain costs in the future. Acquired businesses would show an immediate leap in profit because expenses would be charged against the reserve rather than flowing through the income statement.

The most treacherous category of fraud is failure to disclose liabilities. If financial statements give any hint of the hidden liability, it will be buried in the footnotes. Enron hid billions in liabilities in special-purpose entities, but the footnotes didn't make it easy to connect the dots. The most common sources of footnote mischief include lease obligations, forward commitments, and retirement benefit plans. But if there are too many pages of footnotes, and I don't already own a stock, I conclude that the company must be trying to hide something, and I move on.

EZ Credit, No Payments Ever

Heavy inventories and receivables clearly indicated that Friedman's Jewelers was reaching for sales, even if they weren't fraud clues for the forensics squad. Friedman's served a lower-income customer, locating stores in strip malls near Walmart, mostly in smaller towns in the Southeast. Sales had grown explosively by offering credit to customers who couldn't qualify for it elsewhere. At its peak, Friedman's had 686 stores and was the third largest jeweler in America in 2004. Store managers received bonuses based on improving their store sales, increasing the receivables portfolio, and collecting the receivables. All of Friedman's profits (and more) were plowed back into inventory and receivables, leaving it with almost no cash and rising debt.

Friedman's stock price had bounced between $5 and $10. It had about $10 a share of net working capital, $14 of book value, and a single-digit price/earnings ratio (P/E), making it statistically a cheap stock. Most metal jewelry can be returned or sold for metal value or more, so I figured that the assets put a floor under the value of the company. Because Friedman's was profitable, its value should grow over time. But Friedman's earnings, working capital, and book value were all fake, and the best clues were negative free cash flow almost every year, climbing debt, and increasing shares outstanding.

Zale's, America's largest jewelry chain, makes consumer credit decisions centrally. Friedman's left credit decisions to store managers and salespeople, none of whom were ever formally trained in credit scoring or collections; their job was meeting sales targets. Credit customers were encouraged to pay their balances in the stores, where they might buy something else. Oddly, customers whose accounts were delinquent were sometimes allowed to buy more on credit. As customer credit collections deteriorated, Friedman's changed the definition of current from 30 days to 90 days. And when accounts were delinquent, Friedman's avoided writing them off.

Eventually, in 2003, Friedman's sold off $90 million worth of uncollectible receivables for $1.5 million, less than 2 cents on the dollar. This minimal recovery was improperly credited to reduce bad debt expense. Other misstatements came out, including a software bug (the "X-file accounts") that caused Friedman to age its receivables incorrectly. In 2004, Friedman's filed for bankruptcy. Stockholders lost everything, and some creditors recovered less than 50 cents on the dollar. An attempt to revive the company ended in a second bankruptcy in 2008.

Something Stinky at Allou

Unlike Friedman's, which embellished on a difficult reality, I am not sure Allou Healthcare was ever real. Allou was a wholesale distributor of health and beauty products, with a specialty in perfume. It was a "net-net," which means that net current assets (cash, inventories, and receivables) were of greater value than all of its debts *and* the stock market value of the company. Investors were seemingly getting all of Allou's other assets for free, including an Internet start-up called Fragrance Counter. Allou was trading for about $7 a share in 2002, which was less than its book value of $9 a share. The P/E ratio of eight was also appealing.

In fiscal 2002, Allou reported sales of $564 million, gross profits of $63 million, and net income of $6.6 million. Those work out to be paltry gross and net profit margins of 11 percent and 1.2 percent, respectively. Distribution businesses often have meager margins when sales don't require a lot of assets to support them. If inventories turn briskly and are held only for days, a tiny margin can work out to a decent return on capital invested. For example, Cardinal Health, the leading distributor of pharmaceuticals and medical products, had a gross margin of 5.6 percent and a net margin of 1.2 percent in 2015, with thirty-three days of inventory and twenty-one days of receivables. For Cardinal, quick inventory turnover produced an attractive return on equity of 19 percent, despite narrow margins.

Allou's inventories of $185 million equated to 135 days' supply. Allou indicated that its health care product inventory turned faster than perfumes but had lower margins. I asked Allou's CFO about fashion trends in fragrances and was told that celebrity labels and trendy designers weren't its market. My bigger concern about slow turns was that aged fragrances decay, especially if exposed to heat or light. Perfume turned slowly because it was highly seasonal and could be purchased at big discounts in the off months. Seeking to better understand the reasons for high inventories, I asked public perfume makers about Allou, assuming that it must be a small world. They drew a blank.

When companies report profits but bleed cash, believe the cash. Even though Allou reported net income, it had a net cash outflow from operating activities of $17.4 million in 2002. In the previous two years, Allou had reported net income of $2.5 million and $7 million but had used $34 million and $27 million in cash. In those three years, the company had three auditors: Mayer Rispler, Arthur Andersen, and finally KPMG. While moving to a larger auditor is usually favorable news, switching auditors too often is not. Management seemed worried about their debt covenants. Allou had a $200 million credit line with two lenders: Congress Financial and Citibank. Even when investors were excited about the Fragrance Counter start-up, the market capitalization was only $100 million. Congress and Citi each had exposure matching Allou's market cap.

Around midnight on September 25, 2002, a three-alarm fire broke out in Allou's warehouse in the Williamsburg neighborhood of Brooklyn. Despite 245 New York City firefighters responding, the blaze wasn't fully extinguished until the afternoon. The fire marshals concluded there had been arson at four points in the warehouse. The insurance company denied Allou's claim for $100 million in damages. Senior officers of Allou tried to bribe the fire marshals to alter the report. The fire officials instead notified the police. Allou filed for bankruptcy. Shareholders were wiped out, and lenders lost $177 million.

Shipping Bricks

Most of the time, companies can't squeeze cash out of dubious inventory or receivables, but MiniScribe concocted two ingenious schemes that yielded cash, albeit briefly. The disk drive maker struggled after losing IBM as its largest customer. When it took a physical inventory in 1987, MiniScribe discovered that it was missing $15 million, out of a reported total inventory of $85 million. To fill the gap, MiniScribe began relabeling and repackaging obsolete inventory as current in both its Colorado warehouse and its plants in Singapore and Hong Kong. Three just-in-time warehouses were opened next to distributors. Products would be tagged with a bar-coded serial number, which would be scanned by the distributor when received, and payment would soon follow. MiniScribe abused this automated arrangement by stuffing its distribution channel—shipping products to distributors that hadn't been ordered.

Near year-end 1988, MiniScribe packaged, bar-coded, and shipped *building bricks*—as if they were disk drives—to a warehouse where they would await inspection for a few weeks. After MiniScribe received payment for the shipment, it recalled the bricks and replaced them with disk drives. MiniScribe may have intended to ship bricks again late in 1989 and then have another recall once payment was received, but a large layoff before Christmas included many of the company's packing and shipping workers involved in the brick scheme. Angry workers broke the story to local newspapers; customers who had been shipped bricks informed the authorities. Early on the first business day of 1990, MiniScribe filed for bankruptcy.

Shifting Timing of Expenses

Under its CEO Dennis Kozlowski, Tyco International, a highly acquisitive conglomerate, stretched the limits of GAAP to move expenses out of the current period. Tyco had interests in fire prevention equipment, security monitoring services, electronic components, flow control products, health care supplies, and more. When Tyco bought a company, it was arguably too conservative in accounting for the tangible assets purchased, writing them down to the lowest possible level by increasing reserves for inventory obsolescence, warranty expense, and bad debts. A larger portion of the purchase price would be allocated to goodwill or other intangibles. Instead of ignoring restructuring charges and goodwill amortization, investors should have treated them as yellow flags.

The net effect of this accounting shift was that Tyco increased reported earnings by shifting expenses out of the current period. Depreciation expense was reduced through lower carrying values for property and equipment. The telltale for understated depreciation expense is often that companies must spend more than depreciation to replace worn-out equipment, but Tyco hid capital spending by leasing rather than buying. When a division had a slow quarter, it would instead book a gain by selling inventory or collecting receivables and reversing overly generous reserves tied to them. Fortunately—and atypically—Tyco was trying to make good businesses look better, not cover up a dire situation. For brave investors, officers' indictments afforded a buying opportunity. Kozlowski eventually did go to jail. That's "investing with conviction."

Phony EBITDA

Some say EBITDA can't be faked or manipulated, but phone company WorldCom inflated both EBITDA and earnings. WorldCom improperly classified some of its line costs as purchases of capital equipment. Line cost is the fee one phone company pays another to originate or complete a call when it doesn't own the network at the other end. In 2000, World-Com reported line costs of 42 percent of revenue, while it consumed half of incumbent AT&T's revenues—despite AT&T's much larger network. In fact, WorldCom's true line cost ratio was similar, taking out the improperly capitalized costs. In 2001, the market for long-distance services turned fiercely competitive, and WorldCom slashed its prices; sales fell about 10 percent for the year. At the same time, WorldCom's actual line costs rose by over $1 billion in 2001, crunching margins.

According to the investigative report filed at the U.S. Securities and Exchange Commission, WorldCom's actual line costs were underreported by $3 billion in 2001. Of this sum, $2.7 billion was capitalized as construction-in-process rather than expensed as current line costs. Later, these amounts were transferred to in-service assets and depreciated. Effectively, costs wouldn't show up in 2001 but would appear as depreciation over many years. Line expense is clearly a cost of service and doesn't correspond to any owned equipment, so it shouldn't be capitalized. Even as revenues dipped, the gross amount of transmission equipment rose by 18 percent in 2001. Although EBITDA can be faked, WorldCom's trickery was belied by rising asset accounts and debt. WorldCom's long-term debt surged from $17.7 billion at year-end in 2000 to $41 billion at its bankruptcy filing in July 2002.

Some companies publicly admit their failure to recognize certain costs and present it as a principled disagreement about what constitutes a cost. Most accountants may lean toward certain principles and interpretations, but that doesn't mean that the minority view is wrong. In oil and gas (and scientific) exploration, it is frequently true that the successful efforts would not have been achieved without a series of failed experiments. I don't think that justifies labeling the spending on failed attempts as an asset rather than an immediate cost, but some do, and the FASB permits it. When oil and gas firms use differing accounting principles, they cannot all be compared together, but only as subgroups that follow the same standard.

Although the FASB allows some discretion in applying its standards, it is still not lax enough for everyone, which has spurred a flourishing subculture of non-GAAP accounting. Names have power, and "underlying earnings" or "cash earnings" sound more sophisticated than GAAP earnings. Companies suggest the desired adjustments, and Wall Street analysts follow suit. Technology companies have loudly disputed whether a cost is incurred when employee compensation is paid as stock or stock options. (Talented employees work for free. Right?) Because the life span of intangible assets can be indeterminate and changing, many assert that any form of amortization or write-down is not a true cost.

I grow skeptical in cases like marchFIRST, an Internet professional services company. On an adjusted basis, marchFIRST was profitable in the first nine months of 2000 but lost 6 cents a share for the year. The GAAP loss for 2000 was −$53.27 per share. Less than two months after it reported this huge loss under GAAP, marchFIRST filed for bankruptcy.

Some losses truly are one-time and produce offsetting future benefits. Borrowers may have to pay a premium to retire high-coupon debt early, but in subsequent years, their interest rate will be lower. Severance and plant closures use cash up front but should save money in subsequent years. But what do you conclude about a business that takes big restructuring write-offs every year, yet never seems to reach the Promised Land? Or a rollup that is always buying something and restructuring it? It can be tortuous to determine whether non-GAAP numbers present a truer picture than the FASB-approved figures.

Hiding Liabilities in the Fine Print

The most diabolical species of accounting mischief is hidden liabilities, which leave few traces on financial statements. They can be discovered only in intimidating footnotes, if anywhere. The footnotes to check include pension and retirement plans, capital and operating leases, forward commitments, derivatives, and joint ventures. A company can have three main types of off-balance-sheet assets and liabilities: (1) unconsolidated legal entities, (2) executory contracts, and (3) contingent obligations. Securitizations, joint ventures, and leveraged projects may avoid being consolidated if their debt is nonrecourse to the parent company. Leases and forward purchase agreements are executory contracts in which both parties have yet to perform their obligations. Contingencies include lawsuits, environmental remediation, warranties, and other situations in which a liability isn't yet probable, or its amount can't yet be determined.

Businesses rarely go bankrupt when cash exceeds debt, but Circuit City, America's second-largest consumer electronics retailer in 2008, did just that. If you skipped the footnotes, Circuit City's balance sheet was quite misleading. For the fiscal year ending in February 2008, the audited financials of Circuit City showed $296 million in cash, $57 million in long-term debt, and $1.503 billion in common equity.

In a footnote, Circuit City disclosed future contractual obligations of $5.6 billion, including $4 billion of operating lease payments. Of those massive off-balance-sheet obligations, $637 million had to be paid during the 2009 fiscal year. Add negative operating cash flow into the mix, and it was clear why Circuit City failed. Because of cases like Circuit City, the FASB has updated the accounting standards for leases.

Just before it went bust in 2008, Lehman Brothers elected to use "Repo 105" accounting to show creditors and regulators a stronger balance sheet. A repo is an agreement to sell a security and to repurchase it later at a higher price, while keeping the dividends or interest paid by the security during the period. Effectively, it's a short-term loan backed by a security. The lender has legal title to the security as collateral and lends the value of the security minus a reserve called a "haircut," usually 1 to 2 percent for top-quality bonds. This reserve protects the lender in case the borrower defaults. Lehman might put up $2 to buy a $100 security with a 2 percent haircut. The balance sheet would then show the bond worth $100, and $98 in repurchase liabilities. During the global financial crisis, financial institutions wanted to report more liquid cash and smaller balance sheets.

For lower-grade bonds with larger haircuts (exceeding 5 percent), Lehman used the Repo 105 method. Lehman also used it with stocks with haircuts above 8 percent. To buy a bond worth $100 million, with a 5 percent haircut, Lehman would put up $5 million. It would report this as a forward contract worth $5 million. The repurchase liability would not show up at all on Lehman's balance sheet. Lehman was able to hide tens of billions of dollars of liabilities this way. Even reading the footnotes, these obligations weren't spelled out fully. Unlike most misstatements, Repo 105 did not change reported earnings.

Miss Kitty Did What?!

When I read Enron's 10-K annual report for 2000, I found more questions than answers. The profit contribution of wholesale services was split into assets and investments, on the one hand, and commodity sales and services, on the other. "Assets and investments" doesn't sound like an operating business to me. In 2000, assets and investments provided income before interest and taxes of $889 million, which was more than one-third of Enron's overall profits. But then commodity sales and services included gains on sales of securitization of $381 million, with some of those sales to a 50-percent-owned affiliate named Whitewing. Two affiliates, JEDI and JEDI II, contributed $255 million in equity earnings. It was impossible to sort out whether profits were coming from operating businesses, trading commodities, securitizations, or gains on selling assets.

Enron's balance sheet was ballooning, with investments and other assets totaling $23.4 billion. This was twice as large as property, plant, and equipment. Investments in and advances to unconsolidated equity affiliates totaled $5.3 billion. In a year, assets from price risk management activities jumped from $2.9 billion to $9 billion. Hoping to understand these investments, I studied exhibit 21 of the 10-K, a list of hundreds of subsidiaries and partnerships. No description of activities was provided, so I've never discovered what Bodyflash.com and Merlin Acquisition did or how large their assets were. Percentage ownership was not shown for any entities, but Miss Kitty LLC was listed repeatedly.

My guess was that many Enron entities had small interests in Miss Kitty, which was why it was listed so many times. Enron didn't want to disclose exactly what it owned, and in which entity. Similarly, a half-owned affiliate called Atlantic Water Trust owned 68 percent of Azurix, implying that Enron owned 34 percent. In 2000, Azurix impaired the value of its Argentine water assets by $470 million, which caused a $326 million charge at Enron, which looks like 69 percent of the impairment. Enron encouraged gracious investors to ignore the loss and add 40 cents to its yearly earnings per share. I felt like Enron was trying to bury me with evidence. All that irrelevant disclosure was useless to me as I struggled to figure out how Enron was making money and what its assets were.

Life's too short to wallow in the weeds! There are thousands of stocks to choose from. Some investors do build a career around digging into the minutiae in the footnotes. For banking and insurance analysts, it's mandatory. But as a portfolio manager who didn't own Enron stock,

I didn't need it. Disclosure is a wonderful thing, but I've never had good luck with complex corporate structures that require massive information statements. Not infrequently, companies with complex corporate structures or opaque disclosures are trying to hide something.

Ingenious uses of footnotes aside, the telltales of a company in trouble are usually rapid growth of assets like inventory and receivables. Even when high inventories and receivables do not indicate chicanery, they do suggest that a company is pushing too hard for sales. Rising levels of investments, intangibles, and other assets can also be a warning sign, especially if a company has been a serial acquirer. WorldCom showed that EBITDA can be faked, but its deceit was evident in negative free cash flow and surging debt levels. Investors in retailers should examine the footnote on leases; for unionized industries, the note on retirement benefits matters. If the footnotes are too bewildering, investors should simply step away.

PART IV

Live Long and Prosper

13

Is the End Near?

I don't want to achieve immortality through my work. I want
to achieve immortality through not dying.

—WOODY ALLEN

LIFE IS IMPERMANENT AND SURPRISING, and commerce even more so. Many
forget this when valuing stocks. Often investors neglect the importance
of longevity (or time until corporate failure) and certainty. Earnings and
growth are uplifting topics and readily quantified, while corporate mortality and certainty are less quantifiable and a touch depressing—but
they're all important to the value of a stock. According to the discounted
cash flow formula, the value of a security is the sum of its free cash flows
from now until the end of time, discounted at a fair rate of return; some
use dividends—the free cash flow that is actually distributed—in place of
cash flows to the company. The four elements of value are (1) **profitability
or income,** (2) **life span,** (3) **growth,** and (4) **certainty.**

Some industries are superior. They have higher profits, greater longevity,
faster growth, or more certainty. Although the elements of value are the
same for every industry, they are present at different levels and combine in
varying ways. The next four chapters will explore some of the combinations, with a special focus on the factors that lead to certainty and longevity. In preview, highly profitable companies operating in more certain,
less cyclical industries tend to survive longer. Except maybe in small-ticket
consumer nondurables, certainty and rapid growth rarely go together.

The discounted cash flow method is often used carelessly, treating nearly certain events and nearly impossible events as equals. Some

projections are quite reliable while others are rubbish; investors need to identify the trustworthy information and separate it from conjecture and babble. Descriptions of events that are already happening are generally more credible than extrapolations into the distant future; the further you look into the future, the more likely your forecasts will turn out to be wrong. Conventionally, at the point far enough in the future that nobody has a clue, the remaining prospects for the rest of eternity are bundled up into a number called the terminal value.

I suspect Warren Buffett might deal with uncertainty by minimizing his "**margin of unsafety,**" while he has never expressed it in those terms. This would be the excess of a stock's market price over an extremely conservative present value—a true worst case scenario. Instead of discounting all forecast cash flows—highly probable and somewhat fanciful together—*only the most certain* cash flows would be counted. No terminal value is assumed. In most cases, this is far too gloomy a scenario, because portions of the probable, possible, and fanciful forecast cash flows do emerge. Recognizing this, stocks almost never sell at a discount to their highly certain value. But if your first rule of investing is "Don't lose money," then minimizing the margin of *un*safety is one way to do it.

If corporate life span and certainty were easily measured, I'd like to know how important each of them was to stock returns in different industries. But they aren't, so we're left with more subjective indicators. Industries change over time, and yesterday's industry of the future is obsolete tomorrow, so we're more interested in the attributes and circumstances of industries than the specific industries themselves. Those attributes and circumstances will be more useful in spotting future winning industries than past performance, except where those attributes and circumstances evolve very slowly.

Life Span and Industry Structure: Are Railroads Obsolete?

Elroy Dimson, Paul Marsh, and Mike Staunton (all of the London Business School) have produced panoramic statistical histories of the American and British stock markets, surveying the stock performance of fifteen industry groups from 1900 to 2016. Over that time, the economy has changed dramatically. Something like four-fifths of stock market value in 1900 was in industries that are no longer prominent today. Matches and candles were key industries in 1900; to provide continuity over 116 years, the Dimson studies lumped them into miscellaneous manufacturing.

In the Dimson studies, the best-performing industries in the U.S. market (in order) were tobacco, electrical equipment, chemicals, food, and railroads. The worst (from the bottom up) were shipping, textiles, steel, paper, utilities, and coal. In the UK, the best-performing industry was alcohol. This might have been the case in the United States as well had it not been for Prohibition (1920–1933).

In 1900, railroads *were* the stock market. They accounted for 63 percent of the market value of listed American stocks, and nearly half of the UK market. Today, railroads are a trivial portion of overall market value in both countries at less than 1 percent. Passengers may now fly or drive instead. Freight that once might have moved by ship or rail now travels by truck or air. Despite railroads being displaced by trucks and planes over this period, rail stocks have outperformed truck and airline stocks.

The data series for American trucking and airline shares start in 1926 and 1934, respectively; since then, both have underperformed in the broader market. Despite falling from dominance to insignificance in the stock market, railroads have been the best-performing category of transportation shares. Cumulatively, rails have more or less matched the general market, though not in a straight line. In the early 1970s, there was a flurry of railroad bankruptcies, including the giant Penn Central. Dividends have provided an important part of the total return from railroad stocks.

Intuitively, railroad profits should have been totally knocked out by the new modes of transport. As industries lose customers to substitutes, they generally erode in relative importance, and profit margins shrivel, as happened with shipping, steel, paper, and coal. By the 1970s, passenger trains were such a financial disaster that on May Day 1971, the government nationalized almost all intercity passenger service. Then it seemed that rail freight might crash as well. The most devastating substitutes cost less *and* have at least one feature that is superior. When two or more people are traveling, it's cheaper incrementally to pay for gas to drive a car than to buy passenger rail tickets. Plus travelers depart whenever and wherever they want.

Freight moves faster on trucks and airplanes, but rail has the price advantage. Railroads have reinforced that advantage through massive cost cutting and productivity improvement. Employment at class I (major) railroads plummeted from 1.35 million in 1947 to 152,000 in 2016. With diesel locomotives and double-stacked containers, railroads move almost three times the ton-miles of freight at higher speeds by fewer employees on less track. Behind the scenes, routing, scheduling, safety, and track maintenance have been automated and computerized.

Railroads are local monopolies. This has protected profit margins as their share of passengers and freight has withered. Once one set of track has been laid to connect two points, it's rarely profitable to build a competitive railroad. Customers can choose another mode of transport, but not usually another railroad on their specific route. Air, truck, and shipping lines face competition on identical routes. Despite tremendous growth in traffic moved by trucks and planes, investors' returns on truck and airline stocks have been lower because the competitive dynamics are worse than those of railroads. More passengers are flying every year, but relentless competition has kept airline profits erratic and fleeting. Truckers haven't been devastated by competition like the airlines, but their profitability has been poorer than railroads. International shipping combines the worst of both worlds. It's an increasingly less significant industry with many fierce competitors.

Investors have fared best in industries that cater to daily needs where customers can't or won't switch. The tobacco industry was a monopoly and remains oligopolistic. Brands matter in tobacco and alcohol, which were the top-performing industries in the United States and the UK, respectively. Most drinkers of Jack Daniels whiskey won't accept Pabst Blue Ribbon beer as a substitute, nor will most Marlboro smokers buy Bonus Value instead.

Elsewhere, electrical equipment is an extremely diverse category, with competition on a product-by-product basis. It has been *the* growth industry of the last century, as engines and lightbulbs have replaced manual labor and candles. The strong performance of chemicals stocks is probably because in 1900, the chemicals industry included pharmaceuticals.

Sinking Ships and Lumps of Coal

Industries dragged down by both substitution and competition were terrible investments between 1900 and 2016. Competition was fierce among the many shipping lines and textile, steel, or paper mills. Purchasers of thermal coal reduce their comparisons to the heat content, how clean it is, and the delivered price. If you work in an industry like that, you will claim that there is more to it than that, and occasionally there is. In broad strokes, though, you are talking about commodities. Unless I can show that *customers* don't view a product as a commodity, I assume that it *is* a commodity. On average, commodity industries have mediocre profits. These industries usually are capital intensive and tend to lurch between periods of mass failure and boom. Half of the North American steel industry was bankrupt in 2000; six years later, it was coining money.

Industries with no substitutes and companies with no competitors tend to enjoy the highest returns, survive the longest, and deliver the greatest value. Although the setup for electric utilities seems perfect, they don't fit that theory. Electricity is a consumable with an expanding set of applications and no attractive substitutes. Many utilities are local monopolies. The problem is that many utilities sell at a regulated price, determined by summing up a utility's estimated costs plus a fair rate of return. State regulators assume that a major part of a utility's funding will come from low-cost debt and that a fair return on equity is also low.

In the early days of the industry, electric utilities in fiercely competitive markets lobbied to be consolidated and regulated by the states. Until the early 1900s, some municipalities granted franchises to multiple utilities, which led to a competitive free-for-all. The utilities complained of destructive competition and contended that electricity should be a natural monopoly. In other cities, electric companies merged into local monopolies and hoisted up prices. According to Gregg A. Jarrell of the University of Rochester, the first states to adopt utility regulation did so amid vigorous competition, with electric rates 45 percent lower than average, electricity consumption per capita 25 percent higher, and lower utility profits. Once these utilities were regulated, electricity tariffs increased. Corporate survival and certainty mattered more to these utilities than the remote possibility of high profits.

Profitability: Golden Geese Over 50 Years

The first step to identifying really valuable companies is to find ones with superior profits. If you screened for a selection of especially lucrative businesses, how long did the golden goose keep laying, and does the answer vary by industry? The Dimson studies haven't yet touched on these questions. Most widely available commercial databases get really spotty beyond twenty-five years of history. Using a *Moody's Handbook* from 1965, which had full reports on 1,000 companies, I excluded banks and insurance companies. Then I picked out the ninety companies with operating profit margins of 20 percent or better in 1964. They were not democratically distributed across industries. There were fourteen railroads, a dozen pharmaceuticals, and many consumer products and mining companies. From each of thirty-two industries, I selected one representative company by using an unscientific combination of largest sales, largest market value, and highest profit margin. The retailing, trucking, steel, auto, semiconductor, and unbranded food industries lacked any companies with 20 percent profit margins.

Jumping ahead half a century to 2014, the advantage of these companies had narrowed, but their profits were still superior to the reported S&P 500 average of 10.5 percent. In table 13.1, I list the profit margins of the company or its successor, sorted from the highest in 2014 to lowest. Seven of the companies went bankrupt, many were acquired, and most had to evolve over time. The shorter list of thirty-two is meant to showcase diverse industries. Looking instead at the full list of ninety companies, margins did not revert to the mean as much as in the short list. In industries that had many high-margin companies—drugs, railroads, and consumer nondurables—profits proved more resilient, perhaps the result of some sort of industry-wide competitive moat. The exception was basic materials mining, which is subject to deep commodity cycles.

On average, companies with branded consumer nondurables maintained higher margins over half a century than any other sector. Unless you include photography, none of them went bankrupt. For the most part, their earnings were less cyclical and volatile than average. Of the four indicators of really valuable businesses, nondurables have profitability, life span, and certainty; the only missing indicator is rapid organic

Table 13.1
Profit Margins from Representative Companies in 32 Industries

Company	Successor	Ticker	Industry	1964 Margin	2014 Margin
Brown-Forman		BF.B	Alcohol	27	33
Penn Central RR	BK 1970/Norfolk So	NSC	Rail	27	31
R. J. Reynolds	Reynolds American	RAI	Cigarettes	27	30
Coastal States Gas	Kinder Morgan	KMI	Gas gather	29	27
SmithKline	GlaxoSmith	GSK	Drugs	34	26
Cap Cities	Disney	DIS	TV/radio	34	23
MMM		MMM	Misc. mfg	22	22
Intl Flavors & Fragrances		IFF	Flavors	24	19
IBM		IBM	Computers	27	19
Hershey		HSY	Candy	23	19
Gillette	Procter & Gamble	PG	Razors	24	18
Tampax	Procter & Gamble	PG	Tampons	43	18
Rayonier		RYN	Forest prod	22	16
AMP	TE Connect	TEL	Elec equip	21	15
HarbisonWalker	BK 2002/Halliburton	HAL	Refractories	21	15
Dome Mine	Goldcorp	G.TO	Gold	30	13
Abbott Lab		ABT	Med supply	21	13
Dupont EI		DD	Chemicals	25	12
Caterpillar		CAT	Const equip	21	10
Stone & Webster	BK 2000/Chic. B&I	CBI	Engineering	35	8
Xerox		XRX	Photocopy	30	7
Lone Star Cement	Buzzi Unicem	BZU IM	Cement	20	7
American Commercial Line	Private in 2009	ACLI	Shipping	24	6
Dow Jones	Newscorp	NWS	Newspapers	22	6
Maytag	Whirlpool	WHR	Appliances	25	6
Northwest Air	BK 2005/Delta	DAL	Airline	25	6
British Petroleum		BP	Oil	22	5
Avon		AVP	Cosmetics	27	5
US Gypsum	BK 2001/USG	USG	Wallboard	25	4
Noranda	Glencore	GLEN LN	Mining	22	2
Champion Spark	Fed Mogul/BK 2001	FDML	Auto parts	27	0
Eastman Kodak	BK 2012	EK	Photography	27	−1

Note: BK, bankruptcy.

sales growth. Alcohol stocks were the top performers in the UK market over 115 years, yet per capita consumption of alcohol had actually fallen. Almost every year, cigarette consumption declines. Despite obesity and waste, it's unlikely that food consumption will rise much faster than population growth. Perhaps margins in consumer nondurables like food and alcohol have been resilient precisely because steady demand and gradual product improvements discourage new competitors from entering.

My research found two consumer companies that improved on already superb margins over half a century: Reynolds, the cigarette producer, and Brown-Forman, makers of Jack Daniels whiskey. Other small-ticket consumer products companies also maintained outstanding profitability and enjoyed stronger unit sales growth. Hershey continued to be America's favorite chocolate bar. Procter & Gamble (P&G) bought both Gillette and Tampax, and P&G's profit margin was 18 percent. Gillette and Tampax had brands nearly synonymous with their categories. P&G reports results for its shaving business, which had margins of 24.4 percent in 2014, basically on par with Gillette fifty years earlier. P&G doesn't disclose margins on feminine care but hints that they are well above the corporate average.

Some consumer staples' stocks don't pan out—like Avon and Eastman Kodak. The also-rans among consumer stocks tend to have weak brands or no brands. Interestingly, that wasn't the problem for Avon, which was one of the best-known cosmetics brands, or Eastman Kodak, with one of the most valuable trade names in the world. Avon stumbled because its distribution system was far behind the times. The proliferation of shopping malls and now the Internet meant cosmetics could be purchased anywhere. Avon was also challenged by more women entering the workforce. Working women may use more cosmetics, but they aren't buying them at home from door-to-door salesladies. With more careers open to women, fewer have opted for Avon's low-paying part-time sales jobs.

Growth: Photo Finished

Eastman Kodak was both a branded small-ticket consumer products company and a technology company, but what killed it was changing technology. In the 1960s and '70s, Eastman Kodak was among the most glamorous stocks in the market, with spectacular margins on Kodachrome color film. Kodak's growth was robust despite Polaroid's introduction of instant photography. Polaroid traded at a stratospheric price/earnings ratio (P/E) multiple befitting its founder Edwin Land, an inventor-genius with 533 patents, second only to Thomas Edison. Kodak's margins eroded as Japanese competitors took market share. Ultimately, the chemical photography industry was done in by digital imaging. Polaroid, which had sparked the first round of innovation, collapsed into bankruptcy in 2008, four years before Eastman Kodak.

Explosive growth and fabulous profitability are why traders chase high-tech rock stars. Sadly, rock stars are not known for long life spans or predictability. Of the thirty-two companies in table 13.1, Xerox's P/E ratio of fifty-four was by far the loftiest, followed by IBM. Eastman Kodak was also richly valued. In the 1970s, all three were members of the "Nifty Fifty," the favorite "one-decision" growth stocks. Companies in industries that have changed rapidly survive only if they keep changing. IBM fared best over fifty years because it completely changed its business, from computer hardware to software and services. Xerox has diversified into outsourced services but continues to sell, rent, and service copiers, where margins have collapsed. Kodak went bankrupt in 2012, still focused on film and cameras.

Another victim of a repudiated technology was Stone & Webster, which designed and engineered nuclear power plants. Stone had serviced every nuclear power plant in America. Nuclear power was supposed to make electricity too cheap to meter, but public protests led to massive construction cost overruns. After the Three Mile Island meltdown in 1979, utilities stopped ordering nukes and canceled work in progress. Half of the nuclear plants that had been on the drawing boards were never completed. Stone & Webster coped by diversifying into less profitable lines of work, becoming just another engineering and construction firm and bidding on work to keep staff busy.

Engineers typically are preoccupied with whether a technology serves its intended purpose and not with its side effects. Unexpected consequences can destroy a company. Asbestos lawsuits bankrupted HarbisonWalker, Federal-Mogul, and USG. The public rejected technologies because of their indirect effects, not because they didn't work.

Asbestos still has the flame-retardant and heat-resistant properties that earned it the label of "the miracle mineral." Obviously, asbestos has been replaced by other materials in most applications, including the Micronite filter for Kent cigarettes, where it was once billed as "the greatest health protection in cigarette history." Where safer fire retardants are not available, asbestos is legal in the United States and is still used in gaskets, roofing, and floor tiles.

There were contemporary reports warning of the dangers of asbestos and nuclear energy, but also of tobacco and booze. Does this hint at products future generations may turn away from? Prohibition and its repeal show that in different eras, citizens may feel that the benefits of a product outweigh the social damage, then conclude that the harm is greater, and still later flip-flop back to their original opinion. Some warn that the Internet makes it possible for governments and advertisers to monitor people 24/7 (and electronic currency enables further tracking). Nor do people own data about themselves; still, so far the consensus is that the Internet is a great thing. Genetic engineering has produced amazing advances in agricultural productivity, but doubters are watching for horrible mutants. Really, though, the future's not ours to see.

Certainty and an Unknowable Future

I find a degree of certainty about the future by looking for noncyclical demand, government regulation, monopoly power, brand loyalty, and a relatively unchanging product. For wildly cyclical businesses, an average level of demand may be calculated, but in any particular year, sales and profits may be so far from the trend that predicting is a fool's errand. When regulation or monopoly power shields businesses from competition, the risks of market share battles and price wars are lessened. Strong brands imply loyal customers and a measure of pricing power. Products that evolve slowly (and are not commodities) are less vulnerable to substitution and shifts in market-share.

Contracts, including purchases and sales but also debts and leases, may either increase certainty or reduce it. Some purchases and sales are made under long-term contracts, giving some visibility into a company's revenues or expenses and pricing in future years. Automatic renewals of "evergreen" subscriptions for periodicals, phone service, or software maintenance often continue through inertia, rather than by contract. Cost-plus agreements assure contractors of a level of profit that is known in advance. On the other hand, poorly written contracts can add to uncertainty. During downturns, businesses wish that all of their costs were variable, not fixed. Most companies have debt and lease obligations in which they have promised to pay definite amounts out of their own uncertain future incomes.

Penn Central and Northwest Orient Airlines filed for bankruptcy not just because they had too much debt but also to restructure costly labor agreements. The 1968 merger of the Pennsylvania Railroad and the New York Central gave Penn Central a rail monopoly on many of its routes, but feisty labor unions blocked cost efficiencies. Penn Central's passenger operations had been bleeding profusely through the 1960s as declining ridership left it overstaffed. In 1966, Pennsy had sold the Long Island Rail Road (a commuter line) to the state of New York, but retained other money-losing commuter and intercity passenger lines. Freight has always been cyclical, and Penn Central's cost structure and $3.3 billion of debt seemed to reflect expectations that a buoyant economy would continue indefinitely. Penn Central filed for bankruptcy in 1970, only two years after the merger, without having omitted its dividend.

In 1964, Northwest Orient had a clear path to open-ended growth. More people were flying, and airlines were regulated, so domestic routes were consistently profitable. Northwest had a robust balance sheet, with debt less than half of equity, and a modern fleet. Better still, it had extensive Asian service. Historically, landing slots in the Far East have been tightly constrained. Even today, Asia is a growth market for air travel. Airfares have tended to be costly in Asia, so airlines compete by pampering customers. Lists of the best airlines in the world often include many Asian (and no American) carriers.

In 1978, airlines were deregulated and domestic routes became more competitive. Northwest merged with Republic to reinforce its dominance in the St. Paul and Detroit hubs. Service disruptions ensued. After a leveraged buyout in 1989, Northwest sold many of its planes and leased them back, along with much of its international real estate.

Northwest developed a split personality, offering exquisite service on its Tokyo routes while repeatedly squeezing employees for concessions. For a time, Northwest cut out amenities like peanuts and pillows to reduce costs but, sensibly, not on its Asian flights. By 2005, the leveraged buyout and years of losses left Northwest with billions in debt and leases, a negative net worth, an aging fleet, and few surplus assets to strip out. All of the things that had provided Northwest visibility into its destiny—government regulation, monopoly markets, low debt and lease costs—were gone. Some fliers dubbed it "Northworst."

The fact that ride service Uber has found ways around regulations is bringing an end to a long period of predictability for the taxi business. For more than seventy-five years, New York City has restrained competition by requiring a medallion on each cab and fixing the number of medallions. During the Great Depression, taxi rides slumped, and fares dropped as well. A proposal to create a taxi monopoly in New York was floated but dropped after it was reported that Mayor Jimmy Walker had accepted a bribe from Parmelee Taxi, the largest taxi service. In 1937, New York issued roughly 13,000 medallions at a price of $10 each. By 2013, the medallions were trading at $1.1 million, more than a 15 percent compound annual rate of gain. That's insane, considering that a fully equipped new taxi vehicle costs less than one-tenth of that amount.

Taxi drivers who don't own medallions generally think of the system as a form of legalized shakedown, but to an investor it offered a very certain one-way bet. Most medallion owners rent them to drivers, which produced a steady, growing income of $70,000 a year, or a 6 percent current yield, on top of the capital appreciation. The rental income rarely declined, as it is the drivers who take the risk of slow days and costly fuel. In the 1980s, Checker Motors was a public company. Personally, I was a fan of the spacious gas-hog taxi vehicles that Checker once built, but it also owned thousands of taxi medallions, partly through its holding in Parmelee. I bought some shares, but soon after, Checker went private. At the time, I thought the price was too low; in hindsight, the buyout group absolutely stole the company. Today, Uber and Lyft operate without medallions but offer rides at lower prices, yet driver take-home pay is comparable to that of medallion cab drivers. Meanwhile, medallion prices have tumbled.

For decades, the subscription model and force of habit made trends of newspaper companies like Dow Jones boringly predictable. The government limits competition in broadcasting, but even without regulation, most cities have only one newspaper. Readership chugged along even as electronic media grew. Other than housing and employment, most classes of advertising were not that cyclical. By the time newspaper advertising collapsed, the Internet was old news. Whether your visibility into the future comes from laws, monopoly power, contracts, customs, or habits, it relies on human behavior, with all its foibles.

Indeed, all four elements of value—profitability, life span, growth, and certainty—reflect regular patterns of social behavior. As such, even though we try to attach numbers to the four elements of value, they are nothing like the laws of physics. Elevated profitability reflects a product that buyers want that, for whatever reason, they cannot get elsewhere. Longevity is shortened by periods when the immediate demand for a company's product falls. Whether the sale is lost to a competitive supplier or substitute product or is deferred cyclically, the result is the same. Growth reflects either substitution away from a competing product or a product that allows users to do something that they could not do before. Certainty reflects contracts and the general inertia of institutions and human behavior. The investment challenge is to avoid getting carried away with unrealistic expectations. History suggests that many companies will turn out to have a terminal value of zero.

14

Oil Gushers and Slicks

The top-dollar rooms in capitalism's grand hotel are always
occupied, but not by the same occupants.
—JOSEPH SCHUMPETER

COMMODITY PRODUCERS ARE A SPECULATORS' PLAYGROUND and an investor's minefield. The products are all similar and sold for market prices,
reflecting supply and demand. In buoyant markets, the stories are all
about demand, but investors watch the supply side. The producer with
the lowest costs will have the highest profit margins, which could allow it
to be the fastest grower. If prices were stable, I would (and do, anyway)
search for undervalued assets and lower production costs.

The monkey wrench is that because price is the only basis for competition, commodity prices fluctuate, often violently. Supply comes on
with a lag after high prices. Depending on how competitors react, or
not, to those changes, a producer's relative cost position will shift. In a
buoyant market, lower-cost producers miss opportunities if they don't
add higher-cost, but still profitable, capacity. In a downturn, the low-
cost producer will be the last to die, but the costs of competitors shift at
differing rates. Sustaining low costs is difficult. Asset values can become
shockingly ephemeral.

The cost to discover and produce a barrel of oil, for example, can't
be precisely known in advance. Accountants classify the costs of energy
companies into three groups: (1) finding reserves, (2) developing reserves,
and (3) lifting and producing the oil or gas. Finding oil is a mixed game
of luck and skill. In any single instance, drilling results are unpredictable;

even the best explorers drill dry holes. Measures of finding costs will leap around and so must be considered as a historical average cost of all exploration activity in a geographic area. To explain *why* a company's costs are low, I look to geology, technology, and social institutions.

Development costs are tied to a particular field or project, so explorers budget costs proportionate to the estimated value of the resource. Some reserves are cheap to find but expensive to develop or lift, and vice versa. One rule of thumb for maintaining profitability is that development costs shouldn't be more than one-third of the selling price—for example, costs of $15 a barrel when oil is selling at $45 a barrel.

Lifting costs are more predictable than development costs, partly because they include taxes and royalties, which are often determined by law or contract as a percentage of revenues. The costs of physically lifting hydrocarbons from deep offshore wells are higher than from prolific, shallow land wells. Even in a specific field, the first oil lifted is the easiest and cheapest, with costs rising over time. Fiscal terms and geology vary all around the world. Therefore, not all barrels are equal.

Prices constantly bounce around in anticipation of future supply and demand. Rising prices signal that more of a commodity is wanted, but new supplies of mineral resources take years to develop. The lags are sometimes so spread out that one wonders whether there is any link between price and supply response at all. Oil prices touched a peak of $145 a barrel in July 2008, but American oil production was still rising in 2015. Unlike other minerals, oil cannot be recovered and reused. Unlike agricultural produce, more oil can't be grown. Equilibrium price is a useful idea, but people who take it too seriously will find real-life oil markets treacherous.

Oil traders know that, to make a profit, they must guess the change in the future prices assumed by the market, not the direction of the spot price for immediate delivery. Nearly all of the trading in futures markets is for deliveries within one year, so the implied forecasts for the out years, which matter most to equity investors, are tough to discern. Also, specific oil and gas stocks are priced to anticipate different price decks. (A price deck is a series of price forecasts over time, usually quarterly or annual.)

While I generally avoid commodity businesses, if you must invest in one, go with oil, because of the limit on supply and relatively inelastic demand.

When a resource *can* be renewed, the cost is to find, produce, and replace it. Individual oil companies may be able to replace reserves, but globally, the resource endowment is irreplaceable and depleting. Hubbert's Peak occurs after half of the global oil endowment has been produced; it's possible that it has already occurred. Through improved technology, more oil can be located and extracted, but eventually, Earth's resources are finite.

For now, demand is stable to increasing. In the ten years up to 2015, world crude oil production fell 1.6 percent in its weakest year and rose 2.7 percent in the strongest. Until automotive and alternative energy technologies improve further—and there's a lot of progress happening with that—there are no good substitutes for oil as transportation fuel. Even if climate change is real, it's impossible for the world to quit using oil cold turkey. But just because the oil industry is resilient today doesn't mean individual companies are, or that they will be in the future.

Who rightfully owns a natural resource that cannot be replenished? Depending on the answer, there are different estimates of the cost of producing oil. Because hydrocarbons occur naturally and are depleting, most governments stake a social claim on them. In many countries, national oil companies have a monopoly on ownership. Abroad, oil and gas sales are heavily burdened with taxes and royalties.

At the same time, some costs related to energy production and consumption—like Middle Eastern wars, environmental damages, and road building—are also borne socially. Consider the hundreds of thousands who died in the unending series of Middle Eastern wars. When wars flare up in the Middle East, oil prices tend to jump. Higher oil prices help governments of producing nations fund their wars, but more directly, wars disrupt oil supply lines. After years of intermittent study of Sunnis and Shiites, and of the locations of oil fields, pipelines, and ports, I've not concluded anything very useful for making investments. One could spend a lifetime examining Arab culture and history and never turn up a winning stock. My conclusion is not to invest in war zones.

Taxes, royalties, and profits—what economists call *rent*—claim the majority of oil revenues and are determined by social institutions, not physical inputs. This implies that there may be many prices for oil or no equilibrium at all. Governments, landholders, and businesses would each like as large a cut of the revenue as possible but recognize that if they demand too much, the oil will not be produced, and they may get nothing. However, they accept reality at different speeds.

Between 1980 and 2003, energy prices were flat to down while broad price levels doubled, so oil and gas producers had to slash costs. Since 2008, energy companies again have been forced to cut expenses. All the buckets of costs must be considered together. A project with low finding costs may have high development or lifting costs. "Step out" and "extension" wells, which are adjacent to existing fields, have high hit rates, while high-risk wildcat wells are often dry holes. Many companies dropped traditional exploration in favor of programs with better odds.

New techniques have improved recovery rates and reduced finding costs. In the early 1980s, drillers generally expected to recover 20 percent of the oil in the ground, and 50 percent recovery rates were rare. Now, through secondary recovery methods, 60 percent of the oil in place can often be lifted. More oil can be extracted (with less water and gas byproduct) by drilling horizontally while using measurement while drilling. Hydraulic fracturing ("fracking") cracks open shale rocks to release the hydrocarbons trapped beneath.

Usually, shale and enhanced recovery projects involve higher development or production costs. Infill drilling will generally hit a smaller target, so the per-barrel costs will be higher. As fields get older, it can be costly to inject water, gas, or carbon dioxide and then process and dispose of the wastewater. Many shale wells are relatively short lived, producing the majority of their oil or gas in two or three years. Shale producers will see cash coming in from product sales, but the wells' short lives mean that constant upkeep is needed and new resources must be located. Any shale producer that tries to get off this treadmill will see its output dwindle.

Oil explorers are drawn to regions with promising geology and attractive tax and royalty ("fiscal") terms. They prefer to avoid regions that are corrupt and war torn. Over time, the basins with the most activity become tapped out, even with new drilling technologies. The largest, most profitable fields tend to be found first. Geologists call this pattern of diminishing returns the "creaming curve." The only places explorers can find elephant-sized discoveries are in deep water offshore or in politically dangerous areas.

From Russia with Love

Early in the new millennium, privatized Russian oil companies started to attract the attention of foreign investors, myself included. Russia is the world's largest producer of both oil and natural gas. In terms of reserves, Russia ranks first in natural gas and eighth in oil. Russia's geology puts it low on the world cost curves, even though it uses antiquated technology. Looking around the globe in 2000 (and still today), all of the cheapest energy stocks were in Russia, no matter whether you looked at price/earnings ratios (P/Es), price per barrel of reserves, or estimates of the present value of assets.

In Russia it's not clear who legitimately owns anything, least of all the oil industry. When Russia returned businesses to private hands, influential government officials often wound up as owners. Effectively, Yukos was sold to Bank Menatep and Mikhail Khodorkovsky for $309 million under loans for shares, despite a higher bid. The true profitability and value of Yukos was impossible to determine, but here's a hint: Revenues were $8 billion. In the late 1990s, Yukos shares still traded at a ridiculous P/E of one-half, equivalent to six months profits.

An American depository receipt (ADR) consisting of four Yukos shares began trading on NASDAQ in 2001 at around $10, or a P/E ratio of one and one-half. The stock was also a bargain based on a comparison of Yukos's market capitalization with its barrels of oil reserves. At year-end 2002, Yukos held about $4 billion in cash and marketable securities, which, net of long-term debt of $378 million, equated to cash of $7 per ADR.

Yukos had proven reserves of 5.9 billion barrels of oil that could be recovered before its licenses expired, more than ten barrels per ADR. About two-thirds of the proven reserves had been developed. And if Yukos could get its licenses renewed after they expired, another 4.6 billion proven barrels could be recovered. In addition, it had 4.6 trillion cubic feet of proven natural gas reserves. Even after Yukos's ADR septupled to $68 by October 2003, the stock market value of its proven reserves was $6 a barrel. For comparison, ExxonMobil shares were trading around $40 and were backed by reserves of 1.7 barrels of oil per share and 8.5 thousand cubic feet of gas. Converting the gas to equivalent barrels at a 1:6 energy-equivalent ratio, Exxon had about three equivalent barrels of reserves per share, implying a price of $13 a barrel.

What were Yukos's assets worth? In their U.S. Securities and Exchange Commission (SEC) mandated 10K or 20F annual reports, oil and gas production companies provide an estimate of the value of their reserves, called the "standardized measure of discounted net cash flows." This is the most important table in an oil company annual report; it summarizes the company's best analysis of the value of its proven reserves, including future development. It is a conservative measure, with standards set by the SEC, and excludes speculative projects that lack geological definition, markets, or approvals. Unless oil prices have dropped, downward revisions to reserve estimates from previous years hint at a lack of reporting integrity.

Following SEC standards, Yukos assumed that the 2002 year-end product prices, costs, and tax regime would stay constant indefinitely. Crude oil was trading at $28 a barrel in December 2002. Yukos also assumed certain trends in the economic recoverability of hydrocarbons. Based on that, Yukos calculated the after-tax cash that it would receive by producing out its reserves. These amounts were discounted back at a 10 percent rate of return. This worked out to be $54 per Yukos ADR before its license expiry, and $62 if the license was extended. Arguably, this was a conservative estimate; it included no value for Yukos's cash, refineries, service stations, or probable and possible reserves.

In Russia, bad things happen to those who don't support the *siloviki*, or politicians who were formerly with the KGB or military. In February 2003 at a televised meeting at the Kremlin, Khodorkovsky, by then the richest man in Russia, confronted Russian President Vladimir Putin with accusations that government officials had taken millions in bribes. Soon after, the government presented Yukos with a series of assessments for back taxes totaling $27 billion. The taxes for 2001 and 2002 exceeded Yukos's revenues and amounted to 83 percent of 2003 revenues. The government froze Yukos's assets and auctioned off its largest subsidiary for $9.4 billion even though Dresdner Kleinwort had appraised it at $15–$17 billion. Rosneft, a company much friendlier with Putin, was later revealed as the owner of most of Yukos's assets.

In nations like Russia, where oil is the primary export, there is a real "oil curse." Governments that can be totally funded with oil revenues do not need popular support and are often repressive and undemocratic.

Economic freedom and rule of law are also unnecessary. Actually, kleptocracies work better if no one dares challenge claims on resource wealth. My sense is that oil-exporting nations tend to get into more wars and skirmishes. Saudi Arabia, Russia, Iran, Iraq, Nigeria, Angola, and Venezuela fit this pattern. However, Norway, Canada, and the United Arab Emirates are oil exporters with above-average civil and economic liberties. Until 2013, the United Kingdom was also a net oil exporter.

Carnaval Time in Rio

Around 2003, Brazil was one of the few regions with highly prospective geology that did not have an appalling record on human and property rights. Brazil's military dictatorship ended in 1985 and was replaced by the Brazilian New Republic. The Heritage Institute ranked Brazil as slightly above the world average in economic freedom in 2003, although it has slipped since then. In 2015, The World Justice Project ranked Brazil behind Chile, Costa Rica, and Uruguay on its Rule of Law index, but ahead of a dozen other Latin American nations. Brazil's president, Lula da Silva, was elected in 2003 partly on promises to eradicate the corruption that had led to the resignation and subsequent impeachment of former president Fernando Collor de Mello.

I asked an offshore oil service firm which of its customers was doing the most exciting exploration. They answered Petrobras. Petróleo Brasileiro (Petrobras) was founded in 1953 as the national oil company and, until reforms in the late 1990s, held a monopoly on the business in Brazil. All of the exploration in Brazil until then had been done by Petrobras, and most of it since. Other major oil companies had minimal presence in Brazil. From the oil service company's vantage point, Petrobras was mostly an offshore producer with massive, technically complex fields that required the sort of assistance they could provide.

Petrobras had below-average finding costs for oil and was increasing its reserves briskly, which seemed to bear out the idea that Brazil was underexplored. During the 1990s, Petrobras roughly doubled its oil liquids production, and it continued to grow in the new millennium. From the start of 2000 to year-end 2004, Petrobras had discoveries and extensions of twice the amounts it produced. Most major oil companies replace production and maybe add a smidge more. Over that time, Petrobras's worldwide proven oil reserves grew from 8.3 billion barrels to 9.9 billion. It was as close to a growth stock as you could find among major oils.

On paper, Brazil's tax and royalty regime was competitive with North America's. I pegged Petrobras's finding and development costs for newly discovered oil at about $4 a barrel (remember that costs jump around). In 2003, Petrobras's lifting costs, excluding the government take, were $3.48 per equivalent barrel. For coming years, Petrobras had set a goal of trimming lifting costs to $3.00 a barrel. The government take amounted to $5.14 a barrel, or about one-fifth of the selling price. With world oil prices at around $25 a barrel, Petrobras earned an operating profit margin of just over 50 percent on its exploration and production business. Perhaps because the government owns a majority of the voting stock, Petrobras did little to avoid or defer taxes and paid an effective income tax rate of 31 percent in 2003. An oil producer with great geology, modern technology, and supportive social institutions—like Petrobras—should be a champion.

The bear story was that President Lula was a socialist at heart. Lula's formal education stopped at fourth grade, and he worked for labor unions before he became a politician in the Worker's Party. That was scary stuff, but his Minister of Energy, Dilma Rousseff, was mostly market-oriented. She later became Lula's chief of staff. Petrobras was clearly an instrument of economic policy, with Ms. Rousseff serving as its board chairwoman. Petrobras sold some of its products at controlled prices, even though by law prices were largely decontrolled in 2002. But if the country raised taxes and royalties, one arm of the government would take money from another.

In August 2000, Petrobras ADRs were listed on the New York Stock Exchange, as part of a privatization policy that had been implemented under Brazilian president Fernando H. Cardoso. Investors feared that Lula would roll back privatization and other market-oriented reforms. An analyst quipped, "Brazil is the country of the future, and always will be."

Consequently, despite all the positives, Petrobras stock was seemingly undervalued, with a P/E of between five and six in 2003 and 2004.

By comparison, at its low point, ExxonMobil was at thirteen times 2004 earnings. Between 2002 and 2004, Petrobras stock doubled, but my estimate of value was much higher, and luck lifted it higher still.

Benchmark crude oil prices catapulted from $25 a barrel to $145 a barrel over five years. In 2007, Petrobras discovered the Tupi field (later renamed the Lula field) with 6 billion barrels of oil reserves. Several more billion-barrel strikes followed. These discoveries reversed a three-decade decline in global discoveries of new oil. Brazil seemed to be the only place on earth where drillers could find new fields in the super-giant (over 1 billion barrel) class. Lula became one of the most popular Brazilian presidents ever.

Petrobras stock was unstoppable. Its share price doubled again in 2005, then again in two years to 2007, yet again by year-end 2007, and still further in the first half of 2008. Between 2004 and June 2008, Petrobras stock multiplied tenfold, far outstripping most major oil companies. Petrobras became the largest holding in my fund, even though it had not started that way.

Selling Petrobras shares at this point might look like a mistake, but the stock really wasn't visibly undervalued anymore. In June 2008, with the ADRs at $71, Petrobras had a stock market value topping a quarter of a trillion dollars and a P/E over thirty, both of which exceeded Microsoft's. When I converted the market capitalization into a price per barrel of reserves, the stock looked expensive. A large chunk of Petrobras's reserves was undeveloped, which implied that massive spending lay ahead. On a per-barrel basis, undeveloped reserves aren't worth as much as developed.

To justify continuing to hold Petrobras stock then, I would have had to make ambitious forecasts about probable and possible reserves and future luck. Later events show that exuberance was indeed warranted. In 2010, the Libra field was discovered. At 8 billion barrels of reserves, it was even larger than Tupi. Simultaneously, the Franco field with 4.5 billion barrels was also discovered near the Libra field. There were several other billion-barrel *pre-salt* fields (meaning they were trapped offshore below a shifting layer of salt and rock a mile deep). Brazil might become an oil exporter, perhaps of great size. The financial media doted on Brazil.

When commodity prices are rising, low-cost producers will miss out on profit opportunities if they do *not* bring on capacity at increasing costs. An oil well that had all-in costs of $20 a barrel when crude was selling for $25 should gush cash when oil prices hit $145 a barrel, even allowing that royalties and taxes rise in tandem. At $145 a barrel, any well with all-in costs lower than $145 would be profitable. Adding a well with costs of, say, $100 might reduce a company's profit margin but add to dollars of profit. Petrobras and OGX—a highly leveraged Brazilian driller established in 2007—were both eagerly grabbing higher-cost opportunities. The 6-billion-barrel Tupi field was the largest of these, but there were scores of promising (if costly) prospects in Brazil's offshore basins.

In 2009, two Petrobras economists (Rafael R. Pertusier and Mileno T. Cavalcante) presented a startling report titled "Are Oil Prices and Oil Costs Related?" Their answer was a resounding "Yes!" In 2002, when the price of Brent crude oil was around $25 a barrel, the all-in break-even price for Brent crude was about $20 a barrel. Finding and development costs for the major international oil companies averaged $5.40 per barrel. In 2008, Brent crude spiked to well over $100, but averaged around $97 a barrel. The industry's break-even price was $86 a barrel, as finding and development costs had quintupled to $25.52 a barrel. Oil service contractors hoisted their day rates for using rigs, but at higher oil prices, it was still profitable to spend more to find a barrel of oil.

Petrobras had discovered billions of barrels of oil in the Campos and Santos basins, which faced even greater cost pressures. Some wells were 20,000 feet deep before they struck oil. With well locations two hundred miles offshore, it would take years and great coordination to get the drilling equipment in place. There were no precedents for the scale and scope of the Tupi (Lula) field, and other gigantic projects were anticipated.

The Brazilian government wanted to keep the oil windfall in Brazil and passed a series of laws with that intent. Brazilian content requirements were expanded for equipment used offshore. Less than one-fifth of the rigs used in the Brazilian offshore had been Brazilian, which was increased to three-fifths. High-tech international oil service contractors had to find a local partner or finagle a way around the rules. Petrobras would be the operator of any new fields in Brazil and would own at least a 30 percent interest. Brazil would be assured that "the oil is ours," but the implication was that Petrobras would be borrowing billions of dollars every year for years to come. Net debt exceeded $100 billion by 2015.

Petrobras's slogan is *O petróleo é nosso*, or "the oil is ours," but I kept wondering who was included in the "us." Did the oil belong to the citizens of Brazil, the shareholders of Petrobras, or top government bureaucrats? Were frequent repetition of the slogan and the new laws omens of nationalization? Nor was this an idle fear. Bolivia had nationalized its oil industry in 2006. The next year, Venezuela partly expropriated Orinoco basin wells from foreigners, including Petrobras. I didn't know it in 2009, but Argentina would renationalize YPF in 2012.

Beyond the specter of expropriation, Petrobras was no longer a low-cost producer. It was outspending its cash flow, its debt was rising ominously, and its shares were no longer clearly undervalued. To top it off, oil prices careened from $145 to $36 a barrel over six months in 2008 before hitting a V-bottom and rebounding slowly back to $125 in 2011. In commodity businesses like oil, there will be major cyclical swings. The companies that go bust during a down cycle have either high costs or excessive debt, or both. I bailed out of all of the Petrobras in my funds.

As I gradually exited shares later at much lower prices, I thought wistfully of the peak price of $72 per ADR in 2008. In retrospect, I regret nothing. Oil field development was behind schedule with overruns adding up to tens of billions of dollars. Brazil remains a net oil importer. Dilma Rousseff was elected President of Brazil when Lula's term was up. Plans to build four new refineries were announced, including three in Brazil's poor and less-populated northeast; two of these were partially built and later scrapped. Petrobras's refining operations hemorrhaged billions, as oil had to be purchased on the world market while the gasoline products sold at controlled prices. Today, Petrobras still has more employees than ExxonMobil and less than half the revenues, suggesting overstaffing.

After oil prices crashed in late 2014 and Dilma Rousseff was reelected, Petrobras announced multibillion-dollar corruption losses. Apparently, a surcharge was tacked onto Petrobras's capital projects, with roughly $3 billion funneled to politicians in the Worker's Party. The code name for this was Operation Car Wash, as the cash was laundered through Petrobras filling stations. Evidently, almost no contract in Brazil's oil sector could be secured without a bribe. Dozens of the country's senators, contractors, and prominent officials were indicted, including former president Fernando Collor de Mello, who had been impeached (and acquitted) on corruption charges. President Rousseff was impeached and removed from office in 2016.

From a financial analyst's viewpoint, corruption, mismanagement, steep taxes and royalties, bad geology, and bad luck are all paths to high costs. Corruption is problematic, not only ethically but also because analysts presumably don't know about it and can't gauge how it might change. I can detect mismanagement only with simplistic ratios like revenues per employee. The stable costs of taxes and royalties can shift even in countries with rule of law, as rising prices can make landowners and governments greedier.

Surveys of oil industry finding costs can tell you about the past but should be combined with a forward-looking view of geological opportunity, the stability of fiscal terms, and a company's technological skills. In general, finding and development costs should be lower in underexplored regions with plentiful resources. Tax and royalty regimes are most stable in democracies, provided corruption isn't rampant. Some companies do have superior technology and geological expertise, which results in lower costs.

The variability of commodity prices appeals to speculators but may discourage investors from participating in these industries. It's a fool's errand to predict oil prices, for example, but earnings and asset values can't be estimated without some price deck. An admittedly imperfect way to build in conservatism when calculating asset values and earnings is to assume the *lower* of today's spot price or a ten-year average. I look for indications of safety, including (1) low production costs, (2) political stability, (3) a discount to asset value, (4) a low P/E ratio and (5) little or no debt. Speculators who ignore indications of safety must often conclude, as did Daniel Plainview in *There Will Be Blood* (2007), "I am finished."

15

Tech Stocks and Science Fiction

> Because technology changes a ton, what I focus on is
> what won't change.
>
> —JEFF BEZOS

There Is No Warren Buffett of Technology

BY THAT I MEAN THAT no one on the Forbes 400 richest list made their fortune by investing in publicly listed tech stocks. Yes, dozens of venture capitalists (VCs), technology entrepreneurs, and key employees are billionaires, but they had advantages that you, as a public market investor, don't. They had a bird's-eye view of the path of innovation and some ability to influence it. Often they put all of their capital, plus their heart and soul, into one company. And they held onto most of their stock and let it compound for years and decades.

Billionaire tech insiders benefited not only from superior insight, but more importantly from spectacular luck as holders of an undiversified portfolio of one moonshot investment. Luck's role is hidden because outstanding success is spotlighted; failure is all around but unpublicized and unseen. For every Mark Zuckerberg, there are hundreds of tech entrepreneurs and employees with little to show for years of effort. In another realm, Jennifer Aniston and Sandra Bullock worked as waitresses before they became movie stars. Most of the seventy thousand waiters and waitresses in the Los Angeles area never get a casting call. It is highly unlikely that you will pick just one stock and it will be the next Facebook. Even then, stardom can be fleeting.

To sustain their luck, start-ups need a shifting mix of proprietary technology and low costs, but the actions that support one of these objectives often undermines the other. Technology-focused enterprises spend heavily on research and development (R&D) to stay on the bleeding edge at the expense of current profitability, while financially driven firms minimize costs, including R&D, and trail behind in innovation. The nasty twist is that even the niftiest products eventually mature. Because they become mundane and then obsolete, over time both vision and financial control are mandatory. Investors mirror this divide by approaching tech stocks either as futurists or as financial analysts, when they need both. Financial analysis cannot accurately imagine the course of innovation, while science fiction is equally useless in understanding a commoditizing industry. I start by trying to fill, or at least understand, the gaping holes in my knowledge.

Go Where No One Else Has Gone Before?

Echoing *Star Trek*, most technology entrepreneurs and investors seek to boldly go where no one has gone before. They are drawn to situations with odds that are—strictly speaking—incalculable and the outcomes indefinable. World-changing inventions can't be obsolete and face little competition, so talk of costs and competition bores these visionaries silly. From a tiny base, companies with breakthrough products grow exponentially and earn fabulous profits. But when you explore new frontiers, some of the strange new worlds you discover are disappointment and failure.

The imagination is unlimited, and anything is possible, but investors live in the real world. In science or technology, the constraint is that your vision can't contradict known facts. As physicist Richard Feynman put it: "Imagine something that you have never seen, that is consistent in every detail with what has already been seen, and that is different from what has been thought of; furthermore, it must be definite and not a vague proposition." Successful futurists start with a broad knowledge of the details of relevant observations, focusing in particular on which experiments and proposed solutions have been tried and failed.

One can't assume that the mad scientist with an ingenious idea will be first to turn the discovery into a product that works—or that a working product will lead directly to market acceptance and then to industry dominance, or that top dogs won't quickly be eclipsed by the next next thing. The history of technology is an endless series of stories of geniuses who create inventions but then end up broke while others run with the inventions and make millions. For example, Julius Lilienfeld patented the first transistor, but AT&T's Bell Labs got the credit for the first working device, and Intel earns billions from semiconductors, a product built on the transistor. (Lilienfeld at least has a major physics prize named in his honor.)

The brightest luminaries seem to be motivated by doing something marvelous and worthwhile, not by becoming billionaires. Thomas Edison, the inventor-genius who founded General Electric, anticipated Silicon Valley's mind-set. He said, "My main purpose in life is to make enough money to create ever more inventions." Similarly, Alphabet's mission is "to organize the world's information and make it universally accessible and useful." To prevent any interference with its grand mission and to thwart short-term greedy shareholders, half of Alphabet's shares have no vote while the shares of its two founders (Larry Page and Sergey Brin) have ten votes each.

The greatest scientific glory attaches to the inventors of a building-block technology—one that will be reapplied in countless ways, seeding a multitude of application offshoots. Often the big bucks go to those who create those applications, not the breakthrough. Charles Babbage may have invented the first computer, but IBM perfected it and developed software applications for it, creating an enormous and durable business. The search engine is an application of the Internet, and the Internet an application of computers, but the search engine is itself a building-block invention. Alan Emtage, Bill Heelan, and J. Peter Deutsch invented the Web content search engine, but none of them is as outrageously wealthy as Google's founders.

Research projects that are closest to producing a marketable product are generally seen as the safest bets. Even brilliant tinkering requires trial and error, which looks immensely wasteful to financial analysts. Some companies put into practice the theory that most R&D is squandered.

In China, technology is often simply pirated. Valeant Pharmaceuticals buys drug companies and then slashes their research effort but boosts late-stage development and marketing. Likewise, Apple has seen a great payoff on design and development, but it spends more on patent litigation than it does on pure research.

Expected and Unexpected Inventions

In *Profiles of the Future*, Arthur C. Clarke asserted that progress depends critically on luck, categorizing important inventions as "expected" and "unexpected" (see table 15.1). Clarke defined unexpected to mean that the discoverers weren't searching for it and ancient scientists wouldn't understand its purpose or workings. Black holes are an unexpected

Table 15.1
Unexpected Versus Expected Inventions

Unexpected	Expected
Artificial organs	Airplanes
Black holes	Artificial life
DNA fingerprints	Automobiles
Evolution	Cell phones
Laser	Death rays
Microwave oven	Holodeck
MRI scan	Immortality
Nuclear energy	LSD
Quantum computer	Organ transplants
Radar	Robots
Superconductors	Solar panels
TV/radio	Spaceships
Virtual reality	Steam engines
X-ray	Submarines

Source: kk.org

discovery, as they would perplex the ancients and still baffle scientists today. By contrast, the ancient Greeks and Leonardo da Vinci anticipated flying machines by trying to build them.

This distinction matters to investors in two ways. First, unexpected inventions are more likely to be among the rare building-block inventions. Scientists hadn't expected them because they were on the less-explored frontiers of knowledge. As such, the unexpected discovery often turns out to open up promising areas of inquiry. The lack of competition to make an unexpected discovery likely extends to those adjacent areas and the applications of the new invention. Second, because unexpected inventions are a by-product of research on other topics, you might say they cost nothing. By contrast, billions of dollars are being spent to ensure the forthcoming inventions of driverless vehicles, cheap renewable energy (and storage), intelligent delivery drones, augmented reality, and quantum computing.

Failure is a recurring feature of any research venture. Accountants define a failed experiment differently than scientists do. Accountants consider an experiment that did not reach its goal a failure and write off the cost. Scientists consider an experiment a failure if it did not arrive at a conclusion about their hypothesis—that is, if they didn't learn anything. No one has yet devised a method for assessing the future fruits of today's research.

Serendipity is a by-product of research, but only for those who are flexible enough to find a new context for their observation. Viagra was originally intended to be heart medicine, and it definitely got the hearts of the men in the clinical trials racing. Spencer Silver, a researcher at 3M (formerly known as Minnesota Mining and Manufacturing), tried to develop a super-strong adhesive, which came out as a really weak adhesive; more than a decade later, another 3M researcher, Arthur Fry, turned it into the backing for Post-it notes.

Technologists hate to talk about it, but serendipity can have a very dark side, as unintended consequences become apparent over time. The drug Thalidomide is an example of a discovery in search of an application. Ciba developed thalidomide as an anticonvulsant for treating epilepsy, but it failed in that application. The drug did reduce nausea and was a powerful sedative, so it was labeled for morning sickness in pregnant women. That proved to be a horrific application. In the late 1950s and early 1960s, between ten thousand and twenty thousand children were stillborn or born with missing or deformed limbs to women who had taken thalidomide. Currently, thalidomide is still prescribed to treat the side effects of cancer, HIV, and leprosy.

Many inventions come from recombining known technologies in new ways. For example, the Internet is a mashup of computer and telephone technologies, and Facebook combines the party-line telephone, Internet, and photographs. Driverless vehicles will marry automobiles, sensors, and the Internet. The Xerox copier combined photography with electrostatic printing, but it took twenty-two years to convert the key patent into a marketable product. Instead of using a plate to print, Xerox needed a drum coated with an element that would hold an electrostatic charge in darkness but conduct it away in light. By trial and error, Xerox learned that that element was selenium, and in 1955 obtained a patent granting it exclusive rights to use selenium in copiers.

In some cases, it takes decades to find the missing links needed to turn a brilliant idea into a successful product. A century ago, Nikola Tesla (who died broke) anticipated wireless electricity, which still hasn't quite arrived. Electric cars were invented in the 1800s, and accounted for about three-eighths of the auto market around 1910, but adoption was limited by their short range and the lack of charging stations. Sound familiar? Dr. Ferdinand Porsche created the first gasoline/electric hybrid vehicle in 1900, but few hybrids were sold until Toyota launched the Prius in 1996.

In commerce, being superb and easy to use matters much more than being first.

Luck and Winner-Take-All

Most knowledge-based industries have immense economies of scale. This has the disagreeable implication that a small start-up launching a new product will *not* have the lowest costs. That's why Silicon Valley is obsessed with getting big fast. Gordon Moore, one of Intel's founders, proposed Moore's law, which suggests that the number of transistors on an integrated circuit doubles every two years. As a corollary, the more units of a semiconductor device that have cumulatively been produced, the lower the cost of one more. The strategic implication of this was that Intel should focus on only a few blockbuster products, with each selling millions of units. Variations on Moore's law apply to just about anything electronic, like areal density on disk drives.

Internet and software businesses often benefit from network effects, in which a service becomes increasingly attractive as more customers are added, and information can be reused many times at no cost. As eBay or Amazon marketplace add vendors, they become more attractive to buyers, and more buyers attract more sellers. Visa and MasterCard are accepted everywhere, partly because they are accepted everywhere. Beware of imaginary network effects: America OnLine (AOL) earned more as it added subscribers, but this didn't improve the user experience. Myspace had network effects first, but its users didn't like it as much as Facebook.

Falling costs and network effects give many technology industries a winner-take-all character. In 2015, two-thirds of the technology stocks in the Russell 2000 lagged behind the weighted average performance, and one-third did better; big tech stocks were even more skewed. Less than half of the technology stocks that had been in the Russell 2000 index ten years before were still publicly traded. Some disappeared because of takeovers, but many were failures. The pattern shows many, many losers and a short list of extreme winners (with an unknown life span).

Recognizing the difficulty of picking the ultimate winner, some investors buy exchange-traded fund baskets of stocks in hyper-growth industries like Software as a Service, cloud computing, 3-D printing, Web hosting, or smartphones. This approach will succeed when the collective value of the group of stocks is too low relative to the industry's opportunity. I call this happy case, in which spectacular winners more than cover widespread losses, "exposing yourself to luck." More commonly, the results are akin to buying all of the tickets in a lottery where the sponsor takes a cut. In total, the few gigantic prizes fail to offset a multitude of disappointments. Irritatingly for value investors, the ultimate winners frequently *do* have sky-high expectations. That doesn't mean that all glamour stocks ultimately win. Indeed, most flop.

Table 15.2
Winner-Take-All Lottery Stocks

	Count	Return	End Value
Huge winner	1	9,900%	100
Big winner	1	4,900%	50
Stagnate	50	0	50
Bust	48	−100%	0
Total portfolio	100	100%	200

Assume the following scenario: there are one hundred firms in an industry with equal investments in each of them (table 15.2). Over a decade or two, one becomes the clear leader, and its stock multiplies a hundredfold. There's also a strong contender that advances fiftyfold. Fifty stocks stagnate but maintain their value. Forty-eight go bust. Your overall basket doubles in value. A double that happens in a year is fantastic, but over ten or twenty years, it's mediocre.

That sort of scenario loosely describes the computer hard disk drive (HDD) industry. Today disk drives are a mature category, but in 1990 they were a thrilling play on the young PC industry. Since then, annual shipments of PCs and disk drives are up more than twentyfold. Cumulatively, more than two hundred firms have produced HDDs. Dozens of rivals merged, but many crashed and burned. Seagate and Western Digital are the two dominant remaining players. Over two decades, Western Digital stock has surged more than fiftyfold. From its IPO at a market value of $180 million in 1982 until it went private in 2000, Seagate's market cap expanded a hundredfold. If you had purchased a basket of ten drive makers, at least eight would have been duds, and possibly all of them.

Seagate had the right strategy: Be first to reach high volume production, vertically integrate, focus on enterprise customers, and add software. But the real reason Seagate stock was outstanding was a side bet in software. When Seagate went private in 2000, shareholders received $19 billion in value, roughly one hundred times the market cap at the IPO. Seagate had sold its software business to VERITAS for stock, then worth $17 billion. Effectively, the buyout firm paid under $2 billion for Seagate's disk drive operations—a fantastic bargain. Today HDDs are an oligopoly, and worries have shifted to obsolescence, as solid state drives replace them.

The Game Changes

Once a company grows up and has a best-selling product, the game changes. Someone must assemble the product, market it, collect and count the cash, and most troublesome of all, manage the people in these essential operations. Unlike the creative engineers and designers who led the business to this point, these functions thrive on the average, the recurring, and the conventional. Most computer hardware manufacturing is outsourced to save costs. Perhaps another reason for doing this is to sidestep the culture clash of managing legions of very different sorts of employees. Apple had 110,000 employees in 2015; its contract manufacturer, Hon Hai, had 1.29 *million*. (Outsourcing shifts the location of process innovation to Asia. This matters: Henry Ford's assembly line was a process innovation.)

Engineers are trained to design technical systems rather than to develop people systems, but successful geeks are forced to do both. It really won't do to manage a collection of spiky-haired code-writers in the same way as the buttoned-down accounting department, yet somehow creatives and accountants must collaborate or take turns leading. Joseph Wilson, Xerox founder and visionary who led the company through to a time when it was one of the twenty most valuable companies in America, was succeeded by C. Peter McColough. With a law degree, a Harvard MBA, and experience at Lehigh Coal and Navigation, McColough's business acumen proved beneficial.

Technology firms must fend off both obsolescence and competition, or die. Product people are more intent on innovating to delight customers, while financial officers emphasize low costs and monetizing customers. A company more worried about current profits will aim to be the low-cost producer by producing long runs of the same product and minimizing R&D. At times, managers would rather not build something original, because unit costs fall as more copies of the same old item are produced. But Internet companies that don't continually add new features lose their audience.

Xerox had an attractive financial model focused on leasing and servicing machines and selling toner, rather than big-ticket equipment sales. For Xerox and its salespeople, this meant steadier, more recurring income. With a large baseline of recurring revenues, budgets were more likely to be met, which allowed management to give accurate guidance to stock analysts. For customers, the cost of leasing a copier is accounted for as an operating expense, which doesn't usually entail upper management approval as a capital purchase might. As a near-monopoly manufacturer of copiers, Xerox could reduce costs by building more of a few standard models. As owner of a fleet of potentially obsolete leased equipment, Xerox might prefer *not* to improve models too quickly. As Steve Jobs saw it, product people were driven out of Xerox, along with any sense of craftsmanship.

Nonetheless, in 1969, Xerox launched one of the most remarkable research efforts ever, the Palo Alto Research Center (PARC), without which Apple, the PC, and the Internet would not exist. The modern PC was invented at PARC, as was Ethernet networking, the graphical user interface and the mouse to control it, email, user-friendly word processing, desktop publishing, video conferencing, and much more. The invention that most clearly fit into Xerox's vision of the "office of the future" was the laser printer, which Hewlett-Packard exploited more successfully than Xerox. (I'm watching to see how the modern parallel, Alphabet's moonshot ventures, works out.)

Xerox notoriously failed to turn these world-changing inventions into market dominance, or any market share at all—allowing Apple, Microsoft, Hewlett-Packard, and others to build behemoth enterprises around them. At a meeting where Steve Jobs accused Bill Gates of ripping off Apple's ideas, Gates replied, "Well Steve, I think there's more than one way of looking at it. I think it's like we both had this rich neighbor named Xerox and I broke in to steal his TV set and found out that you had already stolen it."

Once the casual, free-wheeling, and adaptable researchers at PARC had products to sell, they couldn't inspire the suits at Xerox to help with manufacturing and sales. For example, the Alto could have been the first assembled PC on the market, but there was no existing market for it. One proposal was to assemble the Alto in Xerox's Dallas typewriter plant, but changing the tooling and line would be costly and disrupt higher-margin sales. In 1979, Xerox transferred its PC technology to Apple in exchange for Apple shares.

The first PARC invention that Xerox actually sold was the Ethernet network, but the copier sales force wasn't interested. Xerox's sales force wasn't trained in the new products. They would be sold to different customers than those of copiers and weren't an easy add-on sale. The new products would be one-time sales at lower gross margins, while copiers and toner were recurring sales at spectacular margins. It wasn't yet clear exactly how the new technology could be used; figuring out how to apply it would take work. Unpolished, buggy, first-generation technology isn't something you want to foist on stodgy Fortune 500 customers.

Competition and Barriers to Entry

Lucrative industries attract competitors unless there are barriers to entry. Xerox used key patents like the selenium patent to create such barriers. For a while they held up. In 1975, Xerox settled an antitrust case by agreeing to out-license its technology, but serious competitive trouble didn't really start until the early 1980s. By then critical patents had expired, and competitors had found work-arounds for others. Japanese companies like Canon and Ricoh grabbed large market shares from Xerox, especially internationally and with smaller machines.

Unlike consumer staples, brands are strikingly powerless in electronic hardware once a better or cheaper alternative arrives. Compaq and IBM were once leading brands of PCs, but no longer. Just before it exited the PC business, IBM found that its PCs sold better in a generic white box than with an IBM label. Branding works with services only when the service truly is better. Once faster Internet access was available elsewhere, the AOL brand name did not prevent former subscribers from leaving.

By the early 1980s, Japanese competitors were selling copiers for what it cost Xerox to make them. Xerox needed a price premium to cover selling expenses and profit. When Xerox was synonymous with copiers and earning 30 percent operating profit margins, there had been no need to curb manufacturing costs. Doing so might even have been counterproductive, in that Xerox was trying to project a quality, executive suite image. But Xerox found that it had far more manufacturing defects than its competitors, and it stumbled through the 1980s trying to benchmark processes and rein in costs. Although Xerox held onto most of its recurring revenue, it did so at lower prices and margins.

Nothing Endures in Tech

When analysts speculate on the ultimate potential of a product, they often fantasize the crowning moment of glory and assume that it lives happily ever after. But this is a fairy tale, of course. In 1994, AOL had 1 million subscribers, which topped out at 27 million during 2002, roughly a 50 percent compounded growth rate. AOL stock crested two years before the peak subscriber count, collapsing 80 percent in that interval. A decade later, AOL had only about 3 million paying U.S. subscribers. Similarly, Blackberry's sales and earnings grew nearly tenfold over five years before it plunged into a loss, but its stock reached its pinnacle three years before its earnings did. Sales of Internet access and smartphones continued to grow, but AOL and Blackberry were leapfrogged by better products and were devastated.

Xerox and Eastman Kodak shared a common heritage, with roots in the photography industry in Rochester, New York. These brands were among the most renowned in the world until the Japanese arrived, but only Xerox survived digitization. Before the fact, my bet would have been that because chemical photography and print images had been stable for well over a century, they would outlast xerography, which has been around for only several decades. Usually, long-standing physical forms and institutions endure. If it has been around for a while, it will be around for a while. Probably.

Obsolescence has an engineering dimension—Eastman Kodak had great expertise in chemical processes and less in electronics—but the social dimension can't be neglected. With digital camera phones, which are carried everywhere, people discovered endless photo ops that they hadn't noticed when cameras were used only on special occasions. The image quality on early smartphones was mediocre, but customers were price sensitive. I doubt it would have been wise for Kodak—which was known for quality and knew little about electronics—to have competed in smartphones. Perhaps Kodak's best option would have been to emphasize quality in products like rugged, compact cameras, but as GoPro found out, that is a small market. In 2012, Eastman Kodak filed for bankruptcy.

Unintended Consequences

Investors often get excited about inventions without thinking about their ripple effects or society's response to them. Automobiles reshaped population centers, changed how people shopped, and created drive-through restaurants. Print media and music CDs were casualties of the Internet. Nuclear power faded after the Three Mile Island disaster. Science fiction writers have long written extensively about the menaces of pervasive surveillance and polarizing income distributions. The Internet has enabled both on scales not previously imagined, but it does not seem to be under attack. Perhaps it's because the audience for science fiction has found itself on the winning side of the spoils.

Perhaps privacy concerns will interfere with the ability to sell ever larger volumes of ads and data. Governments and businesses have always had databases of personal information, but they have never before been so comprehensive, so valuable, so centralized and retrievable. Much of this information is collected without subjects' knowledge or active consent. This, along with hacking, opens up an unprecedented ability to use it against subjects' interests.

Immense Internet fortunes have been built on the astonishing idea that people do not own information about themselves, with the laws still based on a simpler time. Famously, descendants of Henrietta Lacks learned that her cancerous cells had been taken without her knowledge or consent and cultured as HeLa cells used in medical research. Likewise, using big data, Target stores inferred that a high school girl was pregnant before her father knew. The same techniques that help direct advertising can also be used in undemocratic countries to oppress political, religious, and sexual minorities. In Europe, moves are afoot to protect privacy by changing the legal status of personal information in ways that could hurt ad sales.

Even with 24/7 connection to the Internet, human consciousness can absorb only so many ads. Supposedly, the average American watches more than four hours of television per day, including almost an hour of ads. Whether mobile Internet ads replace TV ads or supplement them, I would have to think that an increasingly distracted consumer will respond less to ads. Also, if the Internet really does promote greater price transparency, goods will be sold at tighter markups, leaving less funding for ad budgets.

What's It Worth?

The premise of present value theory is that one can estimate the future cash flows of an enterprise over its entire life. Admittedly this seems far-fetched given the diverse paths that invention, competition, and obsolescence can take. Most methods in probability, statistics, accounting, and financial analysis are designed for a world of averages, in which repetitive patterns and norms provide a general guide to future events. On average, inventory that costs a company $1 million to produce was worth that amount at quarter-end, and again today, but this is not always true. Because it costs nothing to make an additional copy of Internet software, we need new tools and assumptions.

One way to respond to this dependence on unpredictable paths is to dart in and out of tech stocks as news is reported. When there are too many possibilities, some investors consider only those that are directly in front of them, as in "Will quarterly earnings grow?" and "Will reported earnings beat Street estimates?" Sadly, hyperactive trading doesn't work. In 1972, Xerox stock reached a high price that would not be matched for a quarter of a century—and which was twice its market price in 2016. Xerox's earnings continued to advance, more than doubling between 1972 and 1980, but the stock lost five-eighths of its value. To conclude that Xerox was a sell in 1972, you couldn't have followed earnings growth; you needed some notion of value. Like the notion that forty-one times estimated out-year earnings is a very rich price/earnings ratio (P/E).

A high P/E alone does not mean a stock is overvalued, but to estimate present value, you must return to the unnatural practice of visualizing a company's entire life span. The features to focus on are exactly those that others have put out of mind. If, like Xerox, a company starts with an inspired product, will it be able to make it, sell it, and manage the associated people and finances without becoming so bureaucratic that the opportunity for an encore is thwarted? How quickly will an innovation be eclipsed, and when that happens, will the company be so bloated from success that it is no longer cost competitive?

Rather than scrapping the present value methodology, I look for situations in which it is less ridiculous to think about a company's entire life. Generally, I avoid fad products and others whose obsolescence is foreseeable; I also avoid commodity-like industries with many competitors. Unless there is clear visibility into large profits in the future, I don't invest in loss-making businesses.

ANSYS is an example of a software company that clearly leads in a specialized area where the answers to problems don't change, avoiding both competition and obsolescence. Engineers use ANSYS's multi-physics modeling software to test for defects in product design. For example, aerospace engineers might simulate and test the effects of wind and other stresses on different blueprints for airplane wings. The interactions of stresses from vibrations, temperature, velocity, and air pressure can be modeled. An airplane wing might withstand either extreme temperatures or velocities, but not both together. Because the laws of physics don't become obsolete, this software shouldn't either. Indeed, there are also great new applications in designing medical devices.

Services are less prone to obsolescence and can benefit from technological advances, but check carefully for barriers to entry. Credit card payments processing is an example of a service that does have barriers to entry and oligopolistic pricing. Because banks are regulated and billions of dollars go through the payments system, there is a thicket of rules intended to protect the security of merchants, their customers, and banks. Without this barrier to entry, I couldn't explain why processing should cost small merchants 3 percent of their credit card sales.

Surprise! Low P/Es Work in Tech

Contrary to popular wisdom, picking stocks based on low P/Es and high free cash flow yields often works particularly well with technology stocks. I think it's because tracking competition and obsolescence in fast-changing fields is so all-consuming that many analysts do nothing else. Also, financial analysis calls on a different mind-set: cautious, analytical, and precise. If you are a good financial analyst, you may lack the creativity, flexibility, and adaptability required to be a technology futurist, and vice versa.

I am a better financial analyst than futurist, so I generally prefer the likelihood of a good outcome to the slim chance of a fabulous outcome. I make bets on how big the market can be, but not on whether the science works. My favorites are low-cost producers in slower-changing oligopolies, where I can make rough estimates of the future earnings stream and not be dangerously wrong. Plus, there are moments when exposing myself to luck can pay off.

To expose yourself to luck rather than buy a lottery ticket, it helps to approach tech valuation as both a technology futurist and a conventional financial analyst. When dozens of social media stocks trade at extraordinary valuations, you are buying a lottery ticket, with the runaway winners failing to offset a deluge of losses. Conversely, because of the mood swings of technology investors, sometimes you are paid for daring, and the value of the hits will exceed the misses. Just recognize that the moments when you can expose yourself to luck are rarely posted in blogs or reported on TV.

This approach seems drab and plodding, but few investors can match the skills and knowledge of VCs and tech insiders. Famous Harvard dropouts notwithstanding, years of specialized training are often needed to understand the vectors of change. After careful research, these entrepreneurs invest at low prices (or in amounts small enough that failure would be inconsequential), bring management skill and important customer relationships, can influence business strategy, and can stay with companies for years.

Public market tech investors often ignore value, fail to think carefully enough about competition and obsolescence, and trade frantically—all of which often lead to disappointment. Their results would improve if they focused on companies with current earnings and cash flow, and compared a stock's price with its value, as ephemeral as that may be. Taking a cue from VCs, investors should emphasize software and recurrent services businesses offering something distinctive.

16

How Much Debt Is Too Much?

What matters isn't how well you play when you're playing well.
What matters is how well you play when you're playing badly.
—MARTINA NAVRATILOVA

BUSINESS FAILURE STARTS WITH CYCLICAL FLUCTUATIONS, technical change, or loss of customer goodwill. But it's excessive debt that usually triggers the finale. Borrowers are most eager to borrow, and lenders to lend, when blue skies are in view. Investors and lenders commit capital in good times without contemplating earnings and asset coverage at the bottom of the cycle. Once a downturn is under way, the best protections are large cash cushions, loose covenants, and easy debt-repayment schedules. Liabilities with staggered, distant maturity dates at least defer the pain. A death spiral sets in when the only immediate way to convert operating assets and customer goodwill into cash is by dumping assets at distressed prices.

Most defaults stem from unsound underwriting or failure to observe two matching principles—duration and risk. Bankers consider a loan sound if it can easily be serviced out of discretionary income and, as backstop, the collateral would amply cover repayment. Some lenders accept weaker collateral where income is robust (and require stronger collateral where income is weak). The duration-matching principle is that long-term assets should be funded with equity or long-term debt. The risk-matching principle is that risky assets should be matched with risk-bearing funding (equity), while safer assets are matched with risk-averse funding (debt).

No Net Worth, Great Credit Rating

Dun & Bradstreet, Moody's, and McGraw-Hill (which owns Standard & Poor's) have liabilities exceeding tangible assets—which is one definition of "broke"—yet all are rated investment grade. What these companies do have are strong cash flows and remarkable intangible assets that are largely not carried on their balance sheets. As trusted providers of critical financial information, they're not likely to be disrupted by competition or obsolescence. Nor are they particularly cyclical. The government designates Moody's and S&P as Nationally Recognized Statistical Ratings Organizations, giving their ratings a special legal status—an enduring barrier to entry.

For decades, market-leading newspapers in large cities were expanding cash cows. As daily consumables sold by subscription, they had revenues that were stable and predictable. Newspapers could increase circulation without major capital spending, leaving most of their cash flows free for debt repayment, dividends, or acquisitions. They were perfect for debt-financed buyouts. When media assets are traded, most of the purchase price is typically ascribed to goodwill, such as mastheads or station licenses, and little to the physical plant. As cash flows climb, so too does the value of the goodwill.

Sam Zell acquired the Tribune Company in 2007, contributing a few hundred million dollars, along with money from an Employee Stock Ownership Plan. The rest of the purchase price was borrowed. The resulting liabilities of over $11 billion were nine times Tribune's earnings before interest, taxes, depreciation, and amortization (EBITDA) of $1.2 billion. A ratio of debt/EBITDA exceeding four is usually considered scary unless tangible assets cover the debt, but the *Chicago Tribune* and other media properties were good collateral. To be fair, the plan was to reduce debt by selling some not-so-profitable trophy assets, like the Chicago Cubs.

Only a year after the buyout, Tribune filed for bankruptcy. Advertising revenues faltered in 2008, perhaps because of the recession, perhaps because of Internet cannibalization. Market prices slumped for Tribune's other media assets, even the cable networks and Internet websites. When the Tribune came out of bankruptcy in 2012, Zell's investment was wiped out and employees got a pittance. Creditors received majority ownership of the reorganized company but weren't made whole.

Rolling Over

Competitive moats and powerful brands are truly long-term intangible assets, but absent them, goodwill is highly perishable. The most worrisome cases are "rollups," companies that are constantly on a debt-funded buying spree. In the deal frenzy, buyers have less time to get to know management and the business. It's tough to do a high volume of deals and be too fussy about moats or price. Balance sheet goodwill can reflect enduring long-term intangibles—or having paid too much. Investors have to figure it out, because the accountants won't.

In the late 1990s, Global Crossing bought and built transoceanic fiber-optic cable at a frantic pace, connecting seven continents. Between 1997 and 2000, Global's assets swelled fiftyfold, and total liabilities grew to $15 billion. More than half of Global's balance sheet was in (risky) soft assets, implying a negative tangible net worth. As excess fiber capacity came onstream, the value of Global's tangible assets withered. Global never had net income or free cash flow on an annual basis. The balloon popped more swiftly than it inflated, and Global filed for bankruptcy in January 2002.

In 2008, NCI Building was a slower-moving rollup that not only violated both matching principles, but it also was doubly exposed because its business was sensitive to credit market conditions as well. As the largest metal-buildings firm, NCI had a broader product line, better distribution, and more geographic diversity than its rivals. But it's not difficult to enter the metal-buildings business. Customers are price sensitive, and sales are cyclical, which make the value of goodwill variable and a matter of conjecture.

With hindsight, NCI failed to match long-term assets with long-term funding, as well as risky assets with risk-bearing equity. Intangibles accounted for half of NCI's total assets. Given the cyclicality of metal-building sales, NCI's goodwill was a risky, long-term asset. Using common rules of thumb, debt that was less than equity and under three times

EBITDA was not worrisome. But that ignored the composition of NCI's assets and the timing of debt maturities.

At year-end 2008, NCI's current assets of $466 million were roughly twice current liabilities of $235 million. Most of NCI's current assets were inventories and receivables, not cash. As sales plunged during 2008, unsold inventories rose by two-fifths, consuming cash. And current liabilities didn't include huge debts that would come due in just over a year. As those maturities approached, the debt was reclassified as short-term borrowing, which ballooned from $1 million to $476 million over two quarters. When a debt is due all in one payment, it's called a bullet maturity—aptly, in NCI's case.

In 2009, NCI's operating profits vanished as sales almost halved, casting doubt on the value of its intangible assets, which it wrote down by $623 million. Between restructuring charges, refinancing costs, and operating losses, NCI lost $33.58 per share, blowing away its net worth, and then some. On an "adjusted operating" basis, NCI lost only 39 cents per share.

With most of NCI's debt due immediately, negative working capital, and a negative net worth, lenders held all the cards. Shares were exchanged for debt, and the share count exploded from 20 million to 270.7 million. From high to low, the stock lost 98 percent of its value.

No Fear of Flying

Asset-heavy industries—real estate, energy, utilities, airlines, and finance—attract lenders with their seemingly ample collateral. Without financial leverage, the return on equity in these industries might be lackluster. Following the risk-matching principle, larger fractions of value can usually be borrowed against safer assets (like government bonds) than against riskier assets. But these industries are cyclical, as are perceptions of their risk. Not infrequently, it's when things look rosiest that risks are actually greatest. Lenders feel more secure extending credit for shorter periods and so may push borrowers to mismatch the funding of long-term assets.

At the top of most lists of major corporate failures, you'll find asset-heavy industries, led by banks and other financial firms. The capital-intensive industries favored by highly leveraged billionaires turn out to be disproportionately disaster prone. Other asset-heavy industries like autos, airlines, shipping, steel, and coal have recently produced numerous bankruptcies but few billionaires. In these industries, it is practically impossible to offer anything that competitors won't quickly knock off. The only way to win is to be really, really superb at capital allocation, which includes investing when competitors are not—and vice versa.

In commodity industries, failures tend to cluster together in waves. Businesses are all suffering the same pricing or cost pressures at the same time, and losing money. They're all being pressured by creditors to sell capital assets, depressing their value. Real estate can be repurposed and so is usually more resilient, while highly specialized equipment is devastated. The prices of used dry bulk carriers and oil tankers lurch around between a ceiling of the cost of a newly built vessel and a floor set by scrap metal value. A Very Large Crude Carrier (VLCC) purchased for $137 million in 2008 was sold for $28 million four years later. At any given time, either many shipping lines will be in dire straits, or none will.

Ever since airline deregulation in 1978, the industry has been hit by repeated waves of bankruptcy filings, more than two hundred in total. The largest recent airline insolvency was AMR, which filed in 2011. AMR was losing money, bleeding cash, and had negative working capital and a negative net worth of $7.1 billion. Of the previous ten years, AMR had been profitable in just two: 2006 and 2007. AMR shares had peaked in 2007 at over $40, giving the company an equity market capitalization of more than $10 billion. AMR took advantage of the high stock price to issue shares, temporarily restoring a slightly positive net worth. But as losses resumed, the accounting net worth vanished again, and AMR became a penny stock. Lease obligations and an unhappy unionized labor force sealed AMR's fate. AMR was reorganized in 2013 as American Airlines. Leverage, cyclicality, and a whiff of oligopoly pricing power worked in American's favor in 2014, and its stock more than doubled.

In competitive, commoditized industries, accounting book value, intrinsic value, and market value are often totally disconnected from one another. There is a market for used airplanes, and *Blue Book* prices can be substituted for book values. While landing slots might have been a hidden asset, at the time of bankruptcy they were outweighed by labor agreement liabilities that weren't fully built into the numbers. Even in its profitable years, AMR had scrawny margins. All of this suggests that AMR's (negative) book value was a fair, even generous estimate of its investment value in 2011.

Car Wrecks

In 2005, General Motors' (GM's) sprawling balance sheet was stuffed with opaque assets and indecipherable liabilities. Total assets were $474 billion; adding future contractual commitments caused total footings to top half a trillion dollars. Shareholders' equity was just $14.7 billion, and long-term debt was $32.5 billion; together these summed to 10 percent of footings. Accruals for pensions and postretirement benefits were larger than GM's long-term debt.

GM's balance sheet was dominated by General Motors Acceptance Corporation (GMAC), its insurance and financing operation, with liabilities of $295 billion. GMAC had more than doubled its assets between 1999 and 2005, even as GM sold fewer cars and trucks. All of GMAC's growth had come from mortgages, especially subprime and commercial, with the division earning larger profits than auto finance. In 2006, GMAC sold off its commercial mortgage business as Capmark Financial, which went bust in 2009.

In 2006, GM simplified and shrank its balance sheet by selling a 51 percent interest in GMAC to Cerberus, removing $314 billion in assets from GM's balance sheet. GM's remaining equity stake in GMAC was carried at $7.5 billion. Cerberus also bought control of Chrysler the following year, and subsequently GMAC started to finance Chrysler cars.

Even without GMAC, GM's assets and liabilities were still obscure. In 2006, GM listed $37.5 billion in prepaid pensions as an asset. Liabilities for pensions and other postretirement benefits topped $62 billion. Deferred income taxes were an asset of nearly $45 billion in 2006. Offsetting that were "other liabilities and deferred income taxes" of $16.9 billion. Shareholders' equity had vanished.

In the normal course of business, it's beneficial to have liabilities without collateral, covenants, interest rates, or immediate repayment.

They're commonly called float. Deferred taxes are almost, but not quite, float. The tax code allows some deductions, like accelerated depreciation, to be taken early, reducing taxable income immediately but increasing it later. Accountants accrue for the taxes that will have to be paid later, but there are no covenants, collateral, or interest rates. Timing differences do reverse in a predictable way, so there is a shadow maturity date.

Pensions and retirement health obligations don't have covenants or collateral but must comply with funding and other regulations. The present value of these commitments depends critically on the assumed discount rate or rate of return. Companies with enormous plans, like GM, might be tempted to use an unrealistically high discount rate, which would minimize the present value of these liabilities. For example, a series of annual payments of $1 million a year for thirty years sums to $30 million and has a present value of $23 million discounted at 2 percent. At 8 percent, it's only $12 million.

But GM's financial situation was an ongoing catastrophe; it lost another $68.45 per share in 2007 and $53.32 in 2008. In December 2008, GM and Chrysler received emergency funding from the federal government. In the second quarter of 2009, both companies filed for Chapter 11. Having provided the emergency loans, the government controlled the reorganization processes, which ended thirty-eight days later for GM and forty-one days later for Chrysler.

In legal form, GM's reorganization was a "prepackaged" deal in which the most attractive assets and certain liabilities of "old GM" were sold to "new GM." Under the law, creditors in bankruptcy are paid off in "strict priority," a very specific legal ordering of the seniority of claims. In practice, the actual recoveries of creditors are a product of negotiations, but are seldom as unrelated to strict priority as with GM. Secured creditors are usually paid before uncollateralized creditors—employees, suppliers and junior bondholders. Most of the liabilities on GM's enormous balance sheet were unsecured.

Arguably, the reorganization plan was aiming at fairness for creditors that had not explicitly lent money to GM. The United Auto Workers union recovered most of its unsecured claims, partly through 17.5 percent ownership of the new company and $6.5 billion in preferred stock. In contrast, bondholders felt they had been crammed down with a fraction of the proceeds that would normally go to senior creditors. GM share-holders lost everything.

Don't Bank on It

When it fully owned GMAC, GM had the balance sheet of a financial company, with a thin slice of equity supporting massive borrowings. Financial companies can bear huge leverage as long as they follow the two matching rules—match risk-averse deposit funding with conservative lending, and match the durations of their assets and liabilities. The problem was that GMAC wasn't obeying the first rule, nor, in a pinch, the second. In the run-up to the global financial crisis, GMAC had plunged into subprime mortgages. Home finance became a larger part of GMAC's business than cars, even as it extended credit to dodgier automotive customers.

Explosive growth in a category of lending or by a financial firm is a sure omen of financial explosions. Money is the ultimate commodity. Financial companies can grow rapidly only by offering lower interest rates, or by having lower credit standards, or both. High yields reflect market perceptions of high risks, and you can't blithely assume that the market is wrong without closer study. As GMAC piled into riskier loans, it also borrowed more. In 2000, GMAC held $12 of assets for each dollar of equity; by 2006, it held $20 of assets. It wasn't alone: Washington Mutual, Countrywide Credit, and others did similar things, with tragic results.

Prudent businesses match the contractual duration of liabilities with the duration of assets, but the modern banking system couldn't exist if it did that. Banks take deposits that are payable on demand and use the funds to make long-term loans at higher interest rates. In practice, depositors rarely make major withdrawals simultaneously, and banks estimate their liquidity cushions probabilistically. But an unexpected run on a bank might force it to dump loans and securities at a loss. If the numbers were large enough, a run would threaten both solvency and liquidity. During a run, central banks are mandated to provide emergency liquidity to banks, but not to nonbank financials.

During the 2008 financial crisis, GMAC was in the desperate position of being short of funds, holding dubious collateral, arguably insolvent, and not being a bank. To restore solvency, the U.S. Treasury purchased a total of $17.2 billion in preferred and common shares in three bailouts. GMAC applied to become a bank and was accepted, making it eligible to borrow at the Federal Reserve. GMAC was renamed Ally Bank. (Later, Ally's subprime mortgage subsidiary, ResCap, went bankrupt, but Ally itself avoided bankruptcy.) The U.S. Treasury will probably sustain a loss of a few billion dollars on its bailouts of GMAC/Ally.

Neither Borrower nor Lender?

Debt magnifies the good and the bad, and it's usually optimal to borrow some. The precise level depends on the context. That entails following the risk- and duration-matching principles. Very stable industries like packaged food or regulated utilities can borrow to boost profitability and growth without endangering their life span or certainty. Predictable future cash flows can be matched accurately against future obligations. Even those businesses need a cash cushion to protect against failed forecasts.

For most cyclical businesses, the trade-off between current profits and corporate longevity leads to an impasse. Some investors would rather make hay while the sun shines and not worry about tomorrow until tomorrow. Once a business fails, shareholders no longer get the benefits of profitability or growth. Forecasts of cyclical and volatile businesses are bound to be wrong at some point, and if they involve assets that can't be converted to cash or used by another industry, high debt leaves those businesses vulnerable. My preference is for businesses that can achieve appealing levels of growth and profitability without leverage.

The Corporate "Okinawa Diet"

For investors interested in corporate longevity, Japan is the place to study. According to Arie De Geus, there are 967 businesses worldwide that were established before 1700, with more than half of them in Japan. Today's high-tech marvels are absent from this list, which is dominated by traditional, slow-changing, but not completely commoditized industries like sake, confectioneries, tea, food, restaurants, pubs, and religious artifacts. Change makes life exciting, but companies that must change constantly are destined to make wrong decisions at some point and succumb.

If you view businesses as very long-term assets, and as risky assets, as the Japanese apparently do, it's appropriate to finance them almost entirely with equity. Half of the listed stocks in Japan carry more cash than debt, something you will not find anywhere else in the developed world. On their balance sheets, you'll also find proportionately less reported goodwill than elsewhere, though the Japanese also have their own famous brands and indestructible franchises.

Corporate life span depends on following the two matching principles, but there's also a social explanation: Businesses are communities of people. The companies that survive are communities that customers, employees, and suppliers want to be a part of. They adapted but kept a distinctive character and mission. Nor did they diversify extensively. Most of the businesses that were around in 1700 were family owned, so most of the survivors were also family controlled, making them a very specific form of community. Closer to home, American academics have found that stocks of companies with controlling shareholders, including families, outperform those with dispersed ownership.

For investors, nirvana is a profitable, growing enterprise that is certain to endure. Financial leverage does not destroy companies, but it does create vulnerability. Look for businesses that respect the matching principles: Match borrowings with safe (not risky) assets, and match long-term assets with long-term (not short-term) debt. Businesses that are susceptible to commodity cycles, obsolescence, or shifting consumer preferences should tread lightly. If trouble is foreseeable, look for uncollateralized debt with deferred, staggered repayment dates, few covenants, and friendly lenders. A cash cushion and access to undrawn credit lines also help companies to make it through.

PART V

What's It Worth?

17

Will the Lowest Be Raised Up?

Forecasts may tell you a great deal about the forecaster; they tell you
nothing about the future.

—WARREN BUFFETT

THE QUESTION OF WHAT STOCKS will return, and their implied discount
rate—either as an asset class or for individual securities—is both reasonable and ridiculous. An estimate of value is only as reasonable as
the discount rate used. A perpetual annuity is worth one-third more
if the discount rate is 6 percent rather than 8, and this variance might
create, or destroy, a margin of safety. Investors can't duck the question.
They need some basis for decisions to put money into stocks rather than
bonds, real estate, or whatever. They also need a way to rank and choose
among hundreds of possible opportunities.

Returns on stocks depend critically on the price paid, but as time
passes, they look more like the returns of the underlying business. Active
investors will always seek a return that beats the odds, but they can't
deduce the odds without fathoming the market discount rate. They also
must be wary of using a low discount rate to justify a high value, when
they wouldn't accept it as their rate of return. The estimates of returns
discussed in this chapter are neither certain nor precise, just very long-
term guesses. Unless you are ready for absolutely anything, you should
not invest.

Earnings Yield = Your Return?

I use earnings yield (the inverse of the price/earnings ratio [P/E]) as my first cut in estimating a stock's future returns, but purists turn up their noses at this approach. Later we'll touch on some ways to sharpen this estimate. If at any point this chapter seems too geeky, just remember: Tilt toward low P/E stocks, and veer away from high P/Es. Earnings yield, expected return, and the discount rate all point toward more attractive securities, times to invest, industries, and national markets. Of these numbers, earnings yield is the only one that can be readily observed. Expected return and discount rate require guesswork and calculation, and the extra effort is not always repaid with superior results.

Here's the hang-up: Accounting earnings are not quite the same as economic cash flows, which may not quite equal the gain in present value, which doesn't always match realized shareholder return. Basically, one has to believe that a dollar of reported earnings will translate into a dollar of total return for the investor. For this to be true, a firm's reported earnings would need to reflect its underlying cash flows, and a dollar reinvested in a business would have to be worth a dollar to the company's owner. A lurking assumption is that current income can be maintained indefinitely. Current earnings yield will be misleading for businesses at cyclical peaks and troughs or in terminal decline.

A dollar of profits reinvested for growth is usually worth *more* than a dollar, but it can be less, depending on what it contributes to future earnings growth and cash flows. For companies with skillful, honest management that offer something unique and are in resilient industries, reinvested profits nearly always improve the shareholder's rate of return beyond the initial earnings yield, sometimes tremendously. This is the source of the maxim that time is the friend of the good business and the enemy of the bad one. Look for a moat or competitive barrier to ensure that a good business will still be good by the time the economics of the business become the decisive factor for investor returns. Typically, the stocks showing the most appealing earnings yields suffer from at least one defect, whether a cyclical or commoditized industry, dubious accounting, or even crooked or inept management. These flaws cut into owner returns, so earnings yield is akin to, but not the same as, expected return or discount rate.

Over long stretches of American financial history, returns on stocks have generally exceeded their initial earnings yield. To the extent that businesses can accurately calibrate in advance how growth opportunities will pan out, it *should* work that way. No one deliberately sets out to destroy value. Don't assume it's any sort of universal law, though. Over many five-, ten-, and even a few twenty-year periods, returns on major stock indexes were lower than their starting earnings yield. But for a majority of long periods, a dollar reinvested for growth did produce more than a dollar of value.

Between the oversimplified assumptions and the ready availability of P/Es, the low P/E (high earnings yield) effect seemingly shouldn't exist, but it's well documented with groups of individual stocks. Table 17.1 uses data from Dartmouth professor Kenneth R. French. Basically, when stocks are rank-ordered and categorized by earnings yield, the groups with the highest earnings yields fare best and the lowest worst. Most of these studies have used reported generally accepted accounting principles (GAAP) earnings numbers, especially when long time spans have been covered, but some have used more recent series of adjusted and estimated figures, with similar conclusions.

The low P/E effect is linked to the small-cap stock effect. In table 17.1, value weighting means that if the aggregate market value of U.S. stocks is $20 trillion, the High 10 decile would consist of the $2 trillion worth of stocks with the highest earnings yields. Equal weighting means that if three thousand companies were surveyed, the High 10 decile would consist of the three hundred names with the highest earnings yield. Most of the stocks with extremely high earnings yields are small caps. The equal-weighted high earnings yield portfolio visibly outperforms the value-weighted portfolio by holding portfolios of obscure shares

Table 17.1

Cumulative Percent Annualized Returns by French's E/P Decile (1951–2015)

	Low 10	D2	D3	D4	D5	D6	D7	D8	D9	High 10
Value weight	9.1	8.9	10.4	10.5	11	12.5	13.3	13.9	14.8	15.6
Equal weight	9.1	11.4	12	13	13.7	14.4	15.2	16.2	17.4	18.6

Sources: Kenneth R. French (Tuck), Salim Hart (Fidelity).

that few investors have heard of. Few institutions are willing to own equal amounts of General Motors and Strattec Security, for instance. But even the value-weighted earnings yield portfolios vastly outperform the averages. For both methods, cheaper deciles nearly always return more than more expensive deciles.

On average, over time, high earnings yield stocks have beaten the market, but on average doesn't mean always, or for every stock. In about one-third of the years between 1951 and 2015, the top decile equal-weighted portfolio lagged behind the averages. The disappointments seem to cluster in the late stages of bull markets when speculative favorites rule, and early in slowdowns. Shares in cyclical industries have low P/Es in anticipation of an inevitable economic downturn, but when that happens, their share price still tumbles. Astonishing values can appear only if undervalued assets sometimes become even more so. Eventually, portfolios of high earnings yield shares have produced superior results, but this may be slight consolation while you wait.

Most human portfolio managers, myself included, do not invest entirely in stocks with top decile earnings yields. I don't—because low P/E stocks tend to be small and I limit turnover. In one survey, Kenneth French rebalanced the groups monthly, which seemed unrealistic to me, as it would lead to incessant trading that would be costly and hard to execute with smaller stocks. Instead, the portfolios shown in table 17.1 were rebalanced annually. Annual rebalancing does not mean complete turnover, however, because many stocks remain in the same quintile or decile group at rebalancing.

No Bargain on Walmart

Typically, investors focus on other attributes that are more eye-catching than P/E. Take Walmart in December 1999. Walmart was exactly the sort of business I search for: understandable, durable, and uniquely positioned, with honest, outstanding management. At the time, Walmart was a juggernaut, with a record of many decades of continuous earnings increases and returns on equity of 20 percent or higher. Like Amazon today, it was the merchant that every other retailer feared and respected (with similar stories told about network effects in sourcing and distribution). What could be more indestructible than selling everyone's daily necessities at very sharp prices?

Walmart stock closed out 1999 at $69.13, and later reported earnings per share (EPS) of $1.25 for the fiscal year ending January 2000, up from $0.99 in the previous year. This gave it an earnings yield of 1.8 percent, or a P/E of fifty-five. Obviously, investors were counting on returns that would match the return on equity of 20 percent, or the earnings growth rate, not the tiny earnings yield. For fast growers, I try to tie together the growth rate and the earnings yield. To produce an earnings yield of 8 percent, Walmart would have needed EPS of $5.53 (8 percent × $69.13). Then I calculate how many years of an assumed growth rate it would take to reach that target. In the best case, the crossover is not many years away, I trust my forecast, and I believe that when it is attained the enterprise will *still* be growing dynamically.

I thought Walmart's growth rate would continue, perhaps at a less torrid pace, closer to the 12 percent gain reported the following fiscal year. As the already dominant American retailer in many categories, Walmart couldn't keep grabbing share indefinitely. While Mexico became a stunning success for Walmart, its other international expansion has been a mixed bag. Assuming a 12.1 percent compound earnings growth rate, it would take thirteen years for Walmart's earnings to reach an 8 percent earnings yield hurdle on the initial purchase price. Some analysts were more enthusiastic about Walmart's future growth and believed it would get to the target sooner. But, my calculation ignored the compounding of time value of money for those thirteen years, so the target should have been even higher. Historically, few companies have been able to grow earnings 12 percent *every year* for thirteen years.

Surprisingly, Walmart's earnings *did* advance in an unbroken string at an 11.3 percent compound rate over the next thirteen years, *yet* its stock stagnated. The low price for Walmart in 2012 was $57, which, along with cumulative dividends of just over $10 per share would have summed to a negative total return. The average price of Walmart stock in 2012 was close to its price at the end of 1999, or zero capital appreciation, so its dividends *were* the stock's total return. Cumulatively, the total return and dividend yield were a lot closer to the initial earnings yield of 1.8

percent than the earnings growth rate or return on equity. Uncharacteristically, shoppers of Walmart shares in 1999 had not demanded a bargain, perhaps because it was otherwise an irresistible story.

The realized return on Walmart undershot the discount rate of 8 percent used in my example partly because earnings disappointed, but also because P/Es are prone to mean reversion. Walmart's actual earnings of $5.02 were not that far behind the initial target of $5.53. But over thirteen years the compounded effect of that technical detail about the difference between the required earnings and actual earnings was substantial, which implied a much higher earnings target to produce an 8 percent return. I also had to ask whether I truly believed projections that extended out so many years.

It's not at all intuitive, but the mean to which Walmart's P/E reverts is *not* specific to Walmart but applies to the entire market. Statisticians want the broadest available set for comparison. For much of its life, Walmart grew geometrically and deserved a premium multiple. No one repeats that feat forever. For a company's particular historical multiple to matter looking forward, its future would have to be as brilliant as its past. The S&P 500 index includes businesses at all stages of their life cycles, while the history of Walmart did not. As it happened, in 1999 Walmart was also trading above its own historic multiple. By 2012, the P/E of the S&P 500 had narrowed, and Walmart's P/E collapsed below fourteen, roughly matching it. Walmart closed in on an 8 percent earnings yield—the wrong way. At any given moment, the factors that produce mean reversion are often too discreet to be noticed, but over time, they are decisive.

Great Returns When Market Index P/Es Are Low

The year 1999 was an inopportune one for buying stocks generally, not just Walmart, with the S&P 500 index at a P/E over thirty. When earnings yields are low, subsequent market returns also tend to be mediocre. Ned Davis Research grouped the U.S. market P/E into five valuation quintiles. From the cheapest quintile of starting points, the S&P 500 earned an 11.6 percent real (inflation-adjusted) compounded return over the next ten years. By increasingly expensive quintile, the compounded real returns were 10.0 percent, 9.6 percent, 5.3 percent, and 4.4 percent, respectively. Again, the pattern is very consistent. It's intriguing that if the P/Es are converted into earnings yields, one more percentage point of starting earnings yield often boosts investor rates of return by *more* than one percentage point, assisted by mean reversion.

Bargain-priced stocks (and markets) can still disappoint. In the periods when the S&P 500 was trading in the cheapest quintile of market P/Es, ten-year compound real returns were as high as 19.4 percent, but also as low as 0.3 percent, poorer than the average for the expensive quintile. Of the most expensive quintile of markets, the best period returned 15.7 percent over ten years, far outstripping the average for the cheap quintile. Over a one-year horizon, the market index P/E is slightly predictive, but there are so many miscues that I wouldn't dare to use it for market timing. Mean reversion takes time. A better use is for longer-term asset allocation decisions, which are, I suppose, a slow-moving form of market timing.

In some seasons, as in 1999, very large growth stocks are wildly expensive. Market value–weighted measures best capture the lofty valuations of this sort of market. In other phases, even rank-and-file stocks are all quite pricey. Equal-weighted indexes reflect valuations most accurately in these markets. For an equal-weighted universe, the median is a better measure than weighted average. Examining median P/Es on the 3,000 largest stocks from 1962 to June 2016, I found markets with a median P/E of less than fifteen returned 317 percent over ten years, while markets with a median P/E greater than twenty-five returned just 65 percent over ten years (table 17.2) By reporting the data cumulatively (not annually), I intend to show (1) the power of compounding and (2) that low P/Es were still effective a decade later.

Fund managers are often constrained in how they might use a forecast of unappetizing long-term returns. Asset allocators can move money out of equities into bonds, cash, or whatever they think offers a better prospective rate of return. As a stock manager, I am not meant to do that, but rather to seek out the best of a bad bunch. Instead of chasing the highest potential returns, I emphasize the durability of profit streams and the credibility of forecasts.

At just about every major market top, P/Es were historically elevated, but usually they had been pricey for quite some time. In 1929, the Dow

Table 17.2

Forward Market Returns from Different P/E Starting Points (Median Trailing P/E, 1962–2016, U.S. Top 3,000 Stocks)

	Average	Average	Average
Initial P/E	Median P/E 1-Year Return	Median P/E 5-Year Return	Median P/E 10-Year Return
0–15	18%	102%	317%
15–20	13%	71%	188%
20–25	10%	59%	130%
Over 25	3%	38%	65%

Sources: Factset, Salim Hart (Fidelity).

Jones Industrial Average topped out at twenty-seven times earnings and the S&P 500 at twenty times. The P/E of the S&P peaked at twenty-two in 1962, but remained just under twenty for much of the 1960s, and didn't crumple until 1974. Similarly, before the S&P crested at a P/E of thirty-two in 2000, its P/E had been over twenty in seven years in the 1990s. Although there were corrections in the 1990s, things didn't really fall apart until the new millennium. One still-revered value hedge fund manager acted on his caution. His fund's cumulative underperformance over the decade of the 1990s could have been matched by putting half into an S&P 500 index fund and stuffing the rest under a mattress.

Cyclically Averaged Price/Earnings (CAPE)

The truly catastrophic busts all occurred when earnings and P/Es crested together at extraordinary levels. Based on the multiples of recent decades, it might seem implausible that the S&P 500 P/E climaxed in 1929 at "only" twenty, and this was enough to launch the great crash and Great Depression. But the S&P hadn't traded at a P/E that dear since 1921, when a deflationary recession had crushed earnings. By 1929, S&P 500 earnings had multiplied fivefold from 1921 levels *and* the P/E was high. It turns out the soaring P/E in 1921 should not have been concerning because

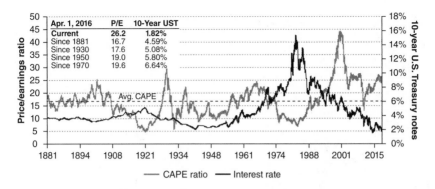

FIGURE 17.1 Historical CAPE ratio versus Treasury note interest rates.

profits were deeply depressed. The slightly lower but still demanding P/E in 1929 should have been worrisome because it was calculated on peaking earnings.

To smooth out the effects of recessions and boom times, Yale economist Robert Shiller proposed calculating P/Es based on earnings averaged over ten years ("Shiller earnings"). Using this method, the S&P 500 in 1921 was not richly priced but actually incredibly undervalued, with a cyclically averaged price/earnings ratio (CAPE) of five, which has only been approached since in 1933 and 1974 (see figure 17.1). In 1929, the CAPE on the S&P 500 peaked out at thirty-three, which was not surpassed until the tech bubble. At the pinnacle of the tech bubble in 2000, the S&P 500 CAPE was forty-four. At extreme points, CAPE is a superb indicator of long-term prospects.

On average, CAPE is a somewhat better predictor of future returns of market indexes than current earnings yield. In the most highly valued decile of the S&P 500 between 1881 and 2015 (figure 17.2), the average CAPE was 30.3, which equates to a 3.3 percent earnings yield. From these starting points, the S&P 500 earned an average real rate of return of 0.5 percent over the next decade. The lowest valued decile had a CAPE of 9.6 or less and returned 10.3 percent, compounded and inflation adjusted, over the next ten years. The warning about this being true on average (but in not every case) applies again.

In recent decades, the CAPE has frequently been expensive compared with its longer historical average. Some say that the world and accounting

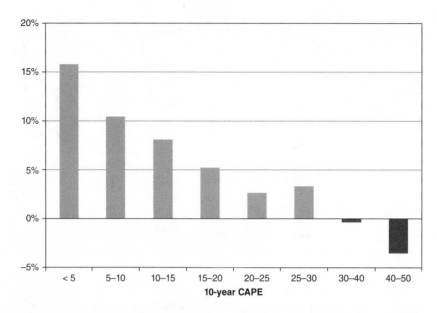

FIGURE 17.2A U.S. stock average real compound returns versus 10-year CAPE, 1881–2011.

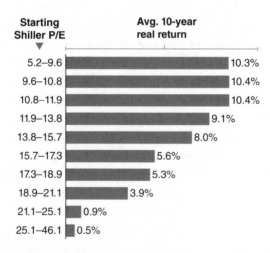

FIGURE 17.2B The power of earnings. Investment returns are better when the market has a lower Shiller P/E (cyclically adjusted price/earnings ratio).

have changed and that CAPE now emits an inaccurate signal. Although these objections are often motivated by refusal to accept that returns could be unsatisfactory for years to come, they might be valid. One claim is that accounting standards have changed over time and, among other things, don't capture the value added by the creation of new technologies, so profits are understated today. Another argument revolves around low interest rates—we've never before in history had widespread negative interest rates—so P/Es should be higher. I don't think much of a third contention that hypergrowth Internet companies have become so central to our economy that higher P/Es are merited. Total gross domestic product growth has not accelerated, so other sectors must be shrinking or growing more slowly. This might warrant a *lower* P/E.

While it's undeniably true that accounting does an abysmal job of tracking the value creation of technological advances, it's not clear-cut to me whether GAAP accounting is more, or less, conservative than in the past. Adjusted earnings are more fanciful than in the past, but GAAP may not be. The cost of stock options was ignored in the past and is now expensed, but still added back to adjusted earnings. Today, the sums involved are much larger—executive compensation has mushroomed, especially in stock options. Before 2001, all intangible assets were considered to have finite lives and were amortized over a maximum of forty years, which is more conservative than today's method. Now, impairments are taken in a big bath, making reported results more erratic.

Banks, insurance companies, and many others took whopping impairment charges during the global financial crisis in 2008–2009, which might unduly punish Shiller (ten-year average) earnings. To the extent that accounting rules allow "marked-to-market" write-downs but not write-ups, this claim is valid. Conversely, it's unreasonable to say that all of the profits from subprime finance were real, yet none of the losses were. Over time, accounting rules for loan securitizations and the treatment of gain on sale have been loosened. In decades past, banks made heavy "unspecified" loan loss provisions, which smoothed earnings but also presented them conservatively. My take is that reported earnings might be more or less aggressively stated today, but they are definitely more volatile. To me, this provides more support for the Shiller formula.

Stocks, Bonds, and Bills

Theoretically, stock earnings yields should ebb and flow in tandem with the returns available on other assets like bonds and Treasury bills, but the historical record shows a series of long regimes and mean-reverting tendencies. Before 1959 (except 1929), stocks almost always offered higher dividend yields than bonds. Profits were also retained for growth, so earnings yields were higher still. The Great Depression, two World Wars, and the arrival of socialism and communism in many countries led many to believe that stocks were dangerous and U.S. government bonds were safe. During the 1940s, bond rates were low (as they are today). This should have justified high stock prices, but actually P/Es were quite moderate. It was a fabulous moment to buy stocks. Was that because earnings yields were high or because of the yield advantage over bonds?

Europeans have long been skeptical of the custom of describing government bonds and bills as risk-free. Investors in German government bills lost virtually everything to inflation in 1923. The upshot was doubtless the same for government *bunds*, but their prices were so chaotic that the data was discarded. In 1948, German *bunds* were largely canceled in the transition from Reichsmarks to Deutsche Marks as currency. Inflation is the most common way for governments to relieve themselves of burdensome debt, but default, restructuring, and moratoriums are also options. At some point, nearly every major nation has resorted to one or more of these expedients, according to Rogoff and Reinhart in *This Time is Different*.

In 1981, the perils of bonds were widely recognized and priced in; consequently bond yields topped stock earnings yields. Confounding expectations, this accurately pointed to higher risk-adjusted returns on bonds. Bonds have much less risk to nominal income than stocks; yet they provided returns that were neck and neck with stocks over the 1980s. In absolute terms, the yield spread favoring bonds was a false omen for stocks. Unprecedented bond yields and generous earnings yields correctly foreshadowed spectacular gains in both stocks and bonds. When inflation-adjusted yields on T-bills have been poor, returns on stocks have followed suit, and vice versa.

Even though inflation continued to abate and tax rates moderated, bond yields remained at a premium to Shiller earnings yields through the 1980s, the 1990s, and up until the global financial crisis. The Shiller earnings yield in 1990 did not indicate that stocks would enjoy record-setting gains in the decade ahead, nor did the earnings yield spread foretell stocks outrunning bonds, but that's how it turned out. Sometimes mean reversion just takes too long! By 2000, the Shiller earnings yield had never been lower, and the shortfall against bond yields had never been wider, both warning against equities.

In the new millennium, bearish predictions came true with a vengeance, but the yield advantage of bonds persisted until 2009. First, technology and growth stocks were smashed in 2001. Bonds rallied as interest rates fell. Declining interest rates fed into a housing boom, with many homes financed by subprime mortgages. In 2007, one prominent brokerage strategist sensed that something was amiss and urged clients to emphasize high-quality stocks. This was a superb call ahead of the global financial crisis. To execute it, he provided a list of top-rated firms, including blue chips like Johnson & Johnson and Microsoft but also a host of financial firms with AAA credit ratings such as AIG and AMBAC. These financial companies and others were devastated as the housing boom turned to bust and a bear market ensued. Again, investors were convinced that stocks were gambles and government bonds were safe.

Most likely minimal interest rates do justify low stock earnings yields, but the equity risk premium has jumped around over time, and gaudy P/Es still produce miserable returns. Wars, depressions, inflation, socialism, and confiscatory tax rates come and go, so there's no reason to suppose that stocks should offer a constant return advantage over bonds. Putting aside these factors, when yields on bonds are negligible and P/Es are high, investors should expect returns that look lousy in historical comparison.

Countries

Provided that investors don't get blown up by macro factors like war, inflation, or socialism, they will normally do well by favoring national stock markets with low P/Es. In figure 17.3, asset manager Grantham Mayo Van Otterloo plotted the national index P/E in 1980 of sixteen developed

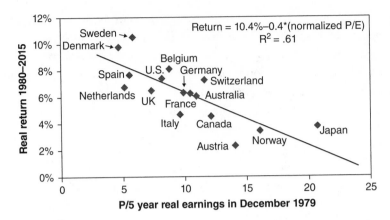

FIGURE 17.3 Average five-year real earnings of selected development markets versus real rate of return over the subsequent thirty-five years.

markets using earnings averaged over five years against the subsequent real rate of return over the next thirty-five years. Rebalancing once in thirty-five years is surely a low-maintenance approach! Japan, Norway, and Austria—the three priciest markets—ended with the poorest performance. All four of the statistically most undervalued markets produced rates of return that beat the median.

This sample set includes only developed nations that were constitutional democracies during a prosperous era of declining inflation and no wars on their soil. The broader, longer set of global investments is not so blessed. Austria, for instance, has the woeful distinction of having the longest continuous period of negative inflation-adjusted stock returns. Over nine decades, many things went awry, starting with the breakup of the Austro-Hungarian Empire during World War I. Hyperinflation followed. Austria was annexed by Nazi Germany during World War II and then was occupied by the Allies for a decade with the Iron Curtain on one border. Toss in high taxes and unwanted government involvement in industry. It's no wonder Austrian economists are so skeptical of grand theories. But Germany, France, and Italy also had stretches of more than half a century of no real returns.

For predicting future returns, it's an open question whether countries that have been lucky, like the United States, will continue their winning streaks, and those that have not, like Austria, will continue their losing streaks. As a U.S. citizen, I absolutely hope that American exceptionalism will continue, but I know that statistically, I should anticipate this only if I can specify forward-looking reasons why America belongs in a unique category. Otherwise, the forecast of future returns ought to be based on the set of all developed capitalist democracies, not the United States alone. Germany's experience with hyperinflation represents a potential risk to investors in every nation. I think the risk of hyperinflation in Germany is actually much lower than elsewhere because the experience was so scarring.

The odds almost certainly differ for stock markets of war-torn, undemocratic, socialist, and developing nations. Also we can't know the true odds. Researchers are drawn to topics for which data are easily available. Basically, none of the widely used histories of American stock prices include the disruptions of the Civil War. How do we factor in lumpy events like markets that went to zero or halts in trading? Russian stocks accounted for 11 percent of world market value in 1900 and were wiped out by the Bolshevik Revolution in 1917. China and Egypt were also among the fifteen largest world stock markets in 1900, and both went to zero. Out of twenty-four national stock markets in 1931, ten were later closed for more than a year, mostly because of war. Seven closed for less than a year and only seven had uninterrupted trading. (Goetzmann and Jorion, *A Century of Global Stock Markets*).

Earnings Yields, Discount Rates and Returns

Calamities and windfalls will drive a wedge between starting earnings yield and realized return, but the moment to have considered this was at the time of investment. Your results will depend on how well you and the market have handicapped the odds. In the late 1990s, shares of the Russian oil company Yukos traded at a 200 percent earnings yield, which foreshadowed precarious property rights in Russia. Yet early investors in Yukos would have more than recovered their investment through dividends, while latecomers suffered a near total loss. Your outcomes also hinge on how you react. Sometimes, if you don't panic, you haven't understood the gravity of the situation.

In a perfect world, one would calculate the frequency and severity of possible events, then dock the demerits and add the tailwinds to create a bridge from earnings yield to expected return. But there is no tidy formula, and one can tell the likely direction of adjustments only from certain factors. Glamour stocks will work as long as the momentum of growth outstrips mean reversion. I buy high earnings yield stocks, hoping for a lift from mean reversion and knowing that slow growth is likely to reduce returns. As long as the business doesn't go splat, and generates cash that it doesn't fritter away, I'm happy. For a longer-term investor, many risks and uncertainties, especially of the macro and industry sort, are best considered as eventualities with unknown timing.

Going back to the notion that most investors need a basis for ranking the appeal of investments, I compare the risks and uncertainties of numerous securities with roughly similar earnings yields and remove the ones that I can't bear. In principle, it's about avoiding situations that would put me out of the game. Sadly, I had small holdings in companies involved in encyclopedias, pianos, newspapers, and photography—all of which I regarded as long-standing amenities of a civilized society. In technology hardware, everything changes constantly. Cyclical commodity producers are bound to hit the wall at some point, as are highly indebted firms. In certain places, kleptocracy, expropriation, and cronyism are just the way things get done. I want no part of it.

Seeking Low P/Es with Good Growth

To recap: When choosing value investments, first eliminate stocks that won't turn reported into realized returns. If earnings don't convert into owner earnings sooner or later, a company's accounting must be overstated, which sets the stage for negative surprises. When cash flows do not correspond to the increase in present value, you have a wasting asset. Local newspapers were an example of this. We will see it more and more as brands and intellectual property become more important. Value can also be lost when firms squander capital on idiotic boondoggles. Present value might not be reflected in realized returns because management channels the gains to themselves.

Next, earnings should be considered as an average using a period with conditions resembling those one imagines will prevail in the future. The Shiller formula takes an average of ten years of reported earnings, which usually covers a couple of business cycles. For specific stocks, an average of reported earnings will make fast growers look overly expensive. Instead, I prefer to estimate normal earnings by taking a ten-year average of profit margins or return on equity; multiply this by current sales or shareholder equity. Beware of using this approach with deep cyclicals—like autos or steel—as sales may be currently high or low. Also, look for a competitive moat that will protect the business against the ravages of time.

Third, check to see whether it's foreseeable that in a few years, a company will grow enough to justify an apparently demanding valuation. Walmart didn't pass this test, but others do. In those cases, the discount rate is generally a better indicator of future returns than the initial earnings yield. Indeed, if there will be plenty of runway after the crossover point, expected returns might be much nicer. This method can also be inverted to assess whether the cash flows of a melting ice cube will shrink so fast that in a few years the cash flows no longer justify the purchase price. For those who fantasize that they can predict cash flows from here to eternity, a precise rate of return can be calculated using a full-blown discounted cash flow model. Knock yourself out!

Finally, I group stocks with similar averaged earnings yields that I can trust and discard the ones with intolerable risks. My risk tolerance is not the same as yours. Your risk tolerance may reflect special knowledge if, for instance, you are Russian, or a venture capitalist. Risk tolerance is also tied in with concentration and diversification. Concentrated portfolios will always produce the best—and worst—performance. But risks that may be worthwhile in small doses can be scary in a focused portfolio. I also try to spot risks that come with a silver lining—for example, slow-growing markets don't attract competitors.

Most investors care about future rates of return as a yardstick for comparing opportunities, and for that purpose, earnings yield is a fair proxy.

You can refine that estimate by cutting out stocks whose earnings may not convert to shareholder return, by averaging earnings, by looking for moats that will protect earnings, by factoring in the value of growth, and by avoiding situations in which you know there will eventually be damaging bolts from the blue. Crisply put, you want low P/E stocks that are also high quality and growing, with a high degree of certainty about the long-term outlook.

18

Which Earnings Number?

CLIENT (POINTING TO PILE OF PAPERS): How much does this add up to?
ACCOUNTANT: What would you like it to add up to?

—OLD ACCOUNTING JOKE

OVER TIME, EARNINGS DETERMINE A STOCK'S VALUE, but many alternative definitions of "earnings" produce radically dissimilar estimates of value. There are reported numbers, and there are forward estimates of uncertain reliability. While many investors fixate on quarterly snapshots of profits, I prefer to view earnings as a moving picture of past and future cash flows. From an owner's standpoint, quality earnings correspond to free cash flows that could safely be paid out as dividends. Analysts adjust reported results in countless ways. Frequently, the costs of stock compensation, restructuring, and amortization are added back to net income to produce higher levels of adjusted results for non-generally accepted accounting principles (GAAP). Earnings before interest, taxes, depreciation, and amortization (EBITDA) is a very broad indicator. While all of these measures are useful in certain contexts, I find GAAP earnings, "owner earnings," and "free cash flow" to be the clearest indicators of value.

Some adjustments can help illuminate a specific issue or to compare a single company's results over time. To analyze whether current profits have improved compared with a prior period, analysts often pull out nonrecurring items. For estimating run rate profits, it makes sense to ignore losses on an activity that is being discontinued, provided that another money pit won't replace it. To judge whether management is doing a good job, some analysts add back stock compensation to profits.

But sometimes yardsticks are intentionally selected to spin the conclusions in a positive direction. Also, those adjustments may become misleading when used out of context.

Adjustments often make comparisons between disparate companies *less* fair. Without an agreed-upon set of rules, like GAAP, the frontrunner will be the one with the most lenient standards. Comparability is reduced in a world where some companies are making certain adjustments, others are adjusting away something else, and a few stick with GAAP. GAAP standards aren't always correct, but mostly they are closer to the real economics of the business than adjusted earnings. When they are not, I am not the one to identify better accounting principles.

While there is some overlap between the concepts of net income and cash flow, there are also distinctions. Net income measures the increase in owners' equity resulting from business activity. Profits don't always mean an inflow of cash. Other assets can increase, or liabilities can decrease. When cash flow is less than net income, it's usually because inventory is piling up or uncollected receivables are mounting. Compare the cash flow statement with the income statement to make sure they tell the same story.

The cash flow statement starts with operating cash flow, which is a measure of the net cash receipts available to sustain the business, to expand it—or to return to owners. The next two sections of the statement, investing and financing, track the actual uses of the operating cash flow. Capital spending ("cap ex") that merely sustains the business ("maintenance cap ex") is lumped together with cap ex that expands the business. An analyst must separate them. Companies in dying industries eliminate sustaining cap ex and suck out cash in excess of net income. At some point these business will wither away; this is not an option most managements favor.

I define *owner earnings* as operating cash flow less sustaining capital spending. For most manufacturing businesses, depreciation is a fair proxy for sustaining capital spending. In the worlds of brands, intellectual property, and monopolies, it's not so clear what it costs to maintain the status quo. Even if newspapers spent their entire operating cash flow on capital improvements, many could not stabilize their operating cash flow. Most newspapers have concluded that the only way to maintain cash flow is by buying broadcast or Internet properties. In this case money spent on acquisitions is properly labeled sustaining cap ex.

Owner earnings serve as a cross-check on GAAP numbers and adjusted earnings, because all three would all be equal in a perfect world. They would signify not only the increase in owners' wealth, but also the cash available for growth or shareholder return (dividends and buybacks). Usually these adjusted earnings numbers are easiest to obtain; they are the common coin of Wall Street and conference calls, while the GAAP numbers are hidden in official public financial documents. Owner earnings are the most obscure because they are not published; they must be calculated and involve judgment calls about the true level of maintenance spending. But owner earnings are the key to value.

One estimate of the value of a noncyclical business is calculated simply by dividing owner earnings by the discount rate, using the perpetual annuity formula. This is based on the assumption that current earnings can be maintained forever, which is absurd in cyclical industries. In those cases, some measure of average owner earnings is needed. These estimates are often overstated because in boom times investors forget how horrible the down cycle can be. I'm also wary of using the annuity formula with businesses that clearly cannot continue forever, like high-tech and fads and fashions. In those industries, investors must do a much more detailed year-by-year estimate of cash flows.

Unless accounting numbers more or less reflect economic reality, none of our estimates of intrinsic value are reliable.

Inflation, Intangibles, and Rollups

GAAP accounting can't keep up with financial reality in certain situations. Be especially wary (1) during periods of rapid inflation, (2) when intellectual property is involved, or (3) with serial acquirers. During inflationary times, low historical costs are mismatched to current selling prices, overstating economic profits. Often research and development (R&D) is written off as incurred, leaving little trace on the balance sheet, even when it produces valuable discoveries. Serial mergers and acquisitions (M&A) leave a cloud of dust that muddies analysis of operating trends of formerly separate entities.

In inflationary times, the accounting dilemma is whether or not to count increased asset prices as profit when no cash comes in. Consider a store that holds two identical items: one purchased recently for $75, the other purchased earlier for $65. The store sells one item for $100, incurring sales and overhead costs of $25, and replenishes the sold item at a cost of $80. On balance, the store loses $5 in cash and holds the same physical inventory. Under the Last In, First Out method, which is no longer permitted, the store would count the unit that cost $75 as sold and break even. Under the standard First In, First Out treatment, the store would be considered to have sold the $65 unit and would report a profit of $10. Taxes might be paid on these phantom profits, which might increase the net cash outflow.

The cumulative effects of decades of inflation distort the accounting for long-lived assets—real estate, broadcast properties, and pipelines. Provisions for depreciation and amortization are based on historical cost—whether the property was purchased recently or decades ago. Buildings acquired decades ago will carry less depreciation than they would if sold to a new owner at today's prices. Generally, maintenance spending consumes only a small portion of EBITDA from long-lived assets, but that fraction differs among types of properties. Hotels and student apartments require far more upkeep than warehouse and storage facilities. For instance, EBITDA makes sense only when used as an intermediate number, from which all maintenance spending is subtracted, along with interest and taxes.

The historical costs of goodwill and intellectual property also often have little to do with their current value. Intangible assets may have short lives, like soon-to-cliff patents, or very long ones, as with brand names like Coca-Cola, Disney, or Louis Vuitton. That said, once-iconic brands like Eastman Kodak, Polaroid, and Sears did fade. Other than patents and licenses with a fixed expiration date, the life span of most intangible assets can't be determined, which in turn makes their value elusive. It's impossible to say how much of an intangible asset was used up in a year. If accountants had the sort of perfect knowledge that economists assume, they would expense the value of the intangible assets that were consumed in the period. Instead, most internal R&D and marketing costs are expensed as incurred and never show up on the balance sheet as assets. When these efforts succeed, companies have an unrecorded (sometimes huge) asset.

The costs of brand-building and R&D can't be matched with the specific sales that result, and that becomes a major issue for acquired intangibles. With M&A, the numbers become an order of magnitude larger. For some companies, intangibles amount to more than half of their total reported assets. Goodwill is no longer amortized for financial reporting purposes, but it does produce a tax deduction. Some intangibles are deemed to have finite lives over which they are amortized. Some companies label intangibles as goodwill rather than finite-life to avoid amortization expense and thus report higher profits. In practice, during recessions accountants flush all at once goodwill that had actually been impaired over a period of many years. Because the loss occurred in years past, the cat is already out of the bag, and investors ignore the write-off. Indeed, many disregard amortization even for short, finite-lived assets.

When there's a whirlwind of activity, as happens with M&A, nobody knows what's really going on. Corporate rollups often combine operations to harvest synergies but, in doing so, lose track of the progress of formerly separate divisions. The financials of purchased businesses are restated, sometimes using numbers chosen for tax reasons, which are then presented to analysts with numbers that are allegedly more realistic. Sometimes the costs of restructuring activities are folded into the purchase price, or disappear into a reserve, which can be a cookie jar for future use.

These are by no means the only circumstances in which accounting numbers fail to reflect economic reality, just some of the most common.

Parallel Universes at Valeant

When an analyst excitedly launched into a pitch for Valeant Pharmaceuticals' new strategy, I stifled my prejudices and asked to hear more. Valeant's predecessor ICN Pharmaceuticals had been investigated by the U.S. Securities and Exchange Commission for insider trading. Biovail (which Valeant would acquire in 2010) had also been investigated for manipulating and misstating earnings, including fiddling with something called "noncash investing and financing activities."

Valeant CEO Michael Pearson conceived a seemingly well-thought-out corporate strategy, focused on durable specialty products, elimination of waste, and growth by acquisition designed to create economies of scale. Dermatology and eye care were regarded as particularly attractive niches. Valeant redomiciled in Canada, Biovail's headquarters, thus slashing taxes on its non-U.S. income. Pearson had been a health care consultant at McKinsey & Co., the strategy consulting firm, for twenty-three years, so of course his strategy presented well. With Pearson at the helm, Valeant executed more than one hundred deals in the next few years.

Using the "cash earnings per share" numbers (aka adjusted earnings) publicized by Valeant, Pearson succeeded brilliantly. From 2008 to 2014, the progression was spectacular: $1.01, $2.19, $2.05, $2.93, $4.51, $6.24, and $8.34, respectively. For 2015, adjusted earnings under the "discontinued tax presentation" were $10.16 per share. The growth came primarily from Valeant's seemingly unstoppable deal machine, which did finally halt when its $58 billion bid for Allergan failed in 2014. But Valeant also had fast-growing products, such as Jublia and Luzu for toenail and toe fungus. Even mature product lines seemed to be reinvigorated, which Valeant attributed to improved marketing, especially through specialty pharmacies.

Valeant's reported GAAP numbers left a disturbingly different impression. Per share annual losses of $1.06, $0.38, $2.70, and $0.85 were reported in 2010, 2012, 2013, and 2015, respectively. The sum of GAAP earnings in 2008, 2009, 2011, and 2014 barely offsets the deficits in the other years. To bridge the gap between cash earnings and GAAP earnings, Valeant provided a laundry list of write-offs of goodwill and intellectual property, restructuring costs, and stock compensation. These adjustments shed light on analytic questions; they were not designed to be used for estimating the stock's value.

To my irritation, Valeant's self-defined cash earnings were a superb indicator of its stock performance for many years. Its share price surged from $7 in 2008 to over $263 in 2015. Any stock that doubles earnings three times in six years is bound to be fantastic, as long as the starting P/E isn't out of this world. As the stock soared, the bullish drumbeat grew louder. At hedge fund stock idea forums, Valeant was *the* hottest tip of a majority of the presenters.

I felt Valeant's definition of cash earnings was far too generous. GAAP operating cash flows were persistently lower than cash earnings. In 2012 and 2013, Valeant's operating cash flow was roughly half the level of its cash earnings figure. Operating cash flow is almost always larger than cash earnings because both add back many of the same charges, but net income reflects some provision for depreciation or capital replenishment. In effect, Valeant's cash earnings ignored some operating costs that used cash.

Restructuring costs were one of the cash items that Valeant asked investors not to count as costs, perhaps to show operating trends more clearly. For example, management can choose the timing of plant consolidations and layoffs, and individual plants are usually only closed once, so associated costs arguably don't belong in any specific period. Otherwise, results will look lousy in the current quarter even if the business is performing well. The costs shouldn't recur in following quarters and so don't help in projecting future earnings. But the streamlining never stops at acquisitive, cost-conscious companies like Valeant. Restructuring costs can't be ignored when valuing this stock.

Investors use operating trends as the basis for forecasts, while boards of directors consider them when setting executive compensation. Executives obviously favor a benchmark that proves they are doing a wonderful job and deserve a handsome paycheck. The board and investors prefer a measure that can't be gamed and that mirrors value creation. Even under GAAP, management can cherry-pick accounting treatments that allow them to report higher earnings, such as classifying intangibles as goodwill, which does not have to be amortized. Restructuring costs can be moved forward or backward and bundled into a big bath in an already crappy year. Shareholders wish for a higher stock price and so go along with the flattering number, despite their doubts.

Although adjusted numbers are meant to avert game-playing, they actually open up new possibilities. Instead of faking the GAAP accounts, managements move expenses into categories that will be ignored. Everyone accepts that interest expense is a cost of doing business, but the up-front or back-end fees for financing are often lumpy. To some extent, borrowers can trade higher fees for a lower interest rate, or vice versa. Valeant excluded financing fees of $199.6 million in 2014 and $179.2 million in

2015 from costs in calculating cash income. Stock compensation is often disregarded in non-GAAP calculations. Even if it's not measured, or not counted, and it doesn't affect cash flows as presented, stock comp does reduce the per share cash flows available to existing owners.

Importantly, patented drugs have finite lives as proprietary products and so must be replenished with new products. Valeant asked investors to disregard some of the costs of renewing its product line by licensing and acquisition. Drug companies traditionally have written off the costs of developing new medications through R&D in their labs. Alternatively, Valeant might license a product that a biotech firm had developed but then ask investors to ignore the GAAP cost of the license. Or Valeant would acquire companies with products on the market and slash R&D. Effectively Valeant bought the cash flows from the products of others' past R&D and cut the means of replacing them. GAAP accounting can't quite keep up when businesses are acquired for their intellectual property. To the extent that GAAP did keep up, Valeant wanted investors to ignore costs.

In 2015, Valeant's cash earnings calculation overlooked $2.44 billion in amortization and impairments of finite-lived intangible assets. It also impaired $248 million of in-process R&D that it had bought.

The bullish story was that Valeant's branded consumer lines didn't depend on patent protection and its patented products were durable, so true product development costs were smaller than the accounting amortization. So I set out to get a fix on what a fairer number might be. There were long schedules of weighted average amortization times—as short as four years for partner relationships and as long as fifteen years for corporate brands. Without product-specific details, I had no way to tell whether these periods were reasonable. I was also concerned that some of Valeant's $18.5 billion of goodwill at year-end 2015 should properly be classified as finite-life intangibles.

I wanted to get a handle on the durability and growth of the product portfolio by checking sales trends for each specific line. Valeant made this almost impossible. Until 2015, Valeant refused to disclose revenues by product, and it still does not provide unit prices and volume levels. In 2011, its operating segments included Branded Generics–Europe and Branded Generics–Latin America, which were combined into Emerging Markets in 2012. The U.S. Dermatology, U.S. Neurology, and Canada and Australia segments in 2012 were bundled into Developed Markets for reporting in 2013. Shifting classifications blocked any attempts to separate out deal-driven growth and track unit sales growth or pricing of individual drugs.

Bits and pieces of disclosure in acquisition documents hinted that Valeant's products were less durable than claimed, and some might be in a tailspin. For example, Solodyn, an acne medication, had sales of $386 million in 2010. Eventually, Valeant disclosed that Solodyn sales had been $213 million in 2015. Valeant doesn't release drug volume data, but there are services that track physician scripts for most drugs through most channels. Solodyn's retail price increased from $700 per month in 2011 to $1,060 in 2015, so with falling revenues, unit sales would seem to have slipped even more. Valeant doesn't itemize realized prices, so we don't know how much of the higher list prices were offset by discounts, allowances, coupons, chargebacks, distribution fees, rebates, returns, and patient assistance programs.

Valeant also reported that it was selling more through "alternative fulfillment," whatever that is. My hunch was that alternative fulfillment was a new means of price discrimination and discounting. Because the data services don't track alternative scripts, their prices are also unknown. What I hadn't suspected was that Valeant wanted "tied" pharmacies that would honor prescriptions for its expensive drugs and not substitute cheaper generic alternatives, as many insurers require.

At first Valeant denied it, but effectively it owned its largest specialty pharmacy customer, Philidor. In December 2014 Valeant had paid $100 million for an option to acquire Philidor at zero cost and agreed to up to $133 million in future earnouts. In the third quarter of 2015, Philidor accounted for $190 million, or about 7 percent of Valeant's sales. Philidor dispensed only Valeant products, and basically all of its sales were in dermatology and by mail order. Apparently, Philidor resubmitted previously rejected insurance claims for expensive Valeant drugs under a different pharmacy ID number after altering some prescriptions to "dispense-as-written," thus precluding substitution of cheaper generics. Philidor may have cheated insurance companies, but *uninsured* cash pay customers received steeply discounted prices, which were not reported in industry pricing and volume surveys.

Once it became known that Valeant contingently owned Philidor, alarm bells went off at insurers and state pharmacy licensing boards. Suddenly, 10-K readers understood the significance of the footnote at the bottom of a six-page list of subsidiaries that did not include Philidor: "In accordance with instructions of item 601 of regulation S-K certain subsidiaries are omitted from the foregoing table." To pacify furious insurers and investors, Valeant terminated its Philidor relationship, which required it to restate its financials. Philidor shut down. Sales of Solodyn and Jublia crashed. Over four months in 2015, Valeant stock crashed 65 percent.

These details left me clueless about how much Valeant would have had to spend to maintain the value of its dermatology line. Zero cost is a ridiculous estimate, given very squishy sales. As an outsider, I can't begin to forecast sales and costs for Solodyn or Jublia over their remaining life, because I do not even have accurate historical data. Nor do I know what Valeant paid to obtain these products. Looking forward, even Valeant insiders are left to conjecture what it will cost to replace the runoff of existing drugs.

If a stock is worth the present value of future cash flows, and Valeant's true operating cash flows, owner earnings, growth rates, and product life spans are unknown, so is its value.

Valeant's debt was real, however, and was ballooning. Between 2009 and 2015, Valeant's long-term debt multiplied one hundredfold, from $0.3 billion to more than $30.3 billion—not to mention $6.0 billion in possible future tax liabilities, plus $1.3 billion in other long-term liabilities. At year-end 2015, these liabilities were balanced precariously against tangible assets that included only $0.2 billion in net current assets and $1.4 billion in property, plant, and equipment. Valeant's ability to repay its debt rested entirely on its future cash flows from its brands and intellectual property. But the crushing debt load might alter the path Valeant chose for reaping those cash flows and its ability to do so.

As Valeant's free cash flow had been chronically negligible compared with earnings, I expected that pattern to continue, unless something had changed radically. The past is our best guide to the future. The future will be different but on average not *too* different. Projections of future earnings and cash flows should echo the consistency and quality of the historical data. Often, adjusted earnings show this pattern even more starkly, because adjusted earnings are typically higher. When earnings have been erratic and cyclical, expect more of the same. In particular, projections rarely take account of the amplitude and length of down cycles.

Forecasts also don't reflect the tendency of extreme numbers to be followed by values closer to the average. Fussy statisticians tell me that reversion to the mean is about variance and errors in statistical sampling, and that effect is partly in play. Businesspeople think of it as competitive pressure, which works somewhat differently. Really profitable industries attract competition, and returns fall. Except for cyclical fluctuations, very unprofitable firms do not revert to the mean, but fail. However, innovative new enterprises are founded on hopes that a bright idea will translate into super-profitability. Investors care about specific entities, not the population average. Because investors are specifically searching for abnormally good businesses, they have to be wary of the ravages of competition and build competitive constraints into their predictions.

I would love to give you an algorithm that spits out the right amounts to plug into a present value spreadsheet, but I can't. Instead of fidgeting endlessly with the numbers, spend more time examining *how* a business plans to grow and *why* its profitability won't be crushed by competition. Valeant declared that it would continue its M&A spree, cut waste, develop product extensions, raise prices, and develop new marketing channels. Pharmaceuticals are a bizarre market in which products are selected by doctors, partly paid for by third parties that do not consume them, with data on efficacy not always available to patients (or doctors!). For conditions with only a few available therapies, drugs often have tremendous pricing power, at least until patents expire.

I feared that both Valeant's deal frenzy and its rapid product price increases had contributed to growth in an unsustainable way. In February 2015, Valeant hiked the prices of two heart medications, Isuprel and Nitropress, by 525 percent and 212 percent, respectively. Later that year, Presidential Candidate Hillary Clinton called for an investigation of drug price gouging, citing Valeant. Massive price increases turned out to be widespread at Valeant. A Deutsche Bank research report in October 2015 indicated that Valeant's weighted average drug list prices had been marked up 19.7 percent in 2012, 31.6 percent in 2013, 52.9 percent in 2014, and 85 percent in the year to date in 2015. Ultimately, Michael Pearson, by then no longer CEO, testified to Congress that some of Valeant's price increases had been mistakes.

By then, Valeant shares had tumbled 90 percent from their highs.

While Valeant's GAAP losses and negative free cash flow provided a strong premonition of the debacle, skeptics will point out that it doesn't prove that GAAP earnings are a more reliable indicator of value than adjusted, non-GAAP figures. After all, Valeant's self-defined cash earnings were the best guide to its stock price performance for many years. There are many situations in which GAAP earnings get out of kilter with owner earnings or economic reality, including when dealing with intangibles and intellectual property, periods of high inflation, and corporate rollups. And I do adjust a company's earnings to improve comparability between periods. Still, I find comparisons between companies untrustworthy without the standardization of GAAP.

Be wary of adjusted earnings. Check cash flow statements to see whether they tell the same story as earnings. Watch for large intangible assets, especially with rollups. In old economy manufacturing sectors, the cost of sustaining the business is relatively easy to determine. Where brands, intellectual property, or monopolies have to be renewed, the cost is more indefinite, and so are owner earnings. Sometimes the discrepancy between reported earnings and owner earnings is just a reminder that inventories and receivables have gotten too high.

Free cash flow measures the cash actually available for acquisitions (if the cost of acquisitions hasn't been deducted as a form of capital spending) or for shareholder return. Unless a business has compelling opportunities with superior returns, I usually expect it to generate some free cash. (In the rare cases where a growing business has free cash flows greater than GAAP earnings, I am willing to concede that the non-GAAP number is closer to the truth.) Value depends on the free cash flows available for growth opportunities and dividends.

19

The Art of Judging Value

As far as the laws of mathematics refer to reality, they are not certain; and as far as they are certain, they do not refer to reality.
—ALBERT EINSTEIN

EVERYTHING VALUE INVESTORS DO TURNS on a comparison of a security's price with its intrinsic value, which is customarily estimated as the discounted value of future cash flows. The theory of discounted cash flows (DCF) ties together current income, growth, life span, and certainty in a way that is precise and true by definition. For example, if an investment will pay $105 one year hence plus $110.25 two years hence and the proper discount rate is 5 percent, then each payment has a present value of $100, for a total of $200. If I can buy this income stream for $150, I will earn not only the fair return of 5 percent, but also $50 in present value because of the bargain purchase price. However, judgments about which numbers can validly be used to drive the model are neither precise nor true by definition. In this chapter, we estimate the value of a stock, and in following chapters, the correct cash flows to discount, the right discount rate to use, and times when prices are far from value.

Taking Out the Garbage

All of the numbers in the present value calculation must come from the messy world of empirical observation, as must the judgments about whether to trust the numbers. There's a snag. We have no data from the future, only from the past. In any human venture, the future that we are trying to predict will be like the past but different, with a varying mix of same and different.

You can estimate DCF for any stock, but in many cases the prediction will be meaningless. When you put garbage estimates in, you get garbage values out. Unless you can accurately forecast earnings, cash flows, dividends, and rates of return into the distant future, it seems pointless, even misleading, to go through this convoluted exercise. The present value of top-quality bonds can be calculated precisely, because the interest and principal payments are set by contract. Although the interest rate estimated for a bond might be slightly off, it's usually nearer to the mark than any stab at an equity discount rate.

Classify the assumptions that go into assessing present value by their believability and reliability, and don't put much weight on those that aren't credible. Forecasts of profits or cash flows over the next couple of years can typically be counted on, at least comparatively. Any prediction of a business's cash flows twenty years out can only be a guess, more so for a tech stock than a food company. Present value math sums up all of these numbers despite their differing trustworthiness, treating each number as equally legitimate. If you have some information that is approximately true and some that is sheer fantasy, it's dangerous to mix them. Everyone has a computer now, so the math is the easy part. What's tough is knowing whether you are using reasonable assumptions. While value investors are wary of the risk of overpaying, in academic financial theory this risk does not exist, as everyone has perfect information and everything is appropriately priced.

In previous chapters, we've reviewed many reasons why estimates of value go awry. Many investors do not bother estimating future cash flows; instead, they run from discomfort and chase the emotional kick of being where the action is. Those of us who do try to value securities are prone to give too much weight to what's happening now and not enough to drab features like the historical nature of an industry. Fraud and colossal ineptitude are uncommon, so we don't model for them.

Commodity-like and highly indebted businesses are especially apt to wind down with a terminal value of zero, often sooner than anyone would have thought. Some analysts do model a variety of scenarios including a "worst case." In the event, the situation often turns out to be way more catastrophic than the worst-case scenario, unless of course the end had already been in view. Optimists will point out, correctly, that at times business cycles turn out unimaginably better than the bullish scenario. In any case, you want to be ready for the worst possible consequences.

Even in more straightforward situations, it's easy to get tangled up in the math of valuation, calculate numbers in error, and pay too much. Aggressive growth investors consider an 8 percent growth rate to be rather drab. If a company will grow 8 percent forever and the discount rate is 8 percent, the DCF formula solves for an infinite value for the stock. The issue is not with the DCF method, but with fallible assumptions. In this particular case, an 8 percent growth rate could be a reasonable supposition for the next few years, but totally unrealistic beyond that, let alone forever.

Warren Buffett is a great proponent of the DCF method, but he also believes in knowing the limits of one's knowledge. He is suspicious of intricate projections that are doomed to be upended by events. He has never shared his DCF analyses, which would show how it's done right, coyly stating that there are some things that people just should not do in public. Here are my conjectures: Buffett thinks the DCF process is a powerful tool for bonds and high-quality businesses, but not elsewhere. He's conservative in his assumptions. He looks for blue sky potential but does not count on it. For the short list of firms with highly certain cash flows, he doesn't need a steep discount rate. In valuing businesses, he uses shortcuts, not painstakingly intricate models.

Present Value and the Annuity Formula

For most stocks, the present value formula that I begin with is the perpetual annuity. The classic perpetual annuities were "consol" bonds once issued by the British government. Consols paid interest every year and were scheduled never to be redeemed. A perpetual income of £3 per year discounted at a rate of 3 percent is worth (£3/.03) or £100. Neatly, the discount rate, current yield, and yield to maturity are all identical, which isn't true of other bonds that aren't trading at par (100 percent of face value). The annuity formula embodies a society in which everyone knows one's place and income, in which incomes neither grow nor shrink and continue for generations.

Commerce lacks the stability that classic British aristocrats once enjoyed, but both stocks and consols have no fixed end date, and calculations are simple with the annuity formula. Divide income by the discount rate (expressed as a fraction) and voilà, you have present value. Some prefer to multiply rather than divide by a fraction. For a 3 percent yield, instead of dividing income by .03, income could also be multiplied by (1/.03) or 33 1/3 to calculate present value. For a stock, the ratio of earnings to price is called its earnings yield, while the ratio of its share price to its per share earnings is its price/earnings ratio (P/E). Personally, I use earnings yield for ready comparison with a discount rate, but on Wall Street P/E is the popular format.

For now, I'll proceed as if income is earnings per share calculated in accordance with generally accepted accounting principles. Some analysts prefer to make adjustments to earnings or average results over multiple years, while others focus on dividends. As I write, I am using 8 percent as my equity discount rate, but I used 10 percent in 2010. It will change in the future as equity risk premiums and Treasury yields shift.

I don't always need to predict accurately to make good decisions. By a good decision, I mean one that will produce satisfactory results most of the time even when I am totally off base about how the world will turn out. At the same time, if I know that I can't foretell a whole category of future outcomes, my best decision is to step aside. By avoiding emotional decisions, avoiding investments that I don't understand well, and avoiding bad people and unstable businesses, I can shorten my list of potential investments considerably—and have done so. After studying which companies fall short in any of the elements of value, I can exclude even more potential investments.

Value Traps in Elements of Value

"Value trap" is a common epithet for stocks that disappoint or are expected to disappoint. It implies that some investing shortcut has indicated that a security is undervalued, yet it hasn't performed well. What I dislike about the term is that it suggests that mistakes were made, but not by me. It doesn't tell me how I screwed up, so I can avoid repeating my mistakes. Shortcuts and DCF analyses fail because of a weak link in one of the four elements of value—(1) profitability, (2) life span (3) growth, and (4) certainty. I use a brief but demanding checklist to pinpoint vulnerabilities.

1. Does the stock have a high earnings yield—that is, a low P/E?
2. Does the company do something unique that will allow it to earn super-profits on its growth opportunities? Does it have a moat?
3. Is the company built to last, or is it at risk from competition, fads, obsolescence, or excessive debt?
4. Are the company's finances stable and predictable into the extended future, or are they cyclical, volatile, and uncertain?

In addressing each of these questions, I examine the company's track record. I also need a forward-looking story that explains why the statistics turned out as they did and whether and how long those factors will continue. The future could be better because of new products or increasing economies of scale, or worse because of rising competition or obsolescence. No matter how glowing the story, I wouldn't confidently assume that a company would enjoy superior future profitability unless it had earned a return on equity (ROE) above 10 or 12 percent in nearly all of the last ten years. I pay close attention to lousy years and special charges, which often reflect adverse factors that the story might have omitted.

When the Affordable Care Act (ACA) or "Obamacare" was passed in 2010, prospects for the health insurance industry were diverging from history. In a rearview mirror, the industry's current profitability and growth were robust. As regulated businesses, health insurers had historically rarely failed. The earnings of the larger companies were generally steady. Their profitability fluctuated with an insurance underwriting cycle, which wasn't tied to the overall business cycle. I decided to focus my attention on UnitedHealth Group (ticker: UNH), the largest managed care operator. All four of the elements of value seemed to support the idea that UNH was undervalued, except for the elephant in the room: Obamacare. If the United States went to a single-payer health system, managed care companies might be superfluous.

Test 1: Low P/E

UNH stock looked quite cheap on current profits, the first element of value. In 2010 UNH earned $4.10 per diluted share, and its stock traded around $30, for an earnings yield of 13.7 percent, or a P/E of 7.3. Applying the annuity formula and a discount rate of 10 percent would produce a P/E of ten. That would indicate that UNH was worth $41 a share, 37 percent more than the market price of $30 per share, indicating a fair margin of safety. There's a lot more to valuation than merely looking for low P/Es—namely, growth, longevity, and certainty—but UNH's low P/E was a strong signal that its shares were undervalued.

Still, I wanted to be sure UNH's current profits wouldn't look like an outlier once the ACA kicked in. Eleven data points and an estimate are too few to be statistically significant, but they do give a notion of the range of past occurrences. In 2010, UNH earned a net margin of 4.9 percent, which placed it a little under the middle of the range of the last dozen years. UNH's highest net margin had been 7.3 percent in 2005; its lowest, 2.9 percent in 1999. Using this small sample, UNH's profit margins appeared to be close to or maybe slightly below their central tendency. I felt comfortable that UNH's then estimated (and later actual) 2010 earnings of $4.10 a share were more or less normal.

Most investors take the central tendency of a probability distribution as a point estimate of value. I consider the entire distribution, which implies a range of outcomes, including some downside scenarios. If UNH's net margin in 2010 had matched its 1999 low of 2.9 percent, it would have earned $2.42 per share, which at a multiple of ten would imply a value of $24.20. Outside of the parallel universe of probability, it would seem inconsistent to say that the best estimate of value is $41 *and* that there are two chances in twelve that the stock is worth less than $30 per share. A sample set of twelve years might provide a useful hint of the shape of a probability distribution under one set of rules, but the rules were changing under Obamacare. I wanted to understand how health insurance companies had failed in the past. For that I needed a longer history.

In the 1990s, health insurers experienced pronounced boom and bust underwriting cycles, and UNH lost money in 1998. Since then, health plans consolidated and the industry structure had changed. Many managed care plans had pushed for rapid enrollment growth in the 1990s, even when it damaged profits. Smaller health maintenance organizations (HMOs) and preferred provider organizations (PPOs) blew up constantly because of surges in various conditions like premature births, but also from expansion into new territories or new categories of covered lives. Medicaid HMOs that had been accustomed to profitably managing a steady stream of normal pregnancies and asthma cases abruptly discovered that special needs populations were actuarially quite different. The billion-dollar question was whether the ACA would revive these issues in a different form.

Under the ACA, every American was mandated to get covered by health insurance or pay a penalty. Historical medical cost data weren't always available for the newly insured population, and what was available might be a poor guide to future claims behavior. To promote more competitive rate-setting, governments established new health insurance exchanges. Rates for younger, healthier members were to be set above economic cost to subsidize rates for older, sicker members. Insurers feared this pricing regime would encourage unprofitable members to sign up first. The law also directed health insurers to spend a minimum proportion of premium income on medical costs or rebate the shortfall to customers. Managed care companies fretted that if they set premiums too low initially, they would be barred from recovering costs in subsequent years.

With so many obvious pitfalls, and no carrots for crazy risk-taking, my take was that most health plans would underwrite to avoid regrets. Where the rules required "guaranteed issue" of policies to populations that were costly to serve, insurers would either set premiums high enough to cover costs or elect not to participate. Exchanges opened up the possibility of geographic expansion, but the larger managed care networks in a region usually have lower costs and better quality. New competitors without networks and medical cost databases would suffer higher costs and little diversification. While exchanges and new competitors would squeeze margins for everyone, the new entrants were more likely than the incumbents to suffer a bloodbath.

Test 2: Profitable Growth

Faster growth usually indicates that a stock is worth more. The catch is that the company must earn incremental profits sufficient to provide an adequate return on the capital involved. No matter how swiftly an enterprise grows, if it only earns a fair profit, its DCF value will not increase. Getting bigger actually reduces shareholder value when the returns on incremental capital are meager. For most businesses, though, growth is a plus for value. The median ROE of S&P 500 companies in 2015 was 14.5 percent, far above the cost of equity capital, which I then estimated at 8 percent.

In theory, unless a business has a moat or competitive advantage that will keep it unusually profitable, changing its growth rate will not change its value much. Many companies don't do anything unique that others can't do, and they don't put capital to work with special skill. For the general run of stocks, this means that the annuity formula works fine without any adjustment for growth. To calculate the value of growth, one must first estimate the period over which a firm maintains a competitive advantage that keeps profits elevated, and then the amount of profits. The period of competitive advantage ends before an enterprise fails, but they are related. Prosperous enterprises survive longer. If we had perfect foresight, what we would aim for is a low current price relative to earnings at some future date.

Based on UNH's combination of consistently attractive ROE and growth, I was sure that growth was a significant positive for its value. In 2010, I was using an equity discount rate of 10 percent, and UNH's returns on invested capital regularly surpassed that hurdle. Even with large amounts of goodwill on its balance sheet and periodic medical cost spikes, UNH's ROE averaged over 20 percent between 1999 and 2010, placing it in an elite group. In its worst year, UNH earned an ROE of 14.4 percent, still superior. I believed that these returns reflected the economies of scale inherent in UNH's position as the largest managed care group, and I expected them to continue. Projecting UNH's growth out ten years, its P/E on future earnings might have been under four, which is to say compellingly cheap.

As America's largest health insurer, covering the nation, UNH had immense negotiating leverage and economies of scale. It could obtain the largest discounts from hospital "chargemaster" fee schedules, and it might be able to dictate reimbursement rates for procedures. Doctors were attracted to UNH by the large volume of patients it could direct to them.

Customers also saw UNH's wide network of doctors and hospitals as a strong value proposition. In recent decades, staff model HMOs have lost market share to PPOs, which offer a broader range of choice of doctors and hospitals. For national employers, UNH provided one-stop health insurance shopping. There might be scale economies in the back office and in selling; UNH's overhead as a percentage of sales was lower than at Aetna and Cigna, but was not the lowest in managed care. UNH's advantages would be hard for competitors to duplicate, and slow to erode, which is to say UNH had a moat protecting its profitability.

I felt the jury was still out on whether UNH's acquisition spree had improved shareholder value. UNH's largest recent deal had been to buy PacifiCare in 2005 for stock and cash. While UNH paid a P/E well into the twenties, which implied that it would earn a low return on its acquisition of PacifiCare, its own shares were also trading at a P/E that was nearly as high. In the years following the acquisition, margins of the PacifiCare plans improved smartly. UNH became a truly national company with the acquisitions of PacifiCare and, in 2007, Sierra Health. With national coverage, the only health plans UNH was still interested in were small tuck-ins.

UNH's major focus for acquisitions shifted to the Optum cluster of faster-growing health care data analytics, pharmacy, and employee assistance businesses. All of these businesses came at steep multiples of earnings, which implied low starting returns on the purchase price. Not surprisingly, in 2010, Optum's ratio of profit to assets was lower than in UNH's managed care business, so I worried that UNH had overpaid. Optum's profits subsequently surged, however, and by 2014, Optum's return on assets would be higher than in managed care. But I didn't know that in 2010.

Even though I hadn't built anything into UNH's value for using its capital productively, UNH had timed its share issuances and repurchases well. Three years after the PacifiCare acquisition, UNH's earnings were higher, but its share price had tanked by two-thirds. UNH stepped up its share buyback program, and in under two years, it had more than offset the shares it had issued to buy PacifiCare. The combination of rising net income and a falling share count turbocharged UNH's earnings per share comparisons.

I was confident that UNH's organic growth would remain vigorous. UNH had never had a down year for revenues. Its slowest year was 2007, with a 5.4 percent increase. Managed care has covered a gradually increasing proportion of the American population, which grows by roughly 1 percent a year. I thought that as health insurance coverage became more universal, volume growth might accelerate. Over the last half-century, health care spending has escalated along with nominal gross domestic product growth *plus* another 2 percent a year. In the new millennium, per capita hospital stays and office visits have actually declined. Whether the increased spending reflected improved care or health-care-specific inflation, it would provide a tailwind for UNH. Then there was Optum, which had growth opportunities that might benefit from Obamacare.

Linear shortcuts don't work when a company's profitability and growth are constantly shifting. But that's the normal state of affairs. To judge the value of growth, you can't avoid a full DCF analysis. In one shortcut, known as the Gordon growth model, dividends or free cash flow are assumed to grow at a stable rate perpetually. A stock's discount rate is the sum of the dividend yield plus its perpetual dividend growth rate. No growth rate lasts forever, but for the next several years, I thought that UNH's earnings and free cash flow could advance 8 percent per year.

Using punchy assumptions, UNH might be worth $123 a share, four times the recent price of $30. Subtracting 8 percent growth from a discount rate of 10 percent implied that the free cash flow yield on UNH should be 2 percent. Assuming that it would earn an ROE of 20 percent forever, UNH would need to reinvest 40 percent of its earnings to grow 8 percent. Out of earnings of $4.10 a share, $2.46 a share in free cash flow would be left. At a 2 percent free cash flow yield, UNH shares would be worth $123 for a P/E of thirty, or fourteen times what I guessed it might earn ten years out.

Using more cautious forecasts for growth, I calculated values for UNH of between $41 and $61 a share. In most cases, I projected growth and incremental ROEs to start at 8 percent and 20 percent, respectively, and taper off. My cheeriest scenario had growth and profitability holding up for fifteen years. In my gloomiest state of affairs, margins would take a step down because of the ACA. Looking forward, no amount of growth would add value, so UNH would be worth its annuity value. The value of a stock should always be considered to be a range, but I went with the geometric average of the two scenarios, or $50 a share. Unless you envisioned a bleaker situation than I had, growth would definitely boost UNH's value.

Test 3: Built to Last

The third component of value, future life span, depends on the period over which an enterprise will sustain exceptional profits. Forever assets with monopoly rents are rare, as competitors will constantly try to knock off the slightest advantage. An average business earns average profits, so most companies never enjoy extended periods of extraordinary profits. Companies with moats protecting their profitability will survive longer. Except in fast-paced businesses like technology and fashion, most companies that have a visible competitive advantage can expect to live long because they prosper.

In present value terms, it hardly matters whether an enterprise will shut down forty years from now or never, as long as the end is not near, in the next decade or two. An income of $8 a year forever, discounted at 8 percent, is worth $100, while the same annual income for seventy-five years would round up to $100. Rounding to the nearest dollar, an annual income of $8 a year for thirty, twenty, and ten years would be worth $90, $79, and $54, respectively. Of course you want to avoid businesses whose lives are nasty, brutish, and short. Beyond a certain point, though, added years provide little benefit; what companies achieve in that interim matters more.

UNH appeared to have competitive advantages that would keep it super-profitable and in business for decades. Managed care firms have failed at a lower rate than the general run of businesses. Health insurers are highly regulated, as it's not in the public interest for them to fail and leave members unprotected, and regulation usually limits competition. Health plans typically run into trouble because they are too small and undiversified to handle a spate of costly claims, which is the opposite of UNH's position. Without doing a full-fledged search, the only sizable HMO bankruptcies that I know of are Maxicare in 1989 and Maxicare's California subsidiary in 2001. Maxicare had become the largest HMO in the country by using a lot of debt to acquire a series of poorly run plans.

While I ranked UNH favorably both in terms of competitive advantage period and overall longevity, my estimate of its value was unchanged at $50 per share. Because the value of the competitive advantage period had already been included in the value of growth, I didn't double count it. I expected UNH to endure longer than most businesses, which in present value terms was nearly as good as perpetual. Effectively, life span operates mostly as a negative filter for investments, screening out companies that aren't very durable. That didn't describe UNH, which had a strong competitive position and finances and provided a vital service.

For many enterprises, the endgame is selling out, not bankruptcy. Often managers will lose their jobs when their company is acquired, so the buyout offer must be too good to refuse—that is, richer than a conservative DCF value. The ability to choose a particularly opportune moment to sell gives managers an option that is most valuable for resilient businesses.

Test 4: Not Certain How to Measure Certainty

Sometimes when uncertainties are categorized together using the outside view, they become risk, meaning uncertainties that have some statistical basis for setting odds in advance. In the *Merck Manual*, I can discover any number of health ailments that I did not know existed. Yet even after reading the pages, I am not certain which infirmities I might personally develop or how I will be stricken next. If you need to know how and when you will fall ill, you are stuck with uncertainty. In contrast, insurers need only know the aggregate cost of health care over millions of lives and so can manage risk rather than the uncertainty of the details.

Managed care is a business with extremely stable, predictable revenues. Members sign up for coverage at premiums set a year in advance. For many people, health insurance is a necessity, so demand is almost economically insensitive. Most enrollees stick with the same plan from year to year, so the number of covered lives changes gradually. Reimbursement rates for doctors and hospitals are contracted for the year ahead as well, giving a forward look at the cost trend. Medical claims are usually filed in a matter of weeks, so any blip will be spotted quickly. When a customer's medical claims surge unexpectedly, his or her premium rates will be hiked the following year. Since the passage of the ACA, major HMOs or PPOs haven't lost money on an annual basis, while several small co-ops have failed.

My opinion was that UNH enjoyed even more certainty than the rest of its industry, but there aren't any really good numerical measures of certainty or of what you don't know. UNH had diversification not only across the nation, but also over types of customers: large commercial, small commercial, individual, Medicare, Part D, Medicaid, and so on. Its investment in technology was meant to help it catch surprises early. Statistically, the variance of UNH's earnings and ROE were lower than its industry peers. If I stopped there, UNH's relatively high operating certainty signaled a low discount rate and a stock worth more than $50 a share.

But I also had to factor in a totally different *existential risk*. The ACA threatened to blow up the business model of health care insurance. If the U.S. government became the "single payer" of all medical costs, insurers might become superfluous. It absolutely could happen. Countries like Britain and Canada do have single-payer health care systems. Under the Medicare system, the U.S. government is already the single payer for people over 65 years old. But then, Medicare disallows some charges and doesn't pay the rest in full, so there's a flourishing business in Medigap coverage. And many people receive their Medicare benefits through a health plan. There are two ways to reflect this risk—subjective probabilities and beta—both of which leave me somewhat uncomfortable.

I subjectively guesstimated a 10 percent chance that Obamacare would kill the managed care business. Truly, it's foolhardy to put a number on unknowable uncertainty, but the whole present value apparatus falls apart if you don't guess the odds. So I carried on. At least one thriving and previously legal industry was shut down by the U.S. government in the past. Exhibit A is the prohibition of alcohol under the Volstead Act. Since the Surgeon General's warning more than half a century ago, the government has arguably been trying to prohibit cigarette sales. The Feds have shut down an industry to protect public welfare, but rarely, and maybe not very quickly.

A 10 percent chance of a total loss and a 90 percent chance of $50 would mean that UNH was worth $45 a share, but I had to be sure I was ready for the worst eventuality. If you own only a few stocks and you lack Warren Buffett's mental calm and wealth, don't buy stocks facing the existential risk that UNH had in 2010. Personally I can't stay objective when coping with the likelihood that one of my main assets will soon be worthless. That's why my funds are widely diversified, some say overdiversified. It allows me to weight risk statistically.

The other way to evaluate risk is to adjust a stock's discount rate depending on its beta—the volatility of a stock's price—using the capital asset pricing model (CAPM) formula. A stock that is as volatile as the overall market has a beta of one. I don't believe that beta measures business risk, but it is readily available and what's taught in school, so in the absence of a better method, it's a perspective worth considering. Business risk has too many facets to be easily reduced to a single number. For traders, beta accurately measures short-term price risk. Investors' valuation risk—the risk of overpaying—has nothing to do with beta. When UNH's stock price collapsed abruptly and its intrinsic value declined less, an investor's risk of overpaying was reduced. At the same time, UNH's beta might increase, which would imply that it had become riskier.

When I plugged a beta of 1.11 into the CAPM formula, it spat out a value of $45 for UNH. Because beta combines all sorts of systemic risk into a single measure, theoretically no further adjustment for Obamacare was needed. Although I thought UNH had a low-risk business model that deserved a much lower beta and discount rate, I accepted this conclusion because it did factor in Obamacare. Perhaps it's a coincidence that both the subjective probability method and beta arrived at the same value of $45 for UNH. Or maybe not. Present value models are fiddly things.

The value estimate served its purpose: Over six years, between 2010 and 2016, UNH's share prices quintupled, from $30 to $150, while the S&P 500 roughly doubled. We will never know the actual probability of managed care's being devastated by the ACA, or the true value of UNH's stock. With hindsight, my expectations for Optum were far too cautious. Other investors would have used assumptions that were more conservative or more aggressive. The contortions can be so awkward and the untruths so bald that I understand why Buffett does not expose his DCF in public.

My favorite investments, then, are those in which undervaluation can be spotted using the basic checklist introduced earlier in this chapter:

1. Does the stock have a high earnings yield—that is, a low P/E?
2. Does the company do something unique that will allow it to earn super-profits on its growth opportunities? Does it have a moat?
3. Is the company built to last, or is it at risk from competition, fads, obsolescence, or excessive debt?
4. Are the company's finances stable and predictable into the extended future, or are they cyclical, volatile, and uncertain?

This checklist does not catch every undervalued stock, but it does cull out the most common sources of disappointment. It does not guarantee that bad things can't happen, but it does improve your odds. When I can fill my portfolio with stocks with all four qualities, I see no need to consider those with defects. Most stocks will fail this screen, but that does not mean they are *not* undervalued. In those cases, you must work through a full DCF, watchful of the risk of forecast error stemming from the known point of vulnerability.

20

Double Bubble Trouble

Bubbles don't grow out of thin air. They have a solid basis in reality,
but reality as distorted by a misconception.

—GEORGE SOROS

A BUBBLE IS WHAT PEOPLE CALL a huge market rally that they are not
enjoying. But that's not a definition you can prove or deny. If you are
going to spot bubbles while they are inflating, you must begin by asking
the right question: "What's it worth?" rather than "What happens next?"
Even die-hard efficient-markets believers will concede that the price is not
right if it's off by a factor of two—that is, if something is selling for twice
(or half) what it's worth. To be a bubble, the price has to be off for a
really major group of assets; otherwise, it's just a few zany prices. There
are always some outliers. If there weren't, value investing wouldn't work.

For better or worse, the value of a stock is unobservable; it's always an
educated opinion. But efficient-markets believers claim that no one can
detect a bubble until after it pops. After stock prices halve, they might
admit a bubble existed. If the observability thing really bugs you, figure
that the historical market average price/earnings ratio (P/E) is fourteen
or fifteen, and twice that is a bubble. Just about any time a highly visible group of stocks has traded at more than thirty times earnings, it has
ended in tears. That goes double for entire markets, like Japan's in 1990.
Even if you don't call it a bubble, it's worth avoiding.

Until you've lived through one, bubbles sound absurd. I had read
accounts of the Roaring Twenties and Swinging Sixties, and ancient
manias in tulips and the South Sea trade described earlier. Financial

captains had manipulated stocks to outrageous, unjustifiable levels, issued wildly intricate securities, and loaded on way too much debt. Company officers paid themselves too much. Sprawling holding companies were thrown together. Herds of crazed people bought and did extravagant, stupid things. It seems everyone suddenly lost their minds at the same time, financially speaking. Based on the stories, you'd think that bubbles happen for no reason. Once you've lived through one, you'll discover that the initial premise of a bubble is usually correct and compelling.

Free Money

Free money, or at least easy money, is a necessary ingredient in every bubble. Although central banks might wish that easy money would support rapid economic growth, it first propels asset prices. When the U.S. Federal Reserve ("Fed") creates money, it shows up as bank deposits, so its first stop is in financial markets. Put cash in the hands of financial people, and they will buy (mostly, at first) financial assets. Depending on the nature of the bubble, the cash might eventually turn into physical assets, as it did with housing. Bubbles last longer if cash stays in the imaginary financial world. If it produces a real asset such as, fiber-optic cable or Las Vegas condos, this may curb enthusiasm. Traders will swap whichever assets are moving the fastest. So much the better if there's no anchor to reality.

At first, because of slowing inflation, the Fed stayed relentlessly easy in the 1990s, providing the financial system ample liquidity. Ten-year Treasury bond yields, which had been near 15 percent at their peak in 1981, had tumbled to 8 percent by 1990 and 6 percent by 1996. The Fed was haunted by the market crash of 1987 and still-high unemployment in the early 1990s. Stock and bond prices go up when the discount or interest rate falls, so this was terrific for financial asset prices. For a stock with a steady yield and no growth, a drop in the discount rate from 15 percent to 6 percent increases its value to (15/6) or 2.5 times its starting level. The share prices of growing companies might jump even more. If you anchored on the starting valuation, that would feel like a bubble.

Later the Fed noticed that a buoyant stock market is politically popular. Every time the economy or stock market threatened to take a spill, the Fed poured money into the system, achieving the desired effect. Unemployment fell, even as the workforce expanded. Inflation stayed tame. Economists suggested that with the "great moderation," business cycles might be a relic of the past. Brokerage strategists eagerly championed the "Greenspan Put," on the assumption that Fed chairman Alan Greenspan would always be there to prop up stock prices if turbulence hit. Just in case he ever did stop helping out, big, actively traded stocks could be dumped in a hurry.

According to Wall Street lore, individual investors always get it wrong; they were piling in. Stock analysts, once seen as boring as accountants, now appeared on TV.

In 1996, Fed chairman Alan Greenspan queried, "But how do we know when irrational exuberance has unduly escalated asset values, which then become subject to unexpected and prolonged contractions as they have in Japan over the last decade?" At last, I thought, Greenspan had noticed that even correct ideas could be taken too far. But his remarks were not an indication of things to come. For decades after the Great Depression until 1974, the Fed would raise stock margin requirements whenever it wanted to cool speculation. After Greenspan's "irrational exuberance" comments, the Fed did not act, and the 50 percent margin requirement is still in force in 2017.

Because of the Greenspan Put, the economy and the stock market seemed to be far safer than in the past. Market strategists talked about the Fed Model, which suggested that the earnings yield on stocks should be the same as the yield on high-quality bonds. In a 1999 book titled *Dow 36,000*, economists Glassman and Hassett extended this thought. Stocks were really *less* risky than bonds over the long run, they argued. Therefore, it was reasonable to have stocks priced to produce the same total return as bonds. One estimate of a stock's total return—and discount rate—is the sum of the dividend yield plus the growth rate of dividends. Usually the total return and growth rate are assumed as given, making the dividend the variable that the formula solves for.

When an investor's discount rate is less than a company's growth rate, this formula doesn't work. With dividends on the S&P 500 stocks growing 6 percent a year and bond yields of 6 percent, no dividend yield was needed at all. This applied particularly to hyper-growth stocks like Cisco. In June 1998, Cisco shares traded at $64, or eighty-six times earnings, but they calculated that it was really worth $399 a share. Glassman and Hassett took a mind-blowing view of the sensible practice of using a range to estimate values. Cisco's value could be as little as $122 and as high as $1,652, they wrote. The top end would suggest a fair P/E of over two thousand. My head was spinning.

So if the Fed was going to endlessly provide liquidity and push interest rates lower, I knew I shouldn't fight it. Savings and loans and small banks were clear beneficiaries of falling interest rates and ample liquidity. There were dozens of financial institutions with single-digit P/Es, trading below book value. Savings and loans turned out to be one of the better-performing groups of stocks in the 1990s. Similarly, companies paying high interest rates could refinance debt at lower rates, giving a boost to earnings. If stocks were cheap even without the extra kick, I snapped them up.

Globalization and America Resurgent

World-changing events were afoot in the 1990s, as they always are in the greatest bubbles. The boom of the 1990s was something of a double bubble, built on two megatrends: globalization and technology. No one could guess just how powerful these trends were, but every projection seemed to be far too low. It became evident that global companies and tech stocks held unlimited profit potential. Anything worth doing was worth overdoing.

Deregulation and globalization of trade had again put America's economy on top; the technological piece was the widespread use of personal computers, cell phones, and the Internet. As for the first, capitalism had won, and America was on top again. The "Evil Empire" collapsed, the Berlin wall tumbled, and Germany was reunified. Governments stopped nationalizing industries and started privatizing them. Many industries were deregulated, most notably telephone and utility companies. Tax rates were cut sharply, and large companies were best positioned to slash taxes further by shifting operations to lower-tax jurisdictions outside the United States, like Hong Kong, Ireland, and Luxembourg.

International trade benefits both trading nations, wrote the British economist Adam Smith in 1776. Each country will produce more of the products in which they have a comparative advantage, and import the products where they are less advantaged rather than producing them. This theory assumed that countries were on a gold standard, which meant that trade ultimately had to balance.

After the oil price shocks in the 1970s, world trade accelerated. In part, the rising value of trade just reflected higher prices for oil. It may also have reflected the response by Germany, Japan, and other countries that had to import most of the oil they consumed. Japan, for example, ran a trade deficit in the late 1970s. To cover the increased cost of oil and balance trade, these countries had to step up exports. Germany and Japan became champion exporters. When Saudi Arabia and other oil producers piled up balance-of-trade surpluses, they often reinvested the proceeds in the United States, or at least in dollar-denominated assets ("Eurodollars")—a pleasant surprise for American capital markets. But it also led to a dilemma identified by economist Robert Triffin. The United States, as a global reserve currency, will be expected to issue dollars to supply the rest of the world. The United States would persistently run a trade deficit, which was terrible for its export industries, but good for financial markets. And borrowing abroad to finance current consumption means that Americans today are able to consume more than they produce.

By borrowing foreign capital, the United States shifted the basis of trade from *comparative advantage* to *absolute advantage*. If an import did not have to be matched by an export, American companies could source products at the lowest possible price globally. Hourly wages are much lower in many countries in the rest of the world. By the 1990s, the shoe, textile and apparel industries shifted to Asia, as did much of the electronics industry. Surging imports brought deflation in the prices of these goods, which allowed the Fed to keep its accommodative monetary stance.

Even if the rest of the world didn't like Americans, it was buying American consumer products and technology. They wanted to be entertained by Mickey Mouse; drink Coca-Cola, Pepsi, and Budweiser; smoke Marlboro; and wear Nike.

This was terrific for American companies with a global supply chain, as it meant they could be price competitive and closer to many new markets. New technologies were connecting people and businesses around the world, opening up new global markets and reducing selling, marketing, and logistics costs. The selling price of new technologies kept plunging, but the cost to produce them dropped even faster. It was possible to have low inflation, rising production, and rising profits all at the same time.

Large companies in the S&P 500 were perfectly placed to benefit from globalization. Walmart, which once promoted the fact that much of its merchandise was "Made in the USA," became the nation's largest importer. In 1998, the share price of Walmart doubled, as did that of several other giants. The S&P 100 outpaced the S&P 500, and the NASDAQ 100 outran the NASDAQ composite.

Many small companies had higher costs, and were part of the increasingly unneeded U.S. supply chain. They also had less exposure to fast-growing international markets. A fund manager who focused on those giants growled at me that small companies were an obsolete and irrelevant asset class. My fund focuses on small caps, so I bought U.S. firms with international operations and foreign small caps. I bought a midsized Finnish TV and telephony company named Nokia which was, rightly, excited about its new cellular phones. As it turned out, even foreign and smaller technology companies often had manufacturing in Asia. If American consumers really liked a product, it would usually sell well in Europe, except for France.

PCs, Phones, and the Internet

Perhaps every great stock market boom rides on the mass application of new technology. The Gilded Age of the 1890s literally rode the rails. Automobiles, home appliances, telephones, and electricity became widely used in the 1920s. The 1960s rolled out computers, color television, xerography, instant photography, and air travel and freight. It was all so dizzying that in 1970, Alvin Toffler wrote the best-selling book *Future Shock*, which described the human effects of too much change.

Every one of these innovations drew legions of competitors. Most of them eventually failed. But from the top of a bubble, even the winners disappoint. Radio Corporation of America (RCA) was a bull market mascot in the 1920s, leaping fivefold in a year and a half. News and music have never been the same since radio. But if you had purchased RCA stock in 1929, you would have lagged behind the market over the next half-century. Similarly, Polaroid, Eastman Kodak, and Xerox, stars of the 1960s, were catastrophic long-term holdings from their peaks. Cisco and America Online (AOL) would meet similar fates.

Even as a child, I knew that computers would be important and transform life in ways that couldn't be fully anticipated. The piece of the future that I totally missed was the telephone network. It started with the breakup of AT&T, which allowed competitive carriers to enter the market. After that came cell phones, fiber-optic cable, networking, and a flurry of other innovations. Fictional TV detectives Dick Tracy and Mannix used cell phones, but why would regular folks ever want to? Long-distance service had become so inexpensive that calls to grandma or my parents were no longer limited to ten minutes and scheduled for weekend evenings. Now that was something rational to be exuberant about.

Technology companies and large global companies were the clear winners from these themes. Tech firms sold the gear that connected the globe, and often the best customers of tech companies were other tech companies. Global companies also had much to gain from cutting their selling and marketing costs, especially across borders. General Electric announced detailed plans to save billions through electronic purchasing and marketing. Companies like Cisco, Dell, Intel, and Microsoft were at the heart of both categories, and were dubbed the Four Horsemen.

Trying to Understand the New World

Things were changing so fast that I couldn't completely grasp what was going on. I couldn't ignore technology and communications because they were major sectors and offered opportunities unlike anything I'd seen. So I set out to learn about and observe technology companies. Newspapers and financial TV didn't help me understand what the emerging products were or study technology road maps. Company annual reports told me about gigahertz and areal density, but left me wondering what they were and why I cared.

Brokerage firms increasingly added specialized salespeople for tech stocks, including "Vinnie." He cheerfully advised me that I just didn't get it. Vinnie repeatedly drove home his key points. This economy is different. Tech stocks are different. Valuing tech stocks is different. You can't learn from the past. The old standards don't reflect the new reality. He told me that in a changing world, the analysts who know the most have the most to unlearn. It wasn't my fault; I was just born five years too early. I wasn't convinced that tech stocks should be valued differently or that the past was useless.

San Francisco–based Hambrecht & Quist (H&Q) was the coolest technology brokerage firm, with deep connections in Silicon Valley. I liked its casual but high-energy vibe. Daniel Case, H&Q's CEO, was born in the same year that I was, making him one of the youngest brokerage CEOs of the time. His brother Steven was the CEO of AOL. H&Q had the best conferences, frenzied gatherings with six companies presenting at the same time for brisk half-hour meetings. The meetings and trading in the stocks had the same feel—two hundred of your closest friends cramming into the same tiny space simultaneously.

I can't prove that ethical standards collapse during bubbles, but I believe it. Investors would congregate between the meetings and talk industry gossip. A few seemed to spend most of their day doing that. At technology conferences, I kept bumping into a smart, friendly woman named Roomy, who worked for Intel. She was especially friendly with Raj Rajaratnam, a hedge fund manager whom I had known as a highly regarded semiconductor analyst at Needham. More than a decade passed without contact, and I forgot about Roomy and Raj. Then I saw news stories about a hedge fund named Galleon Group facing an indictment for insider trading. Roomy Khan was sentenced to a year in prison and Raj to eleven years. I was fortunate to have lost touch with them.

IPOs

Most of all, brokers were eager to educate buyers about their initial public offerings (IPOs), as there was a steady stream of new technology companies coming to market. Investment banks tacitly colluded to maintain the fee for underwriting most IPOs around 6 percent of the offering proceeds. Thus, on an IPO priced at $15, they might earn a fee of ninety cents a share. Vinnie loved these IPOs. On an ordinary stock trade, institutional commissions then might have been five cents a share (and today they are even less). On these deals, Vinnie would earn a much larger commission, and often big blocks were traded. Plus, it's more fun for everyone to deal with a new, exciting story.

In normal times, it's dangerous to buy an IPO knowing only that it's super-hot, but these weren't normal times. Lots of IPOs launch and then drop below their offering price. As the 1990s wore on, almost any IPO offered by the technology boutiques surged. They were hot, hot, hot, but the hotter the stock, the tinier the allocation. For a billion-dollar fund like mine, getting 800 shares of a stock that doubled didn't help much. Hosting the IPO meeting was occasionally a way to get more shares, but in any case it helped me judge whether I really wanted to own the stock.

I had missed the IPO roadshow of Long Distance Discount Services (LDDS) in 1989 but met with its officers later. LDDS was founded in 1983 after AT&T was broken up by the Justice Department. LDDS was much smaller than Sprint or MCI, but it had grown fast and kept acquiring competitors. LDDS stock was trading for a low teens P/E on forecasted earnings. I bought some shares (not many) and didn't hold them long. After it surged, I thought it was too expensive and sold. The stock climbed seventyfold by 1998 when it changed its name to WorldCom Communications.

Over and over, I regretted selling stocks that subsequently were ten baggers, going up tenfold and more. In 1992 I had hosted the AOL IPO meeting. The offering was priced at $11.50 and closed the first day at $14.75. Most investors ignored it. With about 6 million shares, AOL's market value was still tiny, under $90 **million**. The original service had been something called Game Line, which seemed fun but not a bonanza. AOL could be much bigger than that. Executives pointed to Minitel in France, which was meant to handle payments and ticket reservations but had been adapted for romantic hookups and many other uses. AOL was already profitable, revenues were jumping, and I liked management. I decided to give it a go. By 1995, AOL was up twentyfold, but I had again taken only a small slice of that gain.

AOL had been nicked by accounting disputes about how to treat the cost of mailing out diskettes to sign up new subscribers. The company was growing rapidly but burning through a lot of cash to get new customers. How long should AOL take to amortize those costs? That would depend on customer churn rates, which bounced around. The U.S. Securities and Exchange Commission kept going after AOL's accounting process, resulting in repeated fines and financial restatements.

But AOL stock stayed on the gallop. Its sales surged every year, more than doubling in 1994, again in 1995, and again in 1996. By 1999, the stock had split two-for-one six times, making the adjusted IPO price eighteen cents. AOL was worth twice as much as Time Warner. It had a P/E in the hundreds, not that anyone cared. Click-throughs and page views mattered more. When AOL and Time Warner merged in 2000, the new company's market value was more than $300 **billion**.

Other investors had the same regrets I had about being too cautious with IPOs. They did then what they seemingly should have done earlier. They bought trashier and trashier offerings. In 1999, more than three-quarters of IPOs were losing money. In the 1980s and early 1990s, less than a third of IPOs had been losing money. Almost every IPO leapt to a breathtaking premium. For a period in 1999, the average IPO doubled on its first day. There were more than four hundred IPOs in 1999.

In October 1999, Sycamore Networks went public at $38 and closed the first day at $184. In the following four months, its share price tripled again. The two founders became multibillionaires almost instantly. Boston media were all abuzz, because Sycamore was based in Chelmsford, a suburb. By then Vinnie had switched firms three times and had finally started his own hedge fund and venture capital firm. Somehow Vinnie wrangled a massive allocation of Sycamore. His tiny fund took off like a rocket. The money poured in. He kept buying more Sycamore as it surged, rather than taking profits. At the peak, Sycamore had a market value of $44 billion—incredible, considering that in its best year it only had $374 million in sales, and the following year sales crashed by four-fifths. Not that it mattered, but Sycamore hadn't made any operating profit on those sales.

It seems bizarre, but if start-ups can be sold at lavish prices, entrepreneurs will launch businesses they know will never earn any money.

In 2000, among the younger set at Fidelity, the Kozmo.com website was a favorite. Kozmo sold everything twenty-somethings need online at retail prices: DVDs, video games, magazines, food, Starbucks coffee, and more. Best of all, Kozmo delivered the goods within one hour, with no minimum purchase and no delivery fee. One colleague would stay in and cuddle with his girlfriend and have entertainment, soda, and gum brought to his lair for a few bucks.

Everyone with an idea seemed to be getting rich. Suddenly one of my college classmates, who had cofounded an Internet grocery delivery service, was worth tens of millions of dollars. A younger colleague's classmate, who was twenty-eight, hit it even bigger, landing $100 million of untradeable Internet stock. A year or two later, my colleague checked back—that stock had become worthless.

Nonbelievers Are Silenced

On average, my funds have lagged in exuberant bull markets and held up better during downturns. After an extended stretch of nonstop roaring markets, lagging on the upside might look like chronic underperformance. I kept telling myself that unless you are a nasty human being or a crook, you don't get fired in a bull market. Having seen technology analysts demoted because they were insufficiently bullish, I didn't fully believe it.

I kept telling myself that clients are most likely to urgently need their money in a market smashup, and that I should protect them. But my mutual fund shareholders can effectively fire me from their account by withdrawing their assets any time, at once. Many did. Roughly half of my funds went out the door during the Internet bubble.

Shareholder letters and emails were distinctly unhappy. Still, most of the letters were kind, and some were even useful. By useful, I mean that some letters actually included stock pitches that led to good investments. Some of the stocks were new to me; others were existing holdings or at least familiar to me. One of these letters went, "I own some Low-Priced plus 1,000 shares of CMGI. I don't work for CMGI but check it out—you'll make big money." This was a superb and timely tip, coming in 1998, before another year and a half of spectacular gains in CMGI. I already knew about it, but again had held too little and too briefly.

CMG Inc. (CMGI) started as College Marketing Group selling mailing addresses and evolved into a conglomerate of Internet ventures. It went public in 1994 at $8.50 a share, spun off Lycos, and repeatedly split for a total of something like twenty-four for one, so the adjusted price might have been twenty-five cents. By the end of 1999, those split shares had exploded to $238. That's a thousandfold in five years. It was a Massachusetts company, and I knew many people who lived near CMGI's chairman. My colleague Neal Miller was all over CMGI and other Internet stocks; his New Millennium fund more than doubled in 1999.

But I totally missed it. Low-Priced edged up just 5.1 percent in 1999. Many people were sure that I didn't fully comprehend what an idiot I was. Dozens of Internet stocks were in my benchmark, the Russell 2000 index. Not only was CMGI in my benchmark, but it had also become the single most important stock. Everyone told me that it was dangerously risky *not* to hold these stocks. One of my bosses pleaded with me to hold half the index weight in CMGI, but I didn't. If I had, it would have been the fund's largest holding by a factor of three. CMGI had never had positive operating cash flows. I wasn't sure what to make of its ventures with names like Green Witch, Raging Bull, and Tribal Voice.

One value-conscious portfolio manager, a former technology analyst, was in a different position than I was. He was a decade my senior, had a super long-term and mediocre recent record, and always gave excellent advice. Avoid the big loss was one of his touchstones. His fund was larger than mine and was filled with smaller companies and unfashionable but growing companies. I don't know whether his decision to retire was personal or not. He had been vocal about "tulip time," which made his performance a magnet for criticism. In the weeks after he left, the new manager dumped out all the consumer staples, low P/E stocks, and small stuff, replacing them with whizzy, shiny new toys, just as the air started seeping out of the bubble.

In contrast, Vinnie was on top of the world. Although I never cared to know, Vinnie kept updating me on his surging personal net worth. Once I made the mistake of grousing about my fund's underperformance. He told me that I was being justly punished for buying the garbage that

I did. I was an enemy of the future. He agreed with George Gilder's comments in the *Wall Street Journal* (12/31/1999) that "the investor who never acts until the financials affirm his choice [is] doomed by trust in spurious rationality."

The psychology of bubbles brings to mind the diabolical dollar bill auction devised by game theorist Martin Shubik. A dollar bill is auctioned off at penny increments, with the prize going to the highest bidder. The rub is that the second highest bidder also has to pay, but he gets nothing. Even as the bids go past $1.00, the second place bidder keeps coming back with higher bids *to avoid the penalty*. It's a losing game— but they just can't stop. Realizing that something is nuts doesn't mean that it will stop. In the same way, investors who do not hold the inflating asset may feel forced to buy it to keep up. Shubik's game and investment bubbles both eventually end badly for all players.

POP!

With the NASDAQ 100 peaking at more than one hundred times earnings in 2000 and plunging 78 percent over the next two years, few dispute that there was a technology bubble. Although the S&P 500 traded at more than thirty times earnings (exceeding the levels reached in 1929 and 1966) and lost half its value, many dispute that there was a bubble in large growth stocks. As suggested by the authors of *Dow 36,000*, estimates of value can be in a very wide range, but to me it's clear that there was a double bubble. That part is easy. But it's not a very useful conclusion for a value investor because we are trying to buy stocks for less than they are worth and sell them for fair value or more. If a group of stocks is selling for twice its value, we should be long gone.

The hard part is dealing with the crowd psychology of bubbles. It starts with correct premises that the world is changing dramatically. Things have turned out far better than expected, so expectations based on a longer history seem far too conservative. When people pass on misunderstandings of the facts, they build on them, spreading more misunderstanding. It seems pointless to try to value companies. The history of finance is an endless series of booms and busts; anyone who has studied it is apt to wonder whether the herd ever gets it right. The story isn't wrong, but the price is.

No one can tell precisely when a bubble will end. As the professors say, it is arrogant to think that your judgment is correct and that millions of investors are wrong. But it was on the question of timing, and not whether the bubble existed, that millions had focused their attention. As Citigroup CEO Chuck Prince said later, under similar but different circumstances, "As long as the music is playing, you've got to get up and dance." Every bubble in financial history has eventually popped, but the timing will always be a surprise.

You will find the clearest proof that "What happens next?" can't be predicted in the observation that almost everyone got just one side of the boom and bust right. True believers stayed true believers. Doubters remained doubters. Either you rode the boom and lost it in the bust, or you resisted the bubble and collected a windfall later. I was in the second group. Yes, Mark Cuban sold out of Broadcast.com near the top and remained a billionaire. But there were far more traders who missed much of the surge, came late, and got smashed in the aftermath.

When you are in the midst of a bubble, you have to understand that you can't directly control returns. What you can control is how risky your investments are, when you buy them, and what you pay for them. These factors will affect the returns you ultimately earn, but the market does its thing on its own schedule. Cycles swing between greed and fear, and although you can have a sense of where the pendulum is, it is useless to try to guess what happens next, because cycles don't come in standard sizes. It may feel as though current conditions will last for an eternity, but financial memories are extremely brief. Junk bonds had yields in the teens during 2008 and 2009; two years later, their yields fell to the lowest levels on record.

21

Two Paradigms

The unreasonable man adapts conditions to himself. . . . All progress
depends on the unreasonable man.

—GEORGE BERNARD SHAW

My one regret in life is that I am not someone else.

—WOODY ALLEN

THE WISDOM OF WARREN BUFFETT and Jack Bogle, two icons of modern
investing, points in completely opposite directions, yet still converges.
Buffett personifies an utterly idiosyncratic style of active investing, while
Bogle created the Vanguard S&P 500 index fund. Obviously, your portfolio can't look exactly like the market and most dissimilar at the same
time. But both approaches are systems for minimizing regrets of the sort
discussed in this book. The genius of index investing is that being average avoids (by spreading thin) deep regrets brought on by the extremes
of emotions, ignorance, fiduciary malfeasance, obsolescence, overleverage, and overvaluation. And anyone can index! Indexers have no regrets
over missed opportunities, because the index holds a smattering of everything. Buffett's method is much more demanding, as his goal is to avoid
regret altogether. He will not buy a security until he sees ample margins
of safety considered from multiple vantage points.

Buffett and Bogle do not represent the only conceivable ways to invest
safely and some may prefer more speculative approaches. The path you
choose—and sometimes must develop—depends on your emotional
character, knowledge, and curiosity. It is always excruciating to rationally
examine one's own motives, capabilities, and limitations. But it's important to do it. Many people prefer the contentment of the easily practical

to shooting for (and often missing) the stars. Don't torture yourself if you're just not cut out to bend it like Buffett!

Long ago, Buffett said that an investment lifetime scorecard should include just twenty punches. My funds have never, ever held so few stocks. Even when I see nothing on offer that Buffett would completely approve of, my mandate is to act. I don't see the world in black and white, only in shades of gray. Plus, I'm curious and interested in learning, and so I often test the boundaries of my circle of competence. I try to see things from others' perspective and uncover the good in people before I judge them. In the process, I've met a few bad guys. Permanence and resilience intrigue me, but experimentation and adaptability fascinate me. While I'm more patient than many, I'm not immune to the exhilaration of a sudden windfall. Still, I do want to invest safely.

I won't buy an asset unless it is:

1. Safe from rash decisions
2. Safe from misunderstanding of facts
3. Safe from foreseeable fiduciary misuse
4. Safe from obsolescence, commoditization, and overleverage
5. Safe when the future doesn't turn out as imagined

1. Loopy Mr. Market

Bogle and Buffett try to keep their investment decision-making safely apart from their emotions, aiming for fewer, more rational judgments. They cultivate the art of observing mindfully and dispassionately. They don't want emotions to lead to rash actions. To be sure pain won't guide their actions, some Bogle devotees ("Bogleheads") invest preset amounts every month, no matter how the market is behaving. They will buy at market peaks, but also in valleys, believing it should all come out in the wash. Index funds are broad based and bland, and not tasty fodder for hot tips and fantasies that individual stocks can inspire. By analogy, I'd suggest that diets of powdery shakes or celery or tofu might work not only because they contain fewer calories, but also because they make eating less tempting. That said, there are still swarms of day traders in index exchange-traded funds whom Bogle rightly scolds. Minimizing turnover averts bad decisions, commissions, and fees and defers capital gains taxes.

One recipe for happiness is selective inattention and lethargy. The pain of a dollar lost is greater than the joy of a dollar gained, so the more you watch prices bounce around, the glummer you'll be. Spend more time gathering information that bears on your investment's value, rather than tracking the price. If news won't matter in a year, skip it. Sometimes you will miss a real turning point. My permanent resolution is to read more books, annual reports, and publications like the *Economist* and to reduce emails and social media. It's said that a good marriage begins with eyes wide open but continues with almost willful blindness to small flaws; the same applies to stocks. Why rush decisions? You might know more tomorrow.

Buffett not only restrains himself from knee-jerk emotional reactions, waiting until the facts are compelling, but he also profits by buying when others find it uncomfortable, even agonizing. Usually, the most abrupt price reactions come when the moody Mr. Market correctly senses an existential threat. Buffett bought into the *Washington Post* in 1973 after it exposed the story of the Watergate break-in. Allegedly, President Nixon wanted to shut down the newspaper and rescind the company's Florida broadcast licenses. That's not supposed to occur in a functioning democracy, but if everything had been by the book, the Watergate scandal would never have happened. In the meantime, with an ongoing recession, a few advertisers pulled back. It wouldn't have been irrational to have concluded that earnings would be impaired in the near term and that the risk that the *Post* would be shuttered was material. Only with hindsight can we say that these fears were overblown. In fact the *Post*'s stature was actually improved, and its reporters Woodward and Bernstein became folk heroes.

None of Buffett's major investments have had a more terrifying backdrop than his purchase of GEICO shares in the mid-1970s. Unlike Buffett's other coups, GEICO was bleeding profusely, and some thought it was a goner. The losses stemmed from GEICO's expansion outside its original circle of competence—auto insurance for low-risk government employees. Massive underwriting losses meant that GEICO had to dump securities into a slumping market to raise cash to pay claims. The insurance commissioner was poised to declare GEICO insolvent. The CEO was sacked. GEICO's husband-and-wife founders had passed away. Later their son died, apparently by committing suicide. What part of this doesn't scream, "RUN!" to you? But, as with successful cancer surgery, it turns out this patient was mostly healthy, and the noxious parts could be isolated and removed. Still, no one breathed easy for many years.

2. Invest in What You Know

Defining a circle of competence can help keep your investments safe from misunderstanding. Stick with companies where you can identify the key factors that will determine their income out some years, and how those factors interact. For an index investor, these factors are more macroeconomic than they are for individual stocks. Usually, analysts start with an opinion about whether corporate profit margins are cyclically above trend or below, and whether mean reversion will help or hurt. They then factor in a growth rate, often stated as real gross domestic product growth plus inflation. This growth estimate tends to be overstated; it doesn't account for dilution from stock options or the GDP growth coming from start-up and small businesses that weren't in the index. (Think about Google, Facebook, and Uber.) Finally, a reasonable discount rate is needed. If you've read this far, you are probably financially literate enough to include the S&P 500 index in your circle of competence.

Because investors in S&P 500 index funds hold all industries, they don't involve themselves in top-down sector rotation. But as owners of the market, they find that the top-down economic approach opens the door to market-timing. My prejudice is that basically no one is competent to rotate between sectors or time markets, especially on a high-frequency basis. Even the slow-motion timing known as asset allocation is tricky to get right, and few have the requisite patience to stick with it. Economic processes are too complex and have too many hidden links, often involving human behavior that can change, for mechanical systems to work reliably. By disparaging sector rotation and market-timing, Buffett and Bogle are trying to keep you inside your circle of competence.

The S&P 500 index also doesn't have heavy concentrations of foreign-headquartered businesses or mysterious derivatives, which may be outside your circle of competence, but other index funds do. Arguably, you don't need foreign index funds for further diversification because the companies in the S&P 500 have extensive operations overseas. If you do venture abroad, you should consider whether the country has rule of law and political stability sufficient to make forecasts of the intermediate future credible. Consider how financial information will be translated, especially if a country's culture, institutions, and language are unlike yours.

Unlike the S&P index, Berkshire Hathaway is not represented in every industry and apparently considers many to be beyond its circle of competence. Based on his record, Buffett has immense skill in branded consumer products and services, and also insurance and finance. Pharmaceuticals might be in, but not medical devices or services. Other than IBM, technology is absent, almost as if PCs, smartphones, and the Internet never existed! Basic materials and mining are almost completely neglected, as are agricultural commodities. But even in industries that it generally avoids—like automakers—Berkshire finds segments where it does play, like auto dealers. Railroads are in, but not trucking and shipping.

Buffett disclaims any ability to forecast economic data, and does not use economic forecasts to make investment decisions. On average, the businesses under the Berkshire umbrella are not particularly cyclical, so he doesn't need an economic prediction. The economic bet that Buffett does like to make is that over time America will grow, bringing with it, among other things, increased freight volumes on the Burlington railroad, which will spread its fixed costs and boost profits.

Even though Berkshire Hathaway has dealt in complex financial derivatives, Buffett doesn't seem overeager to include them in his circle of competence. He has called them "weapons of financial mass destruction," and spent years winding down a derivative portfolio acquired with reinsurance giant Gen Re. With famously brilliant staff like Ajit Jain, I would think that if any company were competent to trade in derivatives, it would be Berkshire, and only gingerly.

Occasionally, Berkshire has dabbled in shares overseas, mostly in Europe, with investments in Guinness, Glaxo, Tesco, and Sanofi. Again, they were mostly noncyclical, not overly complex businesses with powerful brands, patents, or competitive positions. They are in industries that have been around for decades and seem unlikely to become obsolete. They are in countries with rule of law. Perhaps it's my own leaning, but Buffett seems to fancy English-speaking countries. My take is that he sees vast swathes of the developing world as outside his circle of competence, including Latin America, Africa, and Western Asia.

Both GEICO and the Washington Post Co. were relatively simple, understandable, stable, resilient businesses. Auto insurance is more of a "what-you-see-is-what-you-get" line than many categories of insurance. Insurance premiums are collected before claims are paid, so with proper underwriting, cash flow is almost always positive. Because of its direct sales model, GEICO has lower overhead costs than insurers that use agents. GEICO'S policy limits are small, and while the odd claim may take years, most are settled in months. After an accident, premiums are hiked. Historically, GEICO focused on safe drivers, which gave it below average claims losses. In return, GEICO charged moderate premiums. Most policyholders stayed enrolled, so GEICO had a good fix on its future premium income. It didn't take a management guru to spot what GEICO needed to do to turn around. It needed to get rid of unprofitable policyholders or raise premiums.

In the 1970s, subscription revenues for newspapers like the *Washington Post* were quite predictable, but ad sales bounced around cyclically. Washington, DC had a growing population of government workers, so the trend for circulation and ads was up, quite steadily. As the town's leading newspaper, the *Washington Post* reached the broadest audience, which attracted advertisers from other papers. It could also afford to spend more on a superior newsroom, or spread the costs over more readers and earn a better profit margin—or both. The costs of newsprint and ink were somewhat variable, but the *Post* acquired an interest in a paper mill. Warren Buffett didn't need to build a three-thousand-line spreadsheet to figure out what was happening at the *Washington Post* or GEICO. They were absolutely within his circle of competence.

3. Honest, Capable Intermediaries of Trust

For better or worse, none of us can control the disposition of our capital from start to finish; at some point, we all depend on agents we trust. To reduce it to the absurd, dispensing entirely with agents would mean *you* would have to do the work of *every* employee of the firms you invest in. Obviously, some agents matter more than others. The most heart-breaking situation is to be betrayed by someone you trusted completely. Among other things, the purpose of finance is to connect agents with other agents, and ultimately owners, in a web of trust. When trust is deserved and reciprocated, everything works perfectly. But how does this work for those of us who just want to collect our gains without too much fuss? Everyone may act in his or her own self-interest, but not everyone defines self-interest in the same way.

Owners of index funds are safe from total misappropriation, but instead receive an actuarial slice of trouble. If two CEOs are crooks and twenty are idiots out of five hundred, index owners suffer in line with the averages. Except where the system is deeply corrupt or dysfunctional, these damages get lost in the mix. Management fees on most index funds are around 0.1 percent of assets, a relatively tiny bite out of returns. But even passive investors need to watch to ensure that it is *their* interests that fiduciaries are safeguarding. Appropriately, I think, some sponsors of index funds have increasingly taken these concerns to heart in recent years, voting shares in ways intended to improve corporate governance. When Japanese companies pile up cash, which earns them nothing, and neither reinvest it nor pay it out as dividends, managers are serving interests other than their companies' owners.

On the whole, I think the S&P 500 companies are held to imposing standards. They are among the largest enterprises in America, and presumably wouldn't have reached their dominant position without being well managed, at least historically. Niche companies often have more distinctive product offerings and culture than S&P firms, and are more adaptable. In capital allocation, though, the advantage usually goes to the giants. Being in the spotlight can produce pressures to fiddle the numbers, as with Enron or Valeant, but when combined with requirements for transparency, more often acts as a disinfectant that discourages bad behavior.

Berkshire wholly acquires well-positioned, well-managed companies, and encourages them to stay that way. The main criticism of Buffett's management style is that he trusts too much. Divisions have their accounts audited thoroughly, and excess cash is swept to Omaha for large-scale capital allocation, but otherwise Berkshire has a very light touch. A headquarters staff of twenty oversees operations employing hundreds of thousands. Instead of seeking detailed budgets and targets, Berkshire instructs its managers to "widen the moat, build enduring competitive advantage, delight your customers and relentlessly fight costs." Buffett's ABC enemies are arrogance, bureaucracy, and complacency. The intent is to avoid the pressures and temptations that lead to poor capital allocation or fraud. My takeaway: Don't invest unless the right incentives are in place. It's a good sign when management owns a lot of stock.

Berkshire passes both tests of good management with flying colors—offering something distinctive to customers and allocating capital well. The first is accomplished at separate business units, while capital allocation is highly centralized. Many of Buffett's investments have been nearly synonymous with their category: American Express and high-end credit cards, Gillette and shaving, Disney and family entertainment, Coca-Cola and soda, for example. The wholly owned businesses are also distinctive, but usually in a narrower context. These include Benjamin Moore, Dairy Queen, Duracell, Fruit of the Loom, Flight Safety, and See's Candies. As long as the businesses continue to delight customers, they will throw off more cash than they need for growth. Incidentally, the focus on delighting customers might screen out bad guys, because businesses that abuse their customers will do the same with others, including owners.

4. Avoid Competition and Obsolescence

No one sets out to participate in something that's obsolete, drearily commoditized, and wallowing in debt, but that's how many investing stories end. The S&P 500 will always contain some stocks that are slip-sliding away, but also some of whatever is sparkly and new. I would think that because most S&P 500 companies have been time tested for at least a few decades, they have above average chances of surviving a few more decades.

Around 1960, a stock's average life span as a member of the S&P index was about sixty years; recently, it's been closer to sixteen years. Shorter corporate life spans aren't all bad for investors. They mostly reflect increased mergers and acquisitions. Because the S&P 500 is market cap weighted, it is constantly rebalancing toward stocks that have come up and away from those that have come down. Here again, being average protects you from the ravages at the extremes.

The importance of rebalancing and capital allocation can be illustrated with a hypothetical investment in General Motors at $43 a share in 1958; it might have earned a 9 percent rate of return, or been a total loss. General Motors went bankrupt in 2009, and the shares were canceled. An investor who had reinvested all of his dividends and proceeds from spin-offs in General Motors stock would have lost everything. Over half a century, GM had distributed more than $190 per share in dividends and spin-offs, including Delphi and Hughes, worth another $36 if sold immediately. As long as you spent the income or reinvested in something better, the rate of return was satisfactory. This isn't exactly what S&P index funds do, but they do reinvest income across the portfolio of five hundred stocks.

When Buffett bought into Berkshire Hathaway, it was a doomed textile mill with outdated facilities, selling an insufficiently differentiated product. Without this fiasco, Buffett might have remained blind to the safety provided by moats and unique capabilities. Berkshire was the largest producer of linings for suits, but linings weren't a branded feature that suit buyers sought out. With rising import competition, Berkshire was no longer the low-cost producer and couldn't get a needed price increase. Knowing that closing the mills would destroy the local communities, but also that offshore producers would inevitably prevail, Berkshire did not reinvest in the mills, but kept them open for many years despite losses.

As the United States adopted a permanent policy of tolerating massive trade deficits, anything that lacked a strong brand and could be made more cheaply offshore was doomed. While suit linings and Dexter's line of shoes did not become obsolete, making them in America did. Berkshire had better luck with branded textiles, including Fruit of the Loom underwear and Garanimals children's wear. Insofar as Berkshire has invested in commodity businesses with products that can be traded internationally, it has favored low-cost producers in lower-wage nations. For example, POSCO, the South Korean steel producer, meets the rigorous quality standards of Japanese automakers, yet it incurs lower costs than Japanese mills.

To guard against obsolescence and commoditization, Berkshire tacked toward recurrently purchased branded services and products that are not changing rapidly and don't face import competition. For consumer brands like Disney, Gillette, and Coca-Cola, international markets were a wonderful opportunity, not a threat. The other thing Buffett looks for is a barrier to entry, or moat. Initially, I was baffled by Berkshire's acquisitions in commodity-like services such as railroads and electric utilities, but for a host of reasons these industries are unlikely to see new entrants disrupt the market. Demand is steady and recurrent. Until something like self-driving trucks or renewable energy arrives and becomes commercially profitable, obsolescence will have to wait. By then, rails and utilities may have adjusted to the new world.

Most technology businesses do not fit Buffett's pattern of evolutionary change, differentiated products, loyal habitual customers, and few competitors. The few that have the last three—including Alphabet, Apple, Amazon, Facebook, and Netflix—are spectacular winners. If change is constant, reinvention must also be. At some point, companies that have conquered the world fall prey to Buffett's ABC's of failure: arrogance, bureaucracy, and complacency. Monetizing customers starts to matter more than delighting them. In short, technology is tough. So far, Buffett's only—and not notably successful—technology stock has been IBM.

The *Washington Post* remains one of the national newspapers of record, but Buffett did not foresee that the role of newspapers would be diminished by the Internet, which didn't then exist. In fact, the newspaper was sold in 2013 to Jeff Bezos, the Amazon founder, for $250 million, no more than it was worth four decades earlier. Buffett had correctly identified a durable and growing franchise that threw off cash, which was used to buy broadcast and cable TV properties, addressing the then visible competitive threat to newspapers. Later, Washington Post expanded into educational services by buying Stanley Kaplan. Much later, it acquired *Slate*, the Internet magazine. By the time the *Post* was sold, the proceeds were less than one-tenth of the holding company's assets. While no one could have predicted the Internet, Washington Post survived and prospered by adapting well. Because I'm a mediocre fortune-teller, I look for executives with a learning mind-set.

The Internet was an unexpected boon to GEICO, because it made marketing, rate quotes, and customer service easier and cheaper, reinforcing its cost advantage. It's yet another case of "buy the users of technology, not the technology stock." GEICO has kept gaining on the competition and is now tied for number two in auto insurance. Otherwise, the features of car insurance haven't changed a lot. Until autonomous driving is absolutely foolproof, car insurance isn't going away. With GEICO, Buffett found a business that has resisted obsolescence and commoditization for four decades and even benefited from change. As a part of Berkshire, GEICO has strong financial backing that will allow it to adapt as needed. It's worth noting that if Buffett had not recapitalized GEICO in the mid-1970s, GEICO might not have had the flexibility to take advantage of opportunities as they arose.

Many see Berkshire's low-debt posture as inefficiently conservative, but it prevents being backed into decisions and creates an option to take advantage of unforeseen opportunities. The paradox of cyclical businesses is that at the moments of greatest opportunity, no one has ready money. During the global financial crisis, few others had both the stomach and the cash to buy high-yielding preferred shares with equity kickers. Fast-forward a few years. The 10 percent coupon paid by Goldman Sachs was not available anywhere in good-quality fixed-income securities, and the attached warrants were worth billions. My conclusion: In any industry that is changing fast, or where opportunities come and go, I prefer little debt.

5. Never Ever Pay Full Price

How you think about a safe price for investments depends on how completely you believe in the efficient market hypothesis (EMH). According to true believers, stock prices are always fair, and therefore safe, or at least as safe as equities can be. Manias and bubbles don't exist, or in weaker form, no one can make money from them. Following this logic, investors should instead focus on setting appropriate expectations for returns. The EMH provided the theoretical foundation for developing the S&P index fund. Bogle extended the EMH by proposing the costs matter hypothesis: Investors should expect to earn the market average return, less expenses and taxes.

One implication is that owners of individual securities should expect the same market return, but with far more variability than with the index fund. Bogle would say, given the same returns and lower risk, go for the index fund! Because there is a (low) management fee on the index fund, owners of specific securities could have lower costs if they rarely traded. But for active fund managers like me, it's a shot across the bow. Active funds charge higher management fees, and some have high turnover. (In a recent year, my fund had lower turnover than my benchmark, the Russell 2000 index.) When *all* of the actively managed funds are equally weighted, most surveys find underperformance in line with what Bogle would predict. However, you do noticeably better with funds with low expenses, run by experienced managers, at larger fund groups.

As I see it, on average over time, for an average stock, its price will roughly match its fair value—but what about those extreme outliers? Call it the "sloppy" version of the EMH. The EMH is a cautionary tale warning that securities analysis is hard work, and you shouldn't blithely assume that you know more than the market. As in every human activity, there's a spectrum of ability and application. The average player is average, but at the extremes, some are virtuosos, others ham fisted. Likewise, at the extremes, there are bubble stocks and bubble stock markets and incredible giveaways. Most of the time, things are more or less average, so the Bogleheads will be OK most of the time.

What I worry about is when the market is NOT normal but raving bonkers. The day-to-day collective hallucinations involve a short list of darlings rather than the entire market, but bubbles do appear and can be identified. They do pop—timing unknown. And yes, unless you are ultimately vindicated, a persistent difference of opinion with the world is commonly tagged insanity. If you were thinking about prospective stock returns in 2000, when Treasury yields were over 6 percent, the 3.2 percent earnings yield and 2.3 percent Shiller earnings yield should have howled out a warning. Likewise, at its giddy heights in 1989, the Nikkei had an earnings yield of 1.3 percent, while Japanese government bonds yielded 4.5 percent. And then there are tragic cases like Austria, where human events were more senseless than the markets. In these contexts, indexers are safe only in the sense that there is no shame in misjudgment when it is shared with a crowd.

Buffett has made his fortune off of others' daft behavior, and has said that he is grateful to professors who teach that it is pointless to search for bargains. In particular, he looks for an overreaction to a major problem that can be fixed in an otherwise fantastic business. Such an investment would combine all four elements of value: a high earnings yield, growth prospects, a moat or competitive advantage that protects against failure, and certainty about the future. Except for discontinued activities as in the GEICO case, Buffett's companies are marked by transparent accounting, with few adjustments, and owner earnings that mirror reported numbers. Situations like that don't come around often.

A robot could execute Buffett's first step of buying stocks at low price/earnings ratios (P/Es) on normalized earnings. Washington Post was at eight times earnings when Buffett bought it. Berkshire acquired some GEICO shares at a price that worked out to one and a half times previous peak earnings, and most through a preferred stock that yielded 7.4 percent, which was convertible at the equivalent of 2.5 times previous peak earnings. Wells Fargo came at book value, and less than five times earnings. American Express had a P/E of ten in 1965. Coca-Cola was the glamour stock, at fifteen times earnings. If historical earnings were any guide, the purchase prices afforded margins of safety.

The magical, ineffable part is that in every case, earnings swiftly blew through previous records and made Berkshire's purchase prices look like astounding anomalies. By the early 1980s, GEICO's earnings per share were higher than purchase price for the first batches of stock. Five years later, Washington Post earnings were half its purchase price. Over four years, American Express's earnings soared from $3.33 to $12.00 per share. Coca-Cola's earnings quadrupled over the next decade. And so on. In every case, the problems really were temporary, and the companies were offering something uniquely valuable to an expanding customer base. Apart from their one-time issues, these were fairly predictable businesses.

Putting it all together, their value was much greater than earnings yield alone would indicate. They deserved premium multiples.

For Washington Post, there might have been a 75 percent margin of safety in Buffett's purchase price. There was an active private market for media properties, and appraisals of Washington Post clustered in the $400 million to $450 million range. The company's market capitalization was around $110 million, and touched as low as $75 million. I can only reconcile this with efficient markets by assuming that the odds were three out of four that the *Washington Post* would fold and that its other assets were worthless.

Margins of Safety Reinforce Each Other

A margin of safety in one dimension often supports margins of safety in other dimensions. For example, if you are mindful of thinking rationally, it is easier to see and accept your own limits to circle of competence. If you train yourself to know your limits and admit mistakes, you will also be more able to spot the limited abilities and ethical mistakes of others. If you seek out skilled managers, they may have anticipated the threats of obsolescence, commoditization, and over-indebtedness, and will adapt more successfully. If you have sidestepped the common blind alleys that investors go down when trying to see the future, your estimates of value are more apt to be reliable.

Nothing Is Absolute

Life and investing are inherently unsafe, so all of the margins of safety we've discussed are relative, contextual, and involve trade-offs. Consider rationality. Some refuse to invest in sin stocks like tobacco, alcohol, and gambling, and this doesn't seem irrational to me. They are putting their personal values ahead of any profit they might make on these activities. When Buffett bought a basket of a couple dozen South Korean stocks after minimal research, was that irrational? Or was it rational to conclude that he wouldn't improve outcomes enough to justify deeper research on a group of stocks with good track records in industries he knew were trading at single-digit P/Es? All of us have moments when we are the moody Mr. Market—hopefully, not too many.

Often there is a trade-off between different types of safety, as with Yukos, where a massive discount to calculated asset value implied that property rights in Russia were anything but secure. Conversely, glamour stocks with superstar CEOs and unstoppable growth are typically priced with a margin of *un*safety. The margins of safety that you should not compromise on are the ones you control: your rationality and your circle of competence. If, like me, you are a bit lax on your circle of competence, lifetime learning is the best defense. While you are still gathering facts, small bets and diversification help. (Yes, you also get these through an index fund.) Before investing, you should locate the weakest link in your margin of safety and consider whether it alone could make or break your results.

Whether your path more closely resembles Bogle's or Buffett's, you will reduce your regrets by seeking a margin of safety in five steps. (1) Be clear about your motives, and don't allow emotions to guide your financial decisions. (2) Recognize that some things can't be understood and that you don't understand others. Focus on those that you understand best. (3) Invest with people who are honest and trustworthy, and who are doing something unique and valuable. (4) Favor businesses that will not be destroyed by changing times, commoditization, or excessive debt. (5) Above all, always look for investments that are worth a great deal more than you are paying for them.

Index